The Words of Gardner Taylor

VOLUME 6

The Words of Gardner Taylor

Essential Taylor and *Essential Taylor II*
compact disks or audio cassettes,
featuring excerpts from the multivolume series

THE WORDS OF GARDNER TAYLOR

VOLUME 6

50 YEARS OF TIMELESS TREASURES

Gardner C. Taylor

Compiled by Edward L. Taylor

Judson Press
Valley Forge

The Words of Gardner Taylor, Volume 6: 50 Years of Timeless Treasures

Sermons © 2002 by Gardner C. Taylor
Introduction © 2002 by Edward L. Taylor
Published by Judson Press, P.O. Box 851, Valley Forge, PA 19482. All rights reserved.

Bible quotations in this volume are from *The Holy Bible,* King James Version.

"God's Great About-to-Be," "A Word We Must Never Forget," "The Promise in the Manger," and "Rumor of Life" appeared in *Chariots Aflame,* by Gardner C. Taylor (Nashville: Broadman Press, 1988). Copyright © 1988 by Gardner C. Taylor.
"A Story of Life: A Mother's Day Sermon," "Providence: The Control and Care of God," "Gethsemane: The Place of Victory," "Judgment and Mercy at Palm Sunday," "Two Names in the Morning," "The Power of His Resurrection," and "The Things That Cannot Be Shaken" appeared in *The Scarlet Thread: Nineteen Sermons,* by Gardner C. Taylor (Elgin, Ill.: Progressive Baptist Publishing House, 1981). Copyright © 1981 by Gardner C. Taylor.
"Hearts Waiting for What?" appeared in *Best Sermons,* volume 7, edited by G. Paul Butler (New York: Thomas Y. Crowell, 1959–1960 edition).

Library of Congress Cataloging-in-Publication Data

(Revised for volume 6)
Taylor, Gardner C.
    The words of Gardner Taylor / Gardner C. Taylor ; compiled by Edward L.
Taylor.
        p.   cm.
    Includes bibliographical references.
    Contents: v. 1. NBC radio sermons, 1959–1970. ISBN 0–8170-1339-3
(hardcover : alk. paper). v. 2. Sermons from the middle years, 1970–1980.
ISBN 0-8170-1346-6 (hardcover : alk. paper). v. 3. Quintessential classics,
1980–Present. ISBN 0-8170-1347-4 (hardcover : alk. paper). v. 4 Special
occasion and expository sermons. ISBN 0-8170-1351-2 (hardcover : alk. paper).
v. 5. Lectures, essays, and interviews. ISBN 0-8170-1352-0 (hardcover : alk.
paper). v. 6. 50 years of timeless treasures. ISBN 0-8170-1428-4 (hardcover:
alk. paper).
    1. Baptist Sermons. 2. Sermons, American. I. Taylor, Edward L. II. Title.
BX6452.T39 1999
252'.061–dc21   99–23027

Printed in the U.S.A.
09   08   07   06   05   04   03   02
10   9   8   7   6   5   4   3   2   1

To Gert, aunt and second mother,
who with "flinty-tenderness"
put steel in a little boy's spine
and
in grateful memory of Carl Stewart (1926–1997),
because of whom my preaching was heard regularly
via radio in the bayou country where I was born.

CONTENTS

About the Author

Dr. Gardner Calvin Taylor is presently pastor emeritus of the historic Concord Baptist Church in Brooklyn, New York, where he served as pastor from 1948 to 1990. Dr. Taylor has been widely acclaimed as one of the most outstanding preachers in the nation. He has preached on six continents, delivered the 100th Lyman Beecher Lectures at Yale University, and preached the sermon at the prayer service for the inauguration of President William Jefferson Clinton in 1993. On August 9, 2000, Dr. Taylor received the Presidential Medal of Freedom, the highest honor the United States bestows upon a citizen.

Now retired from the pastorate, Dr. Taylor continues to be in great demand as a preacher and lecturer. He recently concluded an appointment as distinguished professor of preaching at New York Theological Seminary. Dr. Taylor lives in Brooklyn, New York, with his wife, Phillis Taylor.

About the Compiler

Edward L. Taylor is founding pastor of the New Horizon Baptist Church in Princeton, New Jersey. During his ten years of ordained ministry, he has preached at colleges and universities across America and has ministered in Europe, the Caribbean, and Africa. Rev. Taylor has received numerous citations and awards for preaching and congregational ministry. He presently serves as a dean of Christian education for the General Baptist Convention of New Jersey.

A native of Ville Platte, Louisiana, Rev. Taylor currently resides in New Jersey with his wife, Constance La Trice Taylor, and son, Paul Lewis Taylor.

PREFACE

Approximately eighteen months ago, I was summoned to the home of Dr. Gardner Taylor. Driving to Brooklyn's Crown Heights neighborhood has been a joy over the years. I was humored by the notion that I would attempt to teach Dr. Taylor how to surf the Internet during this visit. In addition, I was quite pensive about discussing volume five in *The Words of Gardner Taylor* series. I became a bit sad to realize that the work I had begun as a seminary paper would end within months with the completion of volume five. I have not the vocabulary to describe how I have cherished my afternoon sessions with Gardner Taylor. On each occasion, something special has happened. That day would be no different.

Although I have visited with Dr. Taylor for years, I had never before entered his private study. This day he invited me upstairs. The room was as I suspected it would be. Books on every subject had their place along the wall; pictures of friends and loved ones were everywhere. Sheets of paper covered his desk. Calloway golf clubs stood at attention in their assigned place. My heart grew heavy thinking, "This is where it has been happening for years! Right here in this room!" I thought about the hundreds of thousands of hours in craftsmanship spent here working on the Word.

I followed Dr. Taylor to a closet located in a corner of the study. When he opened the door, my mouth fell open with awe and amazement. Before me, in folders, on bookshelves, in boxes, and in filing cabinets was the much-rumored collection of nearly every sermon Dr. Taylor had preached at Concord Church. As I stared at the treasure trove before me, I felt regret at not having had access to these sermons earlier. Without question, the series would have been organized differently. But, immediately I began to think that a sixth volume of Dr. Taylor's work should be published. This volume is the product of this blessed experience.

Save for the reprinting of a handful of sermons, these messages selected by Dr. Taylor have not been seen or heard, in some cases, for as long as forty years. Each has those elements that have made Dr. Taylor's preaching so widely regarded today: a theologian's thought, a poet's language, a thespian's delivery, and most of all, an engagement with the Eternal.

Not long ago, I was invited by the African American studies department at Princeton University to deliver a lecture about Dr. Taylor's preaching. Upon the conclusion of my presentation, famed historian Nell Painter, department chair, invited Nobel Prize winner Toni Morrison to give remarks. She shared complimentary thoughts about my lecture and about the quality of Dr. Taylor's preaching. She then proclaimed that one of the great traits of black preaching "is that it has the ability to blur the line between practice and performance." She had summed up the whole of my lecture in a few words. A part of the true greatness of Gardner Taylor is that he has the ability to blur the line. I commend these timeless treasures, written in the "blur," to America.

EDWARD L. TAYLOR
Princeton, New Jersey
February 2002

Acknowledgments

I would like to extend my heartfelt thanks to Judson Press for the opportunity to bring these sermons, addresses, lectures, and other works by Dr. Gardner C. Taylor to the American public. The publisher's skill and objectivity have made the process of publication a joy. The technical assistance provided by Mrs. Phillis Taylor, Pamela Owens, Gloria Arvie, Theresa Bailey, Tanisha Hicks, Victoria Hicks, and my wife, Constance La Trice Taylor, along with the contributions of DBS transcription services of Princeton, were invaluable.

A debt of gratitude is owed to the Chicago Sunday Evening Club and to the libraries of Union Theological Seminary of Virginia, Yale University, Harvard University, Howard University, Southern Baptist Theological Seminary, and Princeton Theological Seminary for the invaluable resources provided to me for the compiling of this work.

In addition, I must acknowledge with appreciation the work of Deacon Bernard Clapp of the Concord Baptist Church of Brooklyn. Deacon Clapp has worked diligently for twenty-five years as head of Dr. Taylor's tape ministry and provided the bulk of the materials found in these volumes.

Most of all I wish to thank Dr. and Mrs. Taylor for their understanding, patience, and cooperation in this project. How grateful I am to have been afforded the opportunity to compile *The Words of Gardner Taylor*. I thank God for having so gifted Dr. Taylor that we should be given this rich corpus of material.

EDWARD L. TAYLOR

Introduction

GARDNER C. TAYLOR

America's Twentieth-Century Preacher

by Edward L. Taylor

Early in United States history, the names Cotton Mather, Jonathan Edwards, and George Whitfield begin an exclusive list of American preaching legends. Since then, Henry Ward Beecher, John Jasper, Phillips Brooks, Jarena Lee, C. T. Walker, Lacy Kirk Williams, Sojourner Truth, and Harry Emerson Fosdick are among the names to be added to the roster of those who have displayed excellence in preaching. Many others could be included.

One name, however, deserves singular recognition among Americans who have proclaimed the gospel of Jesus Christ. That name is Gardner Calvin Taylor. Rarely do legends live in their own time, but Dr. Taylor has proved to be an exception to the general rule. His preaching stands as an unparalleled model — indeed a lighthouse — for all who would aspire to preach Jesus.

Gardner Taylor was born on June 18, 1918, in Baton Rouge, Louisiana. His father, Washington Monroe Taylor, pastored one of Louisiana's most prestigious churches, the Mt. Zion Baptist Church, which is registered today in the Baton Rouge Courthouse as the First African Baptist Church.

Washington Monroe Taylor, who also served as vice president at large of the National Baptist Convention, U.S.A., died when Gardner was just thirteen years of age. But under the tutelage of his mother, Selina, young Gardner developed into an outstanding student, eventually enrolling at Leland College, a black Baptist college located in Baker, Louisiana, just ten minutes from Baton Rouge.

As a college student, Dr. Taylor displayed a wide range of interests and talents. He was a star center who led his football team to victory against Grambling University. He was a serious student who devoted much of his free time to reading books. He excelled in extracurricular activities, especially debate. Among the several classmates he regularly engaged in informal, friendly debates was H. Beecher Hicks Sr. The debates, accounts of which have found their way into Louisiana Baptist lore, typically focused on matters of faith. Dr. Taylor made use of several resources, but his favorite text was Robert Ingersoll's *The Mistakes of Moses.*

During his college years, Dr. Taylor looked to Leland College President Dr. James Alvin Bacoats, who succeeded Washington Taylor at Mt. Zion, as his primary mentor. Although surrounded and influenced by ministers his whole life, Dr. Taylor did not at first aspire to become one himself. Instead, he wanted to be a lawyer, and in pursuit of that plan he applied to and was accepted at the University of Michigan School of Law.

A tragic personal experience, however, would change not only his plans for law school but also the entire direction of his life. On a spring night in 1937, Dr. Taylor had taken President Bacoats' car on an errand. On a rural highway, a model-T Ford came out of nowhere and crossed his path. The impact was devastating. Two white men were in the car. One died instantly; the other died later as a result of the crash. In those days, the society's instincts were to regard a black nineteen-year-old participant in such an accident as a murderer.

Thankfully, however, at the court hearing, white Southern Baptist minister Jesse Sharkey, a witness to the accident, testified that young Taylor was innocent of any wrongdoing. Freed from any fear of prosecution, Dr. Taylor put aside his letter of acceptance to law school and began to think about the ministry instead. Out of this tragic experience, he ended up thanking God and offering himself to God for a lifetime of service.

In the fall of 1937, Dr. Taylor enrolled at Oberlin Graduate School of Theology. While there he wooed and later (in 1940) won the hand of Laura Scott, his first wife, who now sits with Jesus. During those years, the soon-to-be Mrs. Taylor, a Phi Beta

Kappa Oberlin graduate, began sharing with Dr. Taylor her love for literature, plays, food, and other elements of the larger culture that would go on to inform Dr. Taylor's preaching. She began her helpful critiques of his work, critiques that would continue throughout her life. During a period in which Dr. Taylor was heavily involved in politics, she said to him, "Your preaching is getting a little thin." That was all the counsel he needed to cut back on his political involvement.

At Oberlin, Dr. Taylor began several practices that, through the years, have greatly influenced his preaching. Most significantly, he immersed himself in the study of preaching as an academic discipline. Like Andrew Blackwood, he realized that every master preacher he respected had made a study of admired preachers.[1] He read sermons constantly, especially those of such early legends as Alexander Maclaren, F. W. Robertson, Frederick Norwood, Leslie Weatherhead, Clarence Macartney, and Charles Spurgeon. He read preaching journals such as *Christian Century Pulpit* from cover to cover.

When a student of preaching inquired of the great expositor Stephen Olford what the difference was between the pastor in England and the pastor in the United States, Olford stated in quick retort, "The pastor in America has an office. The pastor in England has a study." Defying that stereotype, Gardner Taylor has always had a study.

While still a student at Oberlin, Dr. Taylor became pastor of Bethany Baptist Church in Elyria, Ohio. His first pastoral experience, which ended upon his graduation in 1940, affected him deeply and helped him mature in many ways. Since then, he has always shown great love and sensitivity toward those who are starting out in pastorates or going through times of trial in churches across America.

Upon graduating, Dr. Taylor returned to Louisiana to become pastor at Beulah Baptist in New Orleans. In 1943 he returned to Baton Rouge to become pastor of his home church,

Mt. Zion. Just a few years later, he was presented with two rare opportunities, remarkable for a man of just twenty-nine.

The first consisted of an invitation to speak at the six-thousand-member Concord Baptist Church in Brooklyn, New York, whose pulpit had been recently vacated by the death of Dr. James Adams. To the astonishment of many, Dr. Taylor declined Concord's invitation to preach because it fell on Communion Sunday at Mt. Zion. (Some would consider it divine providence that on the date on which Dr. Taylor was originally invited to preach, New York City was besieged by a major snowstorm, among its worst ever.) To Dr. Taylor's surprise, he was reinvited to preach at Concord, and this time he accepted. On the Sunday he preached, Concord was filled to capacity. The sermon, "I Must Decrease, and God Must Increase," captivated those in attendance.

The second of twenty-nine-year-old Taylor's remarkable opportunities was the chance to travel to Copenhagen, Denmark, to attend the Baptist World Alliance. On the Sunday morning of the Alliance, he preached at Second Baptist Church of Copenhagen. Upon returning from his six-week trip to Denmark, Taylor was informed that Concord had invited him to become its next pastor.

No one who knew Taylor doubted that he would accept the invitation. They perceived him correctly as a man of vision whose mind was energized with great and inspiring thoughts and who possessed an immeasurable hope and desire to contribute to the advancement of the Christian faith. Many pastors move on because God has placed before them the challenge of a larger church. For Dr. Taylor, it was more than that. His response to this call entailed fulfilling his role in the destiny of the kingdom of God. As Dr. Taylor's friend David Iles put it, "Gardner was big enough for the field, but the field was not big enough for Gardner."

At the 1948 Baptist State Convention in Alexandria, Louisiana, Taylor announced his intention to accept the position at

Concord. In doing so, he told delegates, "God has called me to preach at the crossroads of the world. I must go." No one in Baton Rouge had to go far to hear Taylor's farewell sermon at Mt. Zion. Radios throughout the black community were tuned to the church's weekly radio program. According to local seniors, it was as if Dr. Taylor were preaching in every home.

At age thirty, Taylor went north, serving the Concord Church from 1948 to 1990, in the process amassing what is among the most respected pastoral records in the twentieth century. Eleven months into his pastorate, Dr. Taylor began serving on a local school board. He went on to become the second African American to serve on the New York City Board of Education.[2] For a short time, he led the Democratic party in Kings County, America's second most powerful political party organization, behind Mayor Daly's Cook County in Chicago.

Nine thousand people were added during Dr. Taylor's tenure at Concord; the church experienced enormous growth. When the building was destroyed by fire in 1952, Dr. Taylor oversaw the building of its present sanctuary, completed in 1956 at a cost of $1.7 million. He presided over the establishment of the Concord Elementary School, where wife Laura served as principal for thirty-two years at no salary; of the Concord Nursing Home, which was founded with 121 beds, along with a seniors' residence; and of the Concord Credit Union that went on to amass assets of $1.8 million. He also helped to establish the Christfund, which was endowed with $1 million to support community development, especially in the area of youth.

Despite these accomplishments, however, it is Dr. Taylor's record as a preacher that has distinguished him in American Christianity. The diversity and sheer number of places where he has spoken are a measure of the respect he has earned as a preacher. He has preached before the Baptist World Alliance on six occasions. He followed Harry Emerson Fosdick and Ralph Stockman on NBC *National Radio Vespers Hour,* which was broadcast on some 100 radio stations. National denominations from ten foreign countries, including China, England, and South Africa, have invited him as a special guest. He has also appeared before eleven U.S. denominations.

Even as an octogenarian, Dr. Taylor continues to receive acclaim and honor for his homiletic skills. He has received eleven honorary degrees. He has served as president of the Progressive National Baptist Convention. A countless number of seminaries and colleges have invited him to preach or lecture. Among them is Yale University, where Dr. Taylor delivered the prestigious Lyman Beecher Lectures. Twice, *Ebony* magazine has honored him as one the greatest preachers in American history. *Newsweek* included an account of Baylor University's distinction of Taylor as one of the twelve greatest preachers in the English-speaking world. In an article on the seven great preachers of the pulpit, *TIME* magazine called him "the Dean of the nation's Black Preachers."[3]

I once asked Dr. Taylor that all-important question, "Are great preachers born or made?" After considering for a brief moment, he remarked, "I think that God gives one natural gifts, but there are some secrets. Those may be learned."

One of the underlying secrets to Dr. Taylor's success is simply hard work. He has read thousands of books, most of which now rest in his own library. Nearly every week he wrote a full sermon manuscript over a period of several days. Typically finishing on Saturday, he would then commit its ideas to memory. Very rarely does he speak without a manuscript of his remarks on file. Given two years' notice before delivering the Lyman Beecher Lectures at Yale University, Dr. Taylor kept up with his regular preaching and writing schedule, teaching appointments, and pastoral and family duties while still finding time to read all of the previously delivered lectures, which numbered about seventy book-length manuscripts.

In Dr. Taylor's preaching can be found a mix that includes a sort of grand nineteenth-century Victorian style, the richness of the African American folk tradition, and a unique interpretation of modern homiletical theory. The richness of his words and sermon design are legendary. Without fail, his introductions whet the listener's appetite. Like an *hors d'oeuvre,* they hold us for a time but make us eager for more. His message moves toward its purpose as a staircase headed to the top floor of a mansion. His rich language and genius for metaphor help to assure listeners that what may appear to be a steep climb is actually an escalator ride.[4] Each message includes thoughtful theological reflection and biblical scholarship, while steering clear of intellectual arrogance and abstraction. To Dr. Taylor, content and delivery are of equal importance. His delivery contributes to his distinctive interpretation of every text, personifying what Phillips Brooks defined as truth through personality.[5] Dr. Taylor embodies the best of what preachers have been and the hope of what preachers should become.[6]

Hearing Dr. Taylor preach opens a window to the essence of his soul. There we gain a glimpse of how his character has been wedded to the text. His legendary marking of the cross with his foot grounds him. His thumbs behind his lapels lift him as he hangs his head in sorrow with Job at his narrow window, enters the dressing room while a freshly bruised Jesus puts on his own clothes, or bathes himself in the blood which is a balm in Gilead. Such skill is unique in preaching. He exhibits his own prescription for sermon building, displaying genuine pathos and ethos through his mastery of African American rhetoric, through eloquence, and by grasping each audience's understanding of the human circumstance.[7] These are the very qualities that endeared Dr. Taylor to Martin Luther King Jr. and that should endear him to us as well.[8]

Dr. Taylor has proven the adage that "diamonds are made under pressure." Many people with similar gifts have faltered at accepting the challenge to greatness in their professions, but Dr. Taylor rose to the occasion. Each invitation became for him an opportunity to be gifted by God for the experience at hand. In part because of who he is as a person, Dr. Taylor is revered as a preacher among preachers. His ministry has never been clouded by personal scandal. He has a unique reputation for not changing his preaching schedule when invited to larger or more prestigious places. All this helps to explain why fellow clergy have granted him the standing he deserves today.

Although retired for a decade, Dr. Taylor still maintains a hectic schedule, spending time with Martha, the daughter of his first marriage, her family, and his new bride, Mrs. Phillis Taylor. Frequently, he crosses the country preaching in pulpits all over the nation and occasionally overseas as well. He recently concluded an appointment as distinguished professor of preaching at New York Theological Seminary.

I am privileged to have had the opportunity to compile *The Words of Gardner C. Taylor* for the American public and, indeed, for all the world. Most of the sermons in these volumes were first preached in the Concord pulpit. Volume One contains sermons preached on the NBC *National Radio Vespers Hour* in 1959, 1969, and 1970. Other volumes contain additional sermons (many of which had never before been published), lectures, articles, interviews, presentations, and special addresses, including his Baptist World Alliance addresses, the Martin Luther King Jr. memorial sermon, his address at the funeral of Samuel DeWitt Proctor, and the sermon delivered at the inauguration of United States President William Jefferson Clinton. (Readers should note that some editorial revision by Dr. Taylor may give these sermons or lectures a modern touch in style or language, but the content of the messages has not been changed in any substantive way.)

For half a century, God has used the words of Gardner C. Taylor to shape lives and develop faith. The purpose of these volumes is to help preserve his legacy. The sermons, lectures, and other selections included in this series are far from exhaustive, but they are highly representative. They are intended for readers' enjoyment, but they can also teach and inspire. Most importantly, it is Dr. Taylor's hope that those who encounter his words, even many years after they were preached, will be drawn to a closer and more intimate walk with God.

Recommended Readings

Susan Bond, "To Hear the Angel's Wings: Apocalyptic Language and the Formation of Moral Community with Reference to the Sermons of Gardner C. Taylor." Ph.D. diss., Vanderbilt Divinity School, 1996.

Gerald Thomas, *African American Preaching: The Contribution of Gardner C. Taylor* (New York: Peter Lang, in press).

Notes

1. William H. Willimon and Richard Lischer, eds., *The Concise Encyclopedia of Preaching* (Louisville, Ky.: Westminster John Knox, 1995), 37.

2. Clarence Taylor, *The Black Churches of Brooklyn* (New York: Columbia University Press, 1994), 118.

3. These remarks may be found in *Ebony* (Sept. 1984; Nov. 1997); *Newsweek* (Mar. 1996); and *TIME* (Dec. 31, 1979).

4. Brian K. Blount, *Cultural Interpretation* (Minneapolis: Fortress Press, 1995), 72.

5. Phillips Brooks, *Lectures on Preaching* (New York: E. P. Dutton & Co., 1907), 5.

6. For discussion of the style and content of African American preaching, see Albert J. Raboteau, "The Chanted Sermon," in *A Fire in the Bones: Reflections on African-American Religious History* (Boston: Beacon Press, 1995); Henry H. Mitchell, *The Recovery of Preaching* (San Francisco, Harper and Row, 1977), *Black Preaching* (New York: J. B. Lippincott, 1970), and *Celebration and Experience in Preaching* (Nashville: Abingdon Press, 1990); Evans Crawford, *The Hum: Call and Response in African American Preaching* (Nashville: Abingdon Press, 1995); Frank A. Thomas, *They Like to Never Quit Praisin' God* (Cleveland: United Church Press, 1997); Bettye Collier-Thomas, *Daughters of Thunder* (San Francisco: Jossey-Bass, 1998).

7. Gardner C. Taylor, *How Shall They Preach?* (Elgin: Progressive Convention Press, 1977), 65.

8. Richer Lischer, *The Preacher King: Martin Luther King and the Word That Moved America* (New York: Oxford University Press, 1995), 50–51.

⌒ 1 ⌒

IT TAKES ALL KINDS

September 21, 1958

But as touching the resurrection of the dead, have ye not read that which was spoken unto you by God, saying, I am the God of Abraham, and the God of Isaac, and the God of Jacob? God is not the God of the dead, but of the living. (Matthew 22:31–32)

We'll call his name Tom, and we talked on a golf course during a morning hour. His contention was that he had once been a part of the church and loved it then and loves it still. He told quite sincerely of how in another place and in the years gone by he had been very active in his church. There followed uprooting; he moved to New York, where the traffic moves fast and the lights burn late and one can turn night into day. Well, honestly, he almost said, he had started working in a club, and there was talk of the horses that run with a dollar, or a thousand, riding on their noses, and the gay, giddy whirl of the girls who are pretty and the fellows who are smooth. So Tom fell by the way, lost his regularity at church, gave up his loyalty to Christ, and started out to "live it up," as they say. But something is haunting Tom, and he talked about it that morning: an awareness, a sense, a feeling, a belief that, though stricken of conscience, he has a part in God's love, is not utterly cast away, may yet turn. He said, "I am coming back. I've got a conscience, and I know I've been wrong. But I am coming back."

How right he was! He does have a place. For it takes all kinds with God. We often hear people say, almost in disgust, if someone has acted in a way of which they do not approve, as they throw up their arms in the air, so to speak, "Well, it takes all kinds to

---

Note: I believe I am indebted to Arthur Gossip for the germ of this sermon. —GCT

11

make a world." It takes all kinds to claim God's love. That's what Jesus was saying in a passage, though this was not particularly the point he was making. Jesus quotes God as saying, "I am the God of Abraham, of Isaac, and of Jacob."

You never would have come upon three more different characters than these, though they were of the same blood lineage. Here is the incontrovertible proof that whoever you are and whatever your life has been, in your own eyes, you are not beyond God's concern. The other day a man, a witty publisher of a periodical dedicated to the complex problem of race in the South, confessed that he had spent time in a federal penitentiary. He told of how he and his wife had dreaded his growing popularity, for fear the fact would come out. He made a public admission of his crime in the public press the other day. Among the telegrams of confidence he received was one from Fannie Hurst that said, "Couldn't care less." Nice, but God has one better than that for you. No matter who you are or what you have done or have not done, his word to you is, "I couldn't care more for you, no matter who you are or what your record is, or how far you've wandered. I couldn't care more."

This is revealed in the quotation of Jesus about God: "I am the God of Abraham." That put God in big business. Sometimes we are of the opinion that when we reach a certain level of vision, of seeing things as they ought to be, that we outgrow God. We are likely to feel when we reach a certain amount of training or a point of sophistication that we belong to a world too big and fine for God. But when this passage says that God is the God of Abraham, that puts the heavenly Father in big business.

Abraham was a great and towering figure. He dreamed in the quiet land of Ur of a new and vaster start, a great and daring new beginning for the human race. He was a man of courage and of faith and gave up the comforts of home and the security of familiar surroundings in order to follow the gleam of a dream whose luminous finger pointed to something big and new and wonderful off beyond the rim of the horizon. He was a man of courage and indomitable will who braved the hazards and faced the dangers undaunted and unafraid, following a faith until he came upon the earnest, the token, the sign of the fulfillment of the promise.

So God is the God of dreamers of big dreams and those men and women who are not willing to drift with the tide but who long in their souls to climb high mountains and to do great things for their day and generation. Those who would change the ways and acts of our democracy need not feel that they must do this without God. The Lord of heaven is the Lord of history, and he stands with those whose cause is just and whose purpose is right. In quietness and confidence, we can work for the better, fairer world, sure that God throws in his strength on the side of truth and goodness and love and righteousness. We shall yet see the "school closers" betrayed by their own evil.

> Mine eyes have seen the glory of the coming of the Lord,
> He is trampling out the vintage
> Where the grapes of wrath are stored.
> He has loosed the fateful lightning
> Of his terrible swift sword,
> His truth is marching on.

"I am the God of Abraham."

"I am the God of Isaac." Well, that's something else again. Now Abraham with his big dreams and his daring pilgrimage — but Isaac — what's so wonderful about him? Not much by human standards. You see, Isaac was a very ordinary figure and very commonplace. They got a wife for him, Rebekah. He dug again the wells his father had dug and which had become clogged with disuse. No new wells, mind you, but the ones that were already there. Isaac reared his children and worked and at last was deceived in his dotage by his son Jacob. There, that isn't much to get excited about.

One thing Isaac did do that we ought to mention. In a well-known marriage prayer there are the words: "May this man and this woman live together as did Isaac and Rebekah." So this man did have a marriage which was a winsome thing of beauty and permanence. But that is hardly anything to become excited about. The truth of the matter is that Isaac's life was very commonplace and very tame.

But God is the God of that kind of person, too. We understate ourselves and downgrade our possibilities by saying, "I would be active in the church, but my talents are so small. I'd volunteer for this or that, but what I can do is so unimpressive." Dr. Martin King and I spoke from the same platform at a huge open-air meeting one night in New York. I think I shall always remember him saying to that gathering of neglected, proscribed humanity: "You may be penniless and broke. You may not have any education, and you may not know the difference between 'You do' and 'You does,' but you've got a soul. You have got either realized or potential spiritual power, and with that you can turn back an army." Right! The most ordinary person is important to God. Charles Darwin wrote once, "I think I could make something of a case against the enormous importance which you attribute to our greatest men. I have been accustomed to think second-, third-, and fourth-rate men of very high importance, at least in science." What he meant was that the great discoveries may belong to the Louis Pasteurs and the Jonas Salks, but behind them always are the ordinary research people, the patient watchers of reaction, the makers of notes and the apprentices who do jobs the meaning of which they do not themselves understand. Gilbert Chesterton puts the case in defense of the ordinary person in another way by saying it is the man in the street who is the great figure in the drama of the world. If you want discoveries about the solar system, said he, you call in the geniuses, but when there is something really serious to be done; when, for example, a life is hanging in the balance, and a man must be tried, you get twelve ordinary men — their minds are likely to be more balanced and poised. If throughout our land we could realize that our citizenship participation is vital, we would give our democracy its most needed impetus. It is important for every one of us to vote, since every election is won by one vote. And to God every person couldn't be more important. When Jesus gathered his disciples, there were some whose names you hear often: Peter, James, John, but there were others whose names are not so familiar, and yet Jesus wanted them with him, Philip, Simon the Zealot, Bartholomew.

"I am the God of Isaac."

Well, let's make one last turn around this idea. "I am the God of Jacob." Ah, you slick, smart ones! Here is your answer as to whether you can ever hope for a place hard by God's side. You've cheated and lied and stolen, and you wonder whether you can ever get near to God. Jacob would tell you that you most assuredly can be close to God. For here was the smart one, Jacob. He wasn't ever going to be left holding a bag. He would get his, he would tell you with a knowing wink. He cheated his father and then set out on a career of fast deals, playing the angles, being one step ahead of the other fellow. He found out at last, of course, that you don't beat the game of life. You play it by the rules, or you suffer the penalty.

If you have been taking advantage of others or are trying to make it by your wits, and now you wish you could make another start, you can. God waits and couldn't care more for you had you been as perfect as angels. "I am the God of Jacob." You see, it takes all kinds to make the heavenly Father happy. Jesus told about how God wants everyone, every member of his family, safely gathered round the hearth. If one, just one, is lost and wandering, there is a shadow around God's throne and a pain in God's heart. There is an emptiness in God's heart that only you can fill. There is a job God has that only you can do. No prophet can fill that place. No saint can fill that place. Neither John the Baptist nor John the beloved disciple can fill that place. It's your place in God's heart, and only you can fill it.

~ 2 ~

BACK TO BETHEL

September 6, 1964

And God said unto Jacob, Arise, go up to Bethel, and dwell there:
and make there an altar unto God, that appeared unto thee when
thou fleddest from the face of Esau thy brother. Then Jacob said
unto his household, and to all that were with him, Put away the
strange gods that are among you, and be clean, and change your
garments: And let us arise and go up to Bethel; and I will make there
an altar unto God, who answered me in the day of my distress, and
was with me in the way which I went. (Genesis 35:1–3)

Behind this passage of Scripture lie the hopes and heartbreaks
of twenty-five years. Behind this passage there is the story of a
man's journey through the years, his high confidence in himself,
his shrewd dealings with family and friends. Behind this passage
rests the experience of a man who found, when all was said and
done, that he needed God if he was going to make life's journey
a victory march.

Jacob, you see, was a rascal, a smooth-talking, quick-thinking
slicker. Now there are reasons why he was that way. He was, to
be honest, partly the victim of a bad environment. There was a
kind of division in his family. His father showed favoritism to
one child while his mother favored the other child. As a matter
of fact, his mother taught him to cheat in order to get ahead. I
mention this to say that a person is never what he is alone. Others
contribute to his faults and failures. Those who are responsible
for warping people ought not excuse themselves; at the same time,
those who are disadvantaged ought not to use their liabilities as
excuses. A person can rise above circumstances and advance to
the stars through difficulties. As my old high school motto had it,
"Ad astra per aspera" — "To the stars through adversity."

16

Jacob was a real smart, smooth, slick operator. It wasn't that he had not met God, but he just believed that he had enough brains and enough shrewdness to make it by himself. Oh, in an emergency Jacob looked to God, but only in an emergency. Like, for instance, that night when he realized he was a fugitive and a wanderer. Jacob's mother had helped him deceive his blind father and rob his brother, Esau, of his heirship as the eldest of the family. Jacob, smooth of skin, had put goatskins on his arms to imitate the hairy arms of Esau. He brought to his father meat prepared to resemble in taste the venison which Isaac, the father, had requested of his hunter son, Esau. The father, old and blind, was suspicious. He said, "The voice is the voice of Jacob, but the hands are the hands of Esau" (see Genesis 27:22). Reassured, he gave Jacob Esau's blessings and rights of precedence and priority. Esau naturally was angry and vowed to kill his brother. Jacob fled his native country as a fugitive and an outlaw.

His shrewdness had trapped him. As night fell, Jacob realized that he was indeed a hunted wanderer. He pitched camp and gathered a stone which he would use as a pillow. Sitting alone in the darkness, a great loneliness came over Jacob and a terrible fear. No friends, no blood family, no home, no comforts, no roots, an uncertain future. Jacob called on the God of his fathers. That night a ladder appeared whose bottom touched the earth and whose top disappeared in the heavens. Angels trafficked between earth and glory. Above the ladder God appeared and spoke to Jacob, "I am the Lord God of Abraham.... I am with thee, and will keep thee" (Genesis 28:12–13, 15). Jacob woke up and said, "Surely the Lord is in this place; and I knew it not.... How dreadful [awesome] is this place! this is none other than the house of God, and this is the gate of heaven" (Genesis 28:16–17). Then Jacob took the stone which had been his pillow, anointed it in an act of dedication, and called that place Bethel, the house of God. In the strength of that experience of God, Jacob traveled on his journey. He found lodging with Laban in Haran and began to prosper. His old wily shrewdness came back to him, and the

memory of Bethel began to fade in his mind. It seemed so long
ago that God was real in his life; the event of God's dealing with
Jacob seemed so far away. Bethel faded from memory.

What a striking similarity this man has to so many who listen to me now. Almost all of us have come to some hard and
nigh impossible hour, and we have called upon God and asked
him to please deliver us. Some of us have said that if from that
circumstance, if out of that pit he would deliver us, we would
serve him all the days of our lives. He would be our God and we
would be his children. And, indeed, he did show us his power.
That was Bethel — house of God, time of the showing of God's
love — that was Bethel, where God was real in our lives. That
was Bethel, where God spoke peace to our troubled spirits. That
was Bethel, where God claimed us for his own. How precious
was that hour, how sweet the experience, what calm crossed our
souls, what buoyant power we felt. That was Bethel!

The emergency passed, as it did with Jacob. So very many of
us have allowed the memory to slip away and to grow dim. It
was a kind of "foxhole religion" we had, an emergency faith, a
vow in extremity. The trouble passed, and our love of the Lord
grew cool and distant. Some moved from some distant place but
found here in a great city the allurements of the world and the
blandishments of pleasure, and the memory of Bethel has grown
dim and hazy. It looks like things might turn out right if we are
smart enough to make them turn out right. It seems that we are
almost able to make it by ourselves. We may still attend church,
but Bethel is dead in our hearts. I mean we sit in church houses,
but we are not experiencing the fiery presence of the living God.
Goodbye, God, I am a New Yorker now!

It has been so long since some of you have heard clearly the
voice of God. Sometimes it seems that he is about to say something in our lives, but there are so many things to do. Sometimes
we hear a knock, but the television is on. Sometimes there is a
sound like the whisper of God, but we've made some other plans.
And we figure we can make it on our own shrewdness. We know

the daily doubles and the numbers and we read the ads and we know a fellow who can get things for us.

It always seemed to Jacob that he was about to make his grand killing, to land his ship, to find his pot of gold at the end of the rainbow. The answer always seemed so close, but he could never quite make it. It seemed that Laban, for whom he worked, was a pretty thick-witted fellow and he could get a wife and fortune from that desert sheikh. But it never quite happens that way. Jacob was disappointed in his bargain to win Rachel, his wife. Seven long years he worked and then had to work seven more. Everything seemed so clear, except that things never quite worked out. Oh, he could see where he had made one slip-up in his strategy — one more chance, though, and with the correction of that minor slip-up he would be in clover. Only it did not work. Some little unforeseen error in judgment kept creeping in. The world leads us that way. It keeps promising, just over the next hill is the prize. Or if it had not been for this or that, everything would have worked out. Why don't you get smart and realize that it never is going to work out until God works it out?

On and on through the years went Jacob with his plans never working out and his soul always restless. He got his wife Rachel, but there was a horrible feud with his father-in-law. He got cattle and property, but he had to keep moving. Laban was pursuing him. He was able at Mizpah to settle his difference with Laban, but he still wanted to go home, but there was Esau whom he had wronged twenty-odd years before. He settled with Esau and thought that everything was well. He settled in Shechem, and then trouble broke out in his family.

A daughter, Dinah, started an affair with a lad of the town. Her brothers, feeling she had been taken advantage of by this young man, killed him. The old fear came over Jacob again. Finally he began seeing it! Things were never going to work out for him; he was never going to have peace because he had wandered so far from God. Oh, he prayed, but only by habit. God was not real in his life. He went through the ceremonies of his fathers, but

God was not real in his life. Then Jacob made the decision which changed his life. He decided he would go back to live at Bethel, where he had found God. He would go back to Bethel, where the light had broken on his pathway. He would go back to Bethel, where the promises were made. He would admit that he was not smart, he needed God, and so Jacob went back to Bethel. It was his way of saying:

> I need thee, O I need thee,
> Every hour I need thee,
> O bless me now, my Savior
> I come to thee.

He said to his family, "We are going back to where God was real. We are going back to where God spoke."

Oh, I know we cannot go back physically to those places and scenes where God spoke to us. Some of us can, but others cannot. For some of us the gates have closed. At the house where I learned of God, I turned the key in the lock one day as the last member of my family to close that door. We can't go back in body. The church in which I first met the Lord is torn down. We can't go back physically, and we mustn't confuse sentimental feeling with a true religious experience. We can go back in Spirit and start over where we left God. We can go back in Spirit and acknowledge we have done wrong and ask that our guilt be pardoned. God draws us back to Bethel. Every person needs a Bethel — a house of God. Every person needs a sanctuary where the world's noise cannot reach. Every person needs a hiding place where the hounds of hell cannot track him. Sometimes it is a place and a church, sometimes a pew. Sometimes the sanctuary is a hymn whose music conducts us into the presence of God. Jesus had a sanctuary. When trouble rose, he would say, "Wait here awhile." Beneath the stars he would renew his covenant with God. "Wait here awhile." God be thanked that there is the house of God. Call it what you will: church, Bethel, Rock of Ages, hiding place, sanctuary, secret altar. Call it what you will. Thank God when trouble is on our trail, we can say to it, "Wait here awhile." Let me go to Bethel — to where

God can talk to me. When problems baffle the soul we can say, "Wait here awhile." Let me go to Bethel, where God can talk to me. God will hear, God will answer me, God will help me, God will deliver me, God will guide. Let us all arise as this September comes and come back to God's house. Let us put aside the idols, bury them, and come to where God is. We can say

> I've wandered far away from God,
> Now I'm coming home.
> The paths of sin too long I've trod,
> Lord, I'm coming home.
> Open wide thine arms of love,
> Lord, I'm coming home.
> Coming home, coming home, never more to roam.

ᮝ 3 ᮝ

MT. NEBO: THE MOUNT OF MYSTERY

May 23, 1965

And Moses went up from the plains of Moab, unto the mountain of Nebo, to the top of Pisgah, that is over against Jericho. And the LORD shewed him all the land of Gilead, unto Dan,... So Moses the servant of the LORD died there in the land of Moab, according to the word of the LORD. And he buried him in a valley in the land of Moab, over against Bethpeor, but no man knoweth of his sepulchre unto this day. (Deuteronomy 34:1,5–6)

Our generation does not like mysteries, other than detective stories on TV or in novels. Once we could truly sing with appreciation, "Ah, Sweet Mystery of Life," but no longer. Recoiling, I suppose, from primitive mystery, myths, superstitions, and the like, we have thrown the baby out with the bathwater. We do not feel comfortable around any mystery. We do not discuss the strange goings-on of hope and fear and worship within us because these are mysterious things. They defy formulation and will not submit to our logic. We are impatient and fretful in the presence of anything we do not understand. We give to such enigmas and puzzles long Latin names, as if we have explained them, and then declare ourselves no longer interested. What ought to give awe and enchantment to our lives, we abhor as being unworthy of so smart a generation.

It is no good. Life is full of mystery, the unknown, and as far as we are presently concerned, the unknowable. Mystery looms large and formidable at both ends of our existence. The biologists, physiologists, and the like have elaborate explanations of cohabitation by our parents, conception by our mothers, and birth following pregnancy. But every birth, how in an act of love

22

characteristics can be transmitted from one generation to another and human life start all over again, is a mystery.

The beginning of the earth is a mystery. The public press this week carried an account of some discovery of particles in the universe which may prove that our universe is ten billion years old. This staggers the imagination and removes by several billion years the primal mystery. How did God bring the earth to pass? What was the implementation in actuality of his word of inauguration, "Let there be light" (Genesis 1:3)?

There lurks, of course, over all humanity the mystery of what lies beyond life. Years ago, as a boy, I read a book by John McNeil, to whose pulpit in Canada I have since had the honor to be invited. It was entitled "Many Mansions." In it he spoke of an incident when the gospel was first carried to the shores of England. Hearing the gospel in the great banquet hall of one of those massive castles whose ruins dot the English countryside, the master of the castle in Northumberland broke in upon the preacher with the question, "Does the new religion have anything to say about death?" "We know," went on the nobleman, "that we are like swallows that enter a room beyond whose threshold there is darkness, fly a bit in the lighted room, and then exit out another door where darkness reigns beyond its threshold. What about the darkness? Does the new religion have anything to say about that?" The old Duke of Northumberland had asked a fitting and proper question, for wherever people have thought seriously about the issues of life, they have brooded upon the mystery of death.

Jesus honored the place of mystery in our lives on at least two occasions. Nicodemus, like most worldly men with scholarly backgrounds, abhorred and shrank back from mystery. "How can these things be?" he asked of Jesus when told about the necessity of a fresh birth of the Spirit. The reply of Jesus was less than satisfying to a purely pragmatic mind, "The wind bloweth where it listeth" (John 3:8). In other words, it moves wherever it will. On another day our Lord confessed a reverent agnosticism, a devout ignorance, an uncynical "I don't know." He spoke of a fearful turn of events when there would be "signs in the sun and in the moon, nations rising against nations, and men's hearts failing them for fear." The graphic description of the onrushing divine drama gripped the imaginations of the disciples. Awestruck, they asked, "When shall these things be?" Jesus honored the presence of the unknown mystery in our lives with His answer, "Of that hour no man knoweth save the Father" (see Matthew 24).

Today we look at Mt. Nebo, rising sheer and majestic above the plains of Moab. It lies but six miles as the crow flies from the land of Canaan, the Promised Land toward which the children of Israel had journeyed so long under the leadership of Moses, the deliverer. But Moses is not to enter the land of promise. He receives from God a message that the old warrior must lay down his mantle of leadership. God promises his servant that he will carry him up into the heights of Pisgah, the summit of Nebo, and let him see the land toward which he had journeyed so long and for whose welcome hills he had labored so long.

God said to him, so runs the old account, that because he had sinned at Meribah, where the children cried for water and Moses, angered, lost his temper before the people, he would not be allowed to go over Jordan. Ah, we protest, how severe a judgment for what appears so trivial an offense. Moses had said to the people, "Drink, you rebels." But there must have been such violent anger and bitterness in his voice that God counted it a barrier to his crossing over Jordan into Canaan's fair and happy land.

Thus Mt. Nebo brings us to the mystery of sin. I do not know how it slipped into the world. In a world made by God, the origin of sin is a mystery. I cannot describe what sin looks like, but I can describe its results. It is fatal like leprosy, if unchecked. Wasn't I being told this very week in San Francisco of a man I knew when we were children as a shy and gentle lad, but who now languishes in a jail cell having murdered his wife, a successful research technician, and how two lovely children are without a mother and a father? Why is it that some persist in ungodliness in our human relations, bigots to bedevil our own land and make what would be a blessed country an ugliness, a stench, a people who dare not stand together? Over and over again, I see in deserted houses and wrecked careers, in broken homes and shattered dreams the results of sin's dreadful work. What is it? A sex impulse, the puritan cries. What is it? A power drive, one school of psychology answers. What is it? A cultural lag, the sociologist says. "An enemy," says Jesus.

Sin is a mystery, but it stopped Moses from entering the land of promise. We may protest that this seemed all too harsh a penalty for the wrong. With Gilbert and Sullivan we appeal, "Let the punishment fit the crime." What we must remember is that the nobler the soul, the more grievous and serious the failing. Let every child of God beware! We cannot afford to be found guilty of acts and practices which those outside the fellowship of Jesus Christ can do without the flicker of an eye. I have prayed to God, and pray to him still, to save me from shaming the people of God and dishonoring dear Jesus Christ in whose service I have received so many blessings. Let us never forget that each of us carries the honor of our Lord and Savior. A spot of mud on a soiled garment will cause no notice; put that spot of mud on a white and laundered cloth, and it will show horribly. So it is with us.

Moses climbs Mt. Nebo to view the Promised Land, but that mount will be his burial place. How sad, we think at first, that this grizzled old leader of his people, his eyes still not dimmed and his back still not bent, should come so close to the land of promise, see it in the distance, behold its fair promise and rugged beauty, only to be denied admission to its happy borders. Here we have the mystery of life's work begun and cut off before we see its fulfillment. When we see Moses standing in Pisgah's lofty height and beholding a land upon which his feet will never walk, we are beholding the mystery of life, our summons to causes so big that we cannot hope to see them fulfilled.

At first, we are sad that Moses did not get to the Promised Land, but, on second thought, a man's reach, as Browning said, "ought to exceed his grasp." We ought to be a part of purposes so huge that we cannot hope to see them all fulfilled. This is the mystery of parenthood. We are made to commit ourselves in our children to a future we shall never see with these physical eyes. We look at them, young and immature now, but sometimes we think of them when they will have come to the full noontide of their powers. We shall not by and large be spared to see them then, but thank God that we can work in that immortal material whose end and flower we cannot see.

It is a mystery, a blessed mystery, of how God does give us the capacity, the unselfishness to participate in efforts and causes whose fulfillment must lie so far beyond our mortal span. We remember those who knew they would not "come to the place for which our fathers sighed." I think now of people I have known here who were with us when fire destroyed our old building. I think of their faithfulness, though the sun or their time in the earth was already sinking on their heads. They knew, some of them, that they would never walk within these walls or worship in this sanctuary, but they gave and served and died without seeing the fruit of their labors. So our dreams must roam far beyond our lifetime, and it must, please God, be said of us, "These all died in faith, not having received the promises, but having seen them afar off" (Hebrews 11:13).

I find endless fascination in the mystery of Moses' unknown grave. The text says that God "buried him in a valley in Moab, but no man knoweth of his sepulchre until this day." Look at this veteran in the service of Jehovah. He is a lonely figure, for his generation lies sleeping in the desert sands. He is surrounded by a new crowd; familiar faces have vanished. Moses' life has been a life of great latitudes with God. At Horeb, Moses and God had been alone when Moses saw the burning bush and heard the voice of God calling him to his life's work. At Sinai God and Moses had been alone when the imperishable law had been delivered. And now God calls him to the mystery of death.

I watch him as he takes his staff and starts his climb up Nebo's side. Look at him as he marches up the mountain. Below stand the people he loves, above God who calls him. "Up the lonely mountain he climbs. Still on he goes as he becomes a tiny figure upon the slope. Higher yet he ascends to where the meteors shoot. Higher yet he climbs to where the clouds form, higher yet to where the lightnings are loosed. Moses lifts his eyes across Jordan and sees the rolling uplands of Gilead; across the deep gash where Jordan's waters roll, glimpses the blue hills of Galilee. His eyes turn southward, and he sees the stony summits of Judea and Jerusalem, and through a gap in distant Mt. Carmel, he sees the gleam of the sea like the glint of sunlight on a warrior's armor. Then in that high moment in the savage uplands, death flings out its long shadow." But God is there in the mystery. The God who called him in Horeb's dusty fields is there. The God who guided him before Pharaoh's face is there. The God whose death angel passed over Israel's huts, where the blood was sprinkled on the doorposts, was there. The God who gave him and his people a pillar of cloud by day and a pillar of fire by night was there. Somewhere in the savage cliffs of Nebo, God rocked his servant to sleep, God dug his grave in a cleft, angels were his pallbearers, and God carried his servant home.

There are mysteries around these lives, but God will be there. There are heights of ultimate solitude where neither family nor friend can go with us, but God will be there. If there will be no hand to clasp ours as we pass through the darkness, God will hold us in "the hollow of his hand" (Isaiah 40:12).

And so Moses, up alone with the stars and the sky and the everlasting mountains, was carried home by God. And so may we pray and march and serve....

> 'Til from Mt. Pisgah's lofty height
> I view my home and take my flight,
> And shout while passing through the air
> Farewell, farewell, sweet hour of prayer.

ᔕ 4 ᔐ

MEN'S SCHEMES AND GOD'S PLANS

August 6, 1967

But as for you, ye thought evil against me; but God meant it unto good, to bring to pass, as it is this day, to save much people alive. (Genesis 50:20)

I have a general rule, as I intimated lecturing to a fine company of preachers at Virginia Union University the week past, that a preacher does not have much going for him in an illustration if it has to be explained. Something is wrong in the first case if it cannot stand on its own. I must violate that rule, somewhat, and try to explain a slight curve in the subject "Men's Schemes and God's Plans."

It all goes back to my childhood; so much does as we get older, doesn't it? That gifted old African preacher under whom I was privileged to sit used to talk much about the "scheme of redemption." I wondered much about that term, since already it was clear to me that the word *scheme* has a sinister and ugly suggestion to the American ear. Among us, "scheme" means some plot, a shrewd plan. In other English-speaking lands, however, the word *scheme* does not hint of anything ugly or underhand. We read in foreign papers of the "government scheme" or a "building scheme," all quite honorable.

I am using the term "men's schemes" in the ugly, American sense of the term. We have little sly and sometimes huge, sinister, self-seeking aims which we plot to bring off. This is "scheme" the way I want to use the word. And our little anthills of schemes are up against the mighty mountains of God's great plans. You have to decide how such a confrontation is bound to end. Men's schemes, sly, devious, selfish, are often up against God's plans, splendid, divine, majestic. It is of such a case I speak today — Joseph, sold into slavery by his envious brethren, becomes a great man and is delivered by the will of God. This sermon was suggested by the play given last Sunday evening at the commencement of our daily vacation Bible school.

Few accounts in the Old Testament are so loaded with the stuff of human life as the story of Joseph. I can still remember summer evenings on a porch where I grew up, and my mother, who is present this morning, reading from a purple-back book, *Great Stories of The Bible: Illustrated for Children,* and a little boy's wild excitement at the story of Joseph.

Joseph's brethren sell him into slavery in a strange and distant land. The lad, so loved by his father, was accustomed to the craggy hills of Canaan and must as a bondservant become accustomed to the alluvial flatlands of Egypt. He perseveres through trials and changing circumstances. He knows favor and disfavor, but bit by bit and step by step the young lad rises to a place of prominence in the life of the land where his lot is cast. A hand, not human, seems to be ordering his destiny and directing his footsteps.

In a great famine, Joseph's foresight, apparently more than the educated guess of a smart man, gains his promotion to chairman of Egypt's food program. The same famine, for in life one man's medicine is another man's poison, which lifts Joseph to a place of power reduces his brothers who had sold him into slavery and their grieving father into abject and desperate need. The father, Jacob, hard put for food to keep his family, hears a rumor along the trade routes borne by Bedouin travelers that Egypt seems to have not been so desperately affected. Jacob tells his sons, "There is corn in Egypt" (Genesis 42:1). He little knows that the man in charge is the lad he loved so much as a child and to whom he had given a coat of many colors.

Some of the children are dispatched to Egypt to seek corn. We never know when we set out on a journey where we are going or whom we are going to meet. For on every journey there is an unseen traveler and at the end of every journey there is an unknown figure, God. He is never absent, though sometimes he seems to disappear. The brothers stand before Joseph pleading for food to carry to their father.

When they have appeared before Joseph, he recognizes them. With great effort, he restrains himself until he can bear it no longer. Joseph then has his aides and servants leave the room. Great sobs shake the well-groomed minister of food in Egypt. Joseph weeps so passionately that his sobs are heard in the house of Pharaoh. He tells these Israelite petitioners, "I am Joseph." And then a question which had haunted him by day and by night leaps from his lips like an anguished cry, "Does my father still live?" How is it with the family? A great moment of reconciliation and forgiveness occurs. He tells them all is forgiven. "It was God who sent me hither to go before you to prepare a great deliverance," he might have said. The father is brought to Egypt.

The family is reunited, but then the circumstances are altered again, the scene changes. Jacob the father dies. The family gathers around. The offices for the dead are performed. The period of mourning proceeds, the brothers carry the father's remains back to the old home place, and they lay him to rest in the cave at Machpelah, where his father Isaac lay with his father, in the cave of the field of Machpelah which Abraham first bought as a place to bury Sarah.

Most funerals are mixtures of many things. Some survivors are thinking of what they are going to get and some about how the passing of their relative or friend will alter their own status. So at Jacob's funeral, Joseph's brothers were wondering whether Jacob's death would affect how Joseph thought of them (Genesis 50:15). They petitioned him about their own status, for though forgiven they were hounded in memory by what they had done long years ago. That old deed of selfish envy continued to haunt them.

The past keeps coming back. Dr. Fosdick long years ago told of a muddy road in Vermont where the sign said, "Choose well your ruts. You will be in them for the next five miles." Those of us who began driving when there were muddy roads will know what he was talking about. It is so important for young people to realize that what choices they make now will affect and influence their lives forever. On the campus of Virginia Union University this week past, I thought of Dr. J. A. Bacoats, my own college president, who was trained there, and how he used to quote George Rice Hovey, whose name is still a legend at Union. "What you are tomorrow will largely depend on what you are today."

Mistakes keep coming back. This is the plight of America. William Styron, commenting upon a new book not yet released, says, "The Negro is the major factor in American history." How strange that a once slave people, only 10 percent of the population, should become the one continuing theme and issue of the nation's reflection and the republic's action. Now we are witnessing a great upheaval variously called "riots," "insurrections," "rebellions," "guerilla warfare." Most of what is transpiring is due to the fact that the past keeps haunting us, unless by some truly costly and purging act, some deed of penance, some act of restitution and cleansing, we are able to expunge the error and make it right. This, at another level, is what the gospel is all about.

C. L. Sulzberger points out in an article posted from Aspen, Colorado, that America is a giant, but a sick giant. There is the gravest uncertainty of whether we are morally right in being in Vietnam at all. A disproportionate number of the young men fighting there are Negroes. Many of them will be coming home, trained to use the most modern weapons, skilled in subversion, having been taught by their country to become accustomed to the sight of violent death. If the nation is still delinquent in its democratic promises by the time they get home and their frustrations are played upon by the merchants of violence, what will happen?

We are hearing increasing talk of repression, antiriot laws, and increased police power as the answer to the national plight. Now this is in the face of the fact that people seem ready to die at the hands of those forces of firepower already at hand. Carry this to its conclusion. Is the white community prepared to follow its policy of containment to its logical conclusion? Extermination of twenty million people could perhaps be accomplished, but what would happen to the nation's soul and what would its enemies do? The black community would hardly accept this without some attempt at defense.

Negroes have a fearful decision to make. Is the plight of black people in America, granting the deprivations, of a nature to warrant the destruction of the whole fabric of the American society? We need some means of cleansing our past within the framework of our common commitment to this land. Under God, whites need to admit their failure to let justice run down as a mighty stream. Black Americans need to confess that they have not employed their opportunity to its maximum. We need them to take each other's hand in this country and openly admit our prejudices and hostility, ask God for guidance and go forward, making black destructionists and white segregationists feel the weight of the nation's condemnation.

Joseph's brethren nervously appeared before him. Their old scheme was still fresh in their memory. They had done wrong. Again Joseph rises to magnificent heights of true greatness. Wronged, he appealed to God. "Fear not: for am I in the place of God?" (Genesis 50:19). We take too much in our hands. God will reward, and God will punish. The issues of life are finally in God's hands. We must learn to appeal to him.

And then Joseph said he had seen through the long years the hand of God. They had schemed, but God had planned. Their schemes and God's plan were not two separate things. God took their scheme and breathed on it his plan. This is why a Christian is unbeatable. My father used to say, "The harder you slam the Christian to the ground, like a rubber ball the higher he bounces." When people try to hurt us, God takes the scheme of hurting and makes it heal. When people talk about God's people, they advertise them and draw attention to the children of God. Like Joseph, we must be ready to say, "That's all right. My case is in God's hand. He can destroy, and he will defend." Like Joseph, we must be able to say, "I'll turn my case over to God. I've left this hurt, that wrong in God's hands. Talk to him." Like Joseph, when the night is darkest we must see preparation for the morning. Like Joseph, when the load of trouble is laid on us, we must see the means whereby we are being stabilized. In all things look to God, expect to see his hand, expect his deliverance.

ᗏ 5 ᗌ

A QUESTION WHICH REQUIRES
A QUESTION

October 12, 1969

And as he journeyed, he came near Damascus: and suddenly there shined round about him a light from heaven: and he fell to the earth, and heard a voice saying unto him, Saul, Saul, why persecutest thou me? And he said, Who art thou, Lord? And the Lord said, I Am Jesus whom thou persecutest: it is hard for thee to kick against the pricks. And he trembling and astonished said, Lord, what wilt thou have me to do? (Acts 9:3–6)

There was this man on the road from Jerusalem to Damascus. He hated Christians, and he put his hate to work. Saul, who was born in Tarsus and trained in the rabbinical school of the celebrated Pharisee scholar, Gamaliel, was an activist. For him to think was to act, and to his mind this new, upstart sect of Jesus followers had to be hounded to earth, exposed, and destroyed by whatever means necessary.

That was why this man was on the road. Saul had already created what havoc he could among the Jerusalem church, entering into the houses in Jerusalem of those suspected of being followers of Jesus, routing the suspects out and hauling them off to prison. This scattered the Christian community in what became the first evangelism campaign, for as they went they told of what a wonderful change in their lives had been wrought since Jesus had come into their hearts.

Hearing that a number of the Christian community had gone off to Damascus, Saul went to the high priest and secured letters of authority, letters which gave Saul the right, if he found any of this way of Jesus, to bring them bound to Jerusalem for trial. This was why this man was on the road to Damascus.

There was another on the same road which Saul traveled. His name was Jesus, the Son of God, the express Wisdom of God the Father. As Saul journeyed, the other waited for him that they might have a confrontation. No one travels any road of life without meeting this other One. Some may say that they have never had any kind of experience of God, but this is not true. There is a light that "lighteth every man who cometh into the world" (John 1:9). On life's road we meet the Lord. He wears disguises. Sometimes he is a beggar like Lazarus at the gates of plenty, but God is on the road we travel. Sometimes he is a poor, beaten Samaritan, but God is on the road. I do not know how many ways or the number of times each of us has been confronted by him, but he is on the road you and I travel. Sometimes he appears as joy, sometimes as sorrow. Sometimes he is present at weddings and when babies are blessed, but he is on the road.

Perhaps that is the key word of our time together this morning. God is on your road. Sometimes he seeks us where the road is smooth and straight and the scenery is green and pleasant. In our blessings and the joy of living, God crosses our pathway that we might remember to give thanks unto him who is the Author of every good and perfect gift. He meets us sometimes on our road where the way is slippery and dangerous and our footing becomes hazardous and uncertain. These are the times when we reach out for a hand to hold ours while we try to keep our balance. Finding that hand strong and steady, we pass on safely to firm ground and are able to say:

> Through many dangers, toils, and snares
> I have already come.
> 'Twas grace that brought me safe thus far,
> And grace will lead me home.

As Saul traveled his road to Damascus, he met another who wanted to put him on the road to life. As the intense light fell bright and blinding around him, Saul was knocked to the ground, likely to his knees. It was beyond question the best fall he ever had. The Scriptures say that "pride goeth before a fall"; sometimes a fall is necessary to get us on our knees so we can really get back on our feet. If you have had a disappointment or your dreams have turned to ashes and dust in your hands, you may right now be in the best condition you have ever been to start really living. Last Sunday commemorated, I started to say celebrated, our fire here years ago which wiped out our old sanctuary. Now nobody would want a fire, and heaven knows we feel that one a lifetime is more than enough. I must say that I do not know anything that did this church so much good, spiritually and materially, as that fire in bringing us together as a people standing in need of prayer, called on to sacrifice, sorting out what was real from what was counterfeit in our congregation's life, yes, and sorting out who was real from who was fake among us. God has his ways, and when the blow falls, flinch, yes, but do try to take it as Jesus took the bitter cup and turned to us with a brave confidence, saying, "The cup which my Father hath given me, shall I not drink it?" (John 18:11).

As Saul fell to the ground he reports that he heard a voice, a question, "Saul, why persecutest thou me?" What identification with his own people! Notice then, if you will, that the question was not "Why do you persecute my disciples?" but "Why do you persecute me?" This makes God as we have known him in Christ not merely interested in us but identified with us. "In all their affliction he was afflicted" (Isaiah 63:9). "Inasmuch as ye have done it unto one of the least of these my brethren, ye have done it unto me" (Matthew 25:40). I must confess that I find it more difficult to visit and minister to people who have been indifferent to the church's needs and obviously lukewarm in their loyalty to Jesus Christ. At such times, I find the will to go by reminding myself that, after all, I am not doing whatever it is because of the person but because of Jesus Christ.

"Why persecutest thou me?" "Who art thou, Lord?" If Saul had wanted to stay on the road to Damascus with the same letters of authority to destroy the church and with the same zeal to stamp out the people of Christ, he should never have asked that question. If you want to steer clear of the Lord, if you do not want to be upset and shaken up and turned around, then stay as far away from that question as you can.... "Who art thou, Lord?"

Who is Jesus? That question will get you in trouble. Historically he has made more difference in the world than anybody who has ever lived. At birth he turned a cattle stall into a royal nursery. At twelve years of age he made learned doctors talk about the eternal things of God which mattered before the sun began to shine or the sea began to roll and which will matter when blazing planets are cold in death, the moon runs down in a crimson stream, and the sun refuses to shine. At thirty, he turned the muddy stream of Jordan into holy water as he bowed to John's baptism. Who is Jesus? He made children centrally important. In his name, hospitals have opened to heal the sick; in his name, schools have opened to lift the veil of ignorance from his children's minds. To this black people must give assent. Hard has been our way in this land. How much harder would it have been if in Jesus' name there had not been colleges like Morehouse, Bishop, Leland, Livingstone, Paine, Wilberforce, Morris Brown, Johnson C. Smith? Where would you be? Could I stand here? Who is Jesus? In his name, men have built hospitals in lands long plagued with disease and women have gone to serve among those with leprous sores.

Who is Jesus? On Friday evening [October 10, 1969], I spoke in the Pavilion Caprice in the Netherland Hilton Hotel in Cincinnati. In the dinner audience were prelates of the church, Catholic and Protestant — one Catholic priest who had been for twenty-three years head of the doctor of sacred theology program at the Vatican — officials of Proctor and Gamble, the president of the University of Cincinnati, the mayor of the city of Cincinnati, the city solicitor, a member of the United States Congress, and maybe above all, hundreds upon hundreds of God's people. No, they were not there primarily to hear me but to honor our friend,

Dr. L. V. Booth. When the ceremonies were over, Dr. Booth stood to respond to the great and glittering reception. He said before all that distinguished assembly that his journey through life had been due mainly to his parents, who led him to the little white church and to the little red schoolhouse. He was talking, really, about Jesus whose church it was and who inspired the school. No, if you don't want to have anything to do with Jesus, don't ask who he is.

Saul made that mistake. He asked, "Who art thou?" The answer came back, "I am Jesus." Oh, what an answer. Whole worlds are contained in that answer, "I am Jesus" — the desire of all nations, the hope of the ends of the earth, the Sun of righteousness risen with healing in his wings, the breath and wisdom of God. "I am Jesus," Mary's baby, the firstborn of many brethren, the man of sorrow and acquainted with grief. "I am Jesus," the first and last, to millions a bright and morning star. "I am Jesus" — the road home for the weary pilgrim, the way back for the lost prodigal. "I am Jesus," the second Adam who is God's answer to the first Adam's transgression, the Resurrection and the Life, the Ransom Price for all believers at the gates of hell. "I am Jesus" — Mediator of a new covenant, a second Lawgiver, greater than Moses, whose day Abraham rejoiced to see. God's answer to sin's charge, God's reply to death's threat, heaven's bridge over hell's troubled waters.

> Jesus, my Lord, I know his name,
> His name is all my boast
> He will not put my soul to shame
> Nor let my hopes be lost.

Well, when Saul got the answer to his question, he was forced to ask a second question. For when one asks who is Jesus and gets an answer, the first question requires a second one. "Lord, what will you have me do?" In other words, Saul was saying that for the first time he had met him who has the right to be his Lord, to own his life and to order his days, to be his Commander and his Master, his Teacher, his Guide, his King, the Object of his devotion and affection. "Lord, I asked the question as to who you are, and having received the answer, I know now where my life ought to be spent and in whose service. Lord, what will you have me to do? Have thine own way. Order me."

Heaven knows it is the greatest day in your life when you say to the Lord, "Take my life." I knew a boy in the cypress swamps forty years ago who said to the Lord, "Take my life. Tell me what you want me to do." I'm not going to hide this thing; I was that boy. It wasn't much, I guess, looking back, to offer the Lord. I never went to a school where there was grass or playground equipment. I had to travel past a school two blocks from my house to get to the school where I could enter the doors, but I said to Jesus, "Take my life." I could not go into any city library to read, though I had a great hunger for books, but I told the Lord to take my life and if he could do anything with it, I'd be willing to try. He has so richly blessed my life. I can say that you don't need to ask any question beyond the second one. Ask the first, "Who art thou, Lord?" and then, receiving that answer, there is the other you must ask, "Lord, what will you have me to do?" I must testify that he answers that and every other question.

\sim 6 \sim

Updating the New Birth

December 7, 1969

Being born again, not of corruptible seed, but of incorruptible, by
the word of God, which liveth and abideth for ever. (1 Peter 1:23)

When television reported the recent sale of a fantastically priced
diamond to whose fame Richard Burton and Elizabeth Taylor
contributed greatly by their bidding and purchase, the man from
Parke Benet galleries was shown holding the diamond in his trembling hand. One of the commentators asked the Parke Benet man
if his hand trembled because the diamond was worth so much
money. With something of a wry smile the man holding the diamond replied, "No, I enjoy moving the diamond about in the
light, which brings out the various sparkles and colors of the
stone." The various angles of light did not change the stone; they
showed different aspects of it.

Truth is like that, for it does not change. Truth is eternal, and
not subject to the vogue of the moment or the voices of the mob.
At the same time we must examine every truth again and again.
For different times will throw differing lights on the same, un-
changing truth, making it show forth varying hues and colors,
though truth's basic makeup continues unaltered and unalterable.

One of the pillars of Christian faith is the doctrine of the new
birth. Many of us heard that doctrine declared with a firm finality by our elders, who spoke of being "borned again." Again
and again in this way and that the New Testament speaks of
a deep and radical change, a fresh and different way of seeing
things, a dismantling and a reconstituting of humanity's nature,
outlook, love, loyalty, and life which we have come to call the
new birth. It was of this Jesus spoke to Nicodemus in the quiet

40

shadows of a Jerusalem evening. The eyes of the doctor of law kept widening incredulously and yet wistfully and hopefully, as Jesus quietly, persistently pressed home the strange, revolutionary, exciting claim that old ways can be traded for new ways. Three times in that fateful conversation in the gentle evening light, the Lord of life pressed home to the man in search of a better life the word that a person can be a new creature, even when he is old. Three times Jesus states this condition for entrance into God's kingdom here and hereafter, "Except a man be born again, he cannot see the kingdom of God" (John 3:3).

Paul takes up that theme of a new birth and reports it with an intensity and an intimacy so vivid and so determined that it sounds like an autobiographical slice of his life, torn loose from the whole loaf of the man's being. To the Corinthians he was saying, "If any man be in Christ, he is a new creature: old things are passed away; behold, all things are become new" (2 Corinthians 5:17). And then to the Galatians the same note is sounded like a trumpet blast, "For in Christ Jesus neither circumcision availeth anything, nor uncircumcision, but a new creature" (Galatians 6:15). And then, there is my text from the epistle of hope, which John Calvin called an epistle "truly worthy of the chief of the apostles." The author of this word of soul pilgrimage speaks to the little Christian community of one sure and stable foundation upon which their discipleship to Jesus Christ is solidly based. He says, "Being born again, not of corruptible seed, but of incorruptible, by the word of God, which liveth and abideth for ever."

Is the new birth some old, musty museum piece of a Christian doctrine hardly worthy of any serious consideration by Christians, or others, as our society hurtles today to within twenty-four days of the end of a decade and into the last thirty years of the twentieth century? Is there any use in our talking about this old and worn phrase, "the new birth," on December 7, anniversary day of the beginning of thirty years of almost interrupted warfare for this nation? Well, Paul Tillich said that if he were asked "to sum up the Christian message for our time in two words," he would say with Paul: "it is the message of a new creation." How so?

We need to be born again, and so many times in so many ways. This past week I spent several days at the triennial assembly of the National Council of the Churches of Christ in America in Detroit. As might have been expected, the proceedings of the assembly were marked by very harsh rhetoric and repeated demonstrations on the part of the black caucus and those opposed to the war in Vietnam, with a great deal of which I was in total sympathy. On Thursday, there was a particularly biting denunciation of the National Council in general and of white Christians in particular. As I got on the elevator in the Pontchartrain Hotel following that session, a man who had been sitting near during the morning asked half-humorously and yet with great puzzlement, "What is a white liberal to do, where does he fit nowadays?"

That man's question belongs in some way to all of us; again and again we have to be born again. The old forms will not work. They wear out, become stale, tired, outdated, and must die. It was my privilege to be a part of the struggle for first-class citizenship in the early 1940s when, in my native state, black teachers were receiving scarcely one-third of what their white counterparts were receiving. School facilities for black children were unspeakably unequal to those for white youngsters. Our great cry then was "equalization." Now this was a right and proper contention, but God help anyone who finding that mold in 1943 could not see that that idea had to die. The times demanded a new birth to the idea of integration. Yes, and these times have demanded another new birth to the idea of self-identity. Time after time, a man must be born again, for as Russell Lowell had it:

> New occasions teach new duties;
> Time makes ancient good uncouth;
> They must upward still, and onward,
> Who would keep abreast of truth.

Yes, and again and again a church must be born again. This was one of the issues at the National Council sessions. All human institutions become self-intoxicated and self-perpetuating. In our preoccupation with our own prosperity and good reputation, a church is likely to reject Jesus Christ. There was a lad at Detroit this week, Jim Rubins by name. He is a member of the Dutch Reformed Church and seemed to me as I looked at him to be of the very highest ideals and devotion to Jesus Christ. He wanted to turn in his draft card to the National Council that it might hold the card in trust. This, of course, would make the council co-responsible, a coconspirator, if you wish to put it so, to Jim Rubins's refusal to participate in the Vietnam war. He and his young colleagues, children of the church of Jesus Christ, repeatedly.said, "We want to follow what you have taught us. We believe the word of Jesus, 'Blessed are the peace makers.' " The council tried, heard somewhere in the cry of these young people the voice of God, but then the voice of the budget, of how things will be supported and all that rose louder, and the council lowered its flag and failed to accept Jim Rubins's card. Sure, there is something to be said on both sides, but a church which ministers to those who fight as chaplains, etc., ought it not to minister to those who will not fight? Can one not hear Peter saying, "We must serve God rather than men"?

Our church here needs time after time to be born again. We tend to think more of our reputation than we do of our loyalty to Jesus Christ. We are likely to put more emphasis upon our size or our facilities than upon our service to the Lord of the church. If this be God's true church, he will give it again and again new birth, by the way of sorrow, by the way of pain, by the way of a blood-red path. We have seen it before in new birth by fire; we shall see it here again. God is going to test this church by trying its old ways and bringing it through great demands and deeper commitment, until we say again:

> Thy way, O Lord, not mine,
> Thy will be done, not mine,

Since thou for me didst bleed
And now doth intercede,
Each day I simply plead
Thy will be done.

Let me press that closer home yet. Each Christian has a time to
"turn, turn, turn," as Peter Jaeger sings. For most of us, we recognize a decisive moment when we publicly commit ourselves to the
way of Christ. It is the celebration of our new birth, of seizure by
spiritual Presence, by God, if you will. Nor would I minimize that
public declaration; we ask for it each Sunday here and will shortly
today. It is a great hour, and many of us can go back in hallowed
memory to when and where it happened, and on what day. Out
of that experience, sudden and dramatic or after long brooding,
there grew the words in our black religious life, "I looked at my
hands and my hands looked new."

Along with that we must die over and over again and be born
again and again. We are told that in the physical world, we are
indeed born once of our mother's wombs, but in the course of a
lifetime, our bodies renew themselves several times, so that at the
last we are indeed different physical bodies from what we were at
the first birth. The old body dies over and over again and is born
again and again.

So in the realm of the Spirit, there are in all of us characteristics
of the old creation: pride in our physical selves, in the beauty of
our countenance, and in the strength of our arms. That must die
in order for that beauty, which time cannot deface, to belong to
us. We must die to our physical attractiveness and be born again
to the beauty of the Lord. The old man who believes in retalia-
tion must die, and the new man must be born over and over again
who believes in the power of forgiveness. The old man who believes in his own knowledge, his own mental resources must die,
and again and again a new man must be born who knows that
"the fear of the LORD is the beginning of knowledge [wisdom]"
(Proverbs 1:7). Over and over again, the old man who believes in

his race alone, or his church alone, or his nation alone, must die, and there must be born again and again a new life who sees life as God sees it, whole, total, a unity.

Pride must die; a humble and contrite spirit must be born. Self-confidence must die, and a new blessed assurance which rests in God must be born. Such a soul will be crying over and over again as the swift rolling years fly by, "New born, new born again."

∽ 7 ∾

A SOUTH LAND AND SPRINGS OF WATER

April 5, 1970

And she said unto him, Give me a blessing: for thou hast given me a south land; give me also springs of water. And Caleb gave her the upper springs and the nether springs. (Judges 1:15)

It took me thirty years of Bible study to see this text and to see it come alive. Israel was in the process of trying to settle the land of Canaan. How interesting that all of these thousands of years later Israel is still trying to find a home in the land of Palestine. (I cannot dwell upon this interesting truth, except to stop to say that there is very little new under the sun.)

George Santayana commented that people who cannot remember the past are condemned to repeat it. It may be that even when we remember the past we still repeat it. At any rate what is happening today in Palestine was happening likewise thousands of years ago. Moses and Joshua were dead, and a new generation was trying to drive out the Canaanites and to take the Negeb, about which we hear, the dry country. Caleb and Joshua were the only ones who brought a report of confidence and hope when the spies had been sent by Moses to view the land. The Lord then said that only Joshua and Caleb would go over.

Now Joshua is dead, and only Caleb is left, and he is in the years of his old age. Caleb has a daughter, Achsah, whose hand in marriage he promises to that young man who would lead the Israelites to victory over the Canaanites. Othniel succeeded, and Caleb made a gift of the south land to his daughter as a dowry for her.

The south land which Caleb gave his daughter was very dry land. It lacked water and vegetation. It was rocky, not fertile. Perhaps Caleb did not have other available land for his daughter.

Perhaps he wanted Achsah and her husband, Othniel, not to have too much with which to start. In either case there will be many parents here who can understand Caleb's difficult situation.

Many parents have wanted to do, but lacked the means. Louise Merriwether's first novel will soon be published. I have had the privilege of reading an advance edition for review. It is called *My Daddy Was a Numbers Runner* and describes the heartbreaking story of a poor Harlem family who lived in and around 118th Street in the days of the Depression. It is the story of a young black girl growing up in the gutsy, raw life of a black ghetto. It is, also, the story of how a proud, and basically good, father's spirit is broken in his vain attempt to bring up his children and to keep his family together.

There will be parents here who have experienced in their own homes what it means not to be able to give to children what you would like for them to have. Others will remember the homes of their childhood where parents desperately desired to do for their children but just did not have the means. So! we can sympathize with Caleb if he did not have better to give his daughter.

It may be, as I have suggested, that Caleb did not want to ruin these young people by starting them off with too much. Perhaps Caleb was a wise father and realized that too much can ruin as well as too little. Diana Barrymore, whose life ended so disastrously, wrote a soul-searing autobiography, *Too Much Too Soon.* Here is a problem parents face, especially those who have risen to where they can do a little more for their children than was done for them. It is a worthy thought when we say, "I do not want my child to have it as hard as I did." It may also be a dangerous thing, for all of us need to put forth effort in order to reach our goals.

Well, parent or no, we can understand Caleb's daughter's situation. She had been given land which was less than the best. It was harsh, dry, barren, unproductive land which needed water in order that the young family's herd might have a place to drink. We can all understand and appreciate the plight of this young family which has been given a set of circumstances less than ideal.

This is the story of every person — a set of conditions less than ideal. I do not know anybody in the world who has everything the way he or she would like it to be. Granted, for some of us the lines have fallen in more pleasant places than for others, but no one has everything in perfection. Everyone who ever lived and who fought the way to some eminence had to climb against odds. For whenever you start upward the force of things, the law of gravitation works against you. I get rather tired of black people always blaming somebody else for why we do not forge ahead.

Look, all of us know things have not been right with us in this country. Everyone knows that there was slavery and that there has been brutal discrimination. In my own family years ago an examination was taken in New Orleans, and when the person placed second and was called in, she was openly told, "This is not a job for a Negro." It's all right to complain to people who are responsible for the outrages, but we must stop excusing ourselves and start demanding of ourselves.

We all have to work out some way with which to deal with dry, barren land, south land which leaves us at a disadvantage. Some resent their circumstance and turn bitter. Now there is a place for a disciplined bitterness, if it is going to spur us and drive us toward a goal. There is little place in life for bitterness that does nothing more for us than to make us sullen and nasty and resentful. Resentment, unsmiling meanness of countenance, the perpetual scowl which I have seen on some people who call themselves tough can be a form of self-pity.

Others given south land, hard and dry and barren and un-watered, resign from effort. Now among black people today there are two kinds of men and women who have resigned because they were given south land. There are those on the left who talk of nothing but destruction, who want to pull down all that is but who have nothing to lift in its place. The only hope is serendipity, something good coming through unsought and unplanned, like the Princess of Serendip in Horace Walpole's novel. There is another group who have resigned, the winos and trip takers and heroin shooters who have resigned from reality and who see in each day only a chance to get out of it all. How interesting that the two groups resigning because of south land should be those who claim to be most determined and those who are least determined.

Now there is a third thing which can be done when we have been given south land circumstances that are unfortunate and unpleasant. It was the course that Caleb's daughter took. She did not go off into some corner sullenly to resent the fact that she and her family had been given circumstances that were hard and trying. She did not throw up her hands and resign from all effort. Mark well what this young woman did. She went to her father. Mark that, for I will be coming back to that in a moment. She went to her father.

She made her request. Listen to her as she addresses Caleb. She must have said, "Father, I have come to ask a blessing of you. You have given me a south land. It is dry and barren. Nothing will thrive there as it is. There is no watering place for the cattle. I cannot do anything with the land as it is, but I've come to ask you to fix it so the land you have given me will be a blessing and a boon. You have given me this dry south soil, now give me springs of water, also." Caleb, so runs the account, received his daughter's request and granted her the upper and lower springs surrounding the dry south land, the Negeb.

I know a greater Father than Caleb. He is our heavenly Father. I do not know why we are given south land, hard conditions, bitter circumstances. I know we all have to adjust to things not being all they ought to be and all we would like to have them. It may be that God knows what it takes to make us humble, and it may be God knows what it takes to make something splendid out of us. Muscles are strengthened by climbing high mountains and steep hills; sight is lengthened by looking toward far horizons.

Today we remember the life and labors and leaving of that man who may well emerge as the greatest American ever produced on these shores, Martin Luther King Jr. Already he must be counted as the only authentic spiritual genius this nation has produced. He did not come from a people of great privilege. His soul was shaped in compassion by generations of the black experience. When you listened to him you heard the heartbreak mixed with hope of a people long in bondage. So God gave black people in this country the south land of hardship and heartbreak and Martin King.

I know that some of you have been given south lands of trouble and sorrow. Everything is not as it ought to be. It's a dry place, unwatered and barren, which you are given to till. Don't you give up. I had to make adjustment early. My father died when I was twelve years old. I had no big brother or older sisters to help me along. Many were the nights I cried myself to sleep. It was a south land dry and barren. O yes, there were many good things, but there was this central south land — a fatherless child.

I know, I know a great heavenly Father. I asked him to take my loneliness and to make something out of me. Give me springs of water. Oh, everyone who has asked the Lord that will tell you that God made it all right. He makes sorrow sweet, fills human loneliness with divine presence. God makes it all right. He makes weakness the way his strength is made perfect. He makes high, lonely hills fine places from which to see the distant city. He makes enemies a spur to help us on to victory. He makes troubles lift us up to a throne of grace. He makes our shortcomings the instruments which bend our knees and humble our hearts and sweeten our spirits.

This is why Jesus is so sweet to the saved sinner's soul. Good people cannot truly appreciate the Lord, for they that are well need no physician. One who has been forgiven little loves little. Ah, but sinners so ashamed, so bowed down in the dry south land of barren guilt and blistering condemnation have found in Jesus a living spring of everlasting water. He is water in dry places, a river ever flowing.

$$\backsim 8 \backsim$$

A Touch of Greatness

May 24, 1970

And Saul said unto Samuel, I have sinned: for I have transgressed
the commandment of the LORD, and thy words: because I feared
the people, and obeyed their voice. Now therefore, I pray thee, pardon my sin, and turn again with me, that I may worship the LORD.
And Samuel said unto Saul, I will not return with thee: for thou
hast rejected the word of the LORD, and the LORD hath rejected
thee from being king over Israel.... Then he said, I have sinned:
yet honor me now, I pray thee, before the elders of my people, and
before Israel, and turn again with me that I may worship the LORD
thy God. (1 Samuel 15:24–26,30)

There is a touch of greatness in every person. In some it is out in
the open in all they do, in the way they walk and talk and bear
themselves. This strange attractiveness, this winsome greatness is
what we have come to hear so much about as charisma. In other
people the touch of greatness does not lie in open view, easily
observable, clear for all to see. It lies covered by layers and layers
of what we call ordinariness, like fatty tissue over firm muscles
and hard bones, but it is there. In many people, this touch of
greatness lies silent and unseen like unborn music in the belly of
a violin, waiting for some master hand to touch the bow and call
forth previously unheard harmonies.

Following the Kent State killings which triggered the savagery
of the American people at Jackson State, the Oberlin College
choir, of such blessed memory in my own life, journeyed all night
by bus to the nation's capital. They were traveling in order to sing
Mozart's Requiem Mass in Washington Cathedral. The students
themselves said that the requiem was done "as a witness to their
deploring all war and violence and their affirmation of faith in
nonviolent means to peace and brotherhood." Reporting on the

51

great feeling of the presentation, Paul Hume said in the *Washington Post* of May 11, 1970, that "it was not in the 'how' of the performance, which was superb, authoritative technique. It was in the 'why' (the feeling of the critical moment), the emotion of the day, that the 250 singers and instrumentalists reached beyond Mozart's notes to sound their deepest meaning." In all of us there is a touch of greatness, and some moment of joy and sorrow will call it forth in music which lies beyond what is written and what is expected.

Saul, Israel's first king, might well instruct us this morning, in the bright uplands and the low valleys, the high qualities and the base failures which make up the lives of most of us. Saul was crowned king at Gilgal, and it was at Gilgal, the same place, that he heard the fateful words of Samuel informing him that God had rejected him as king and had taken the realm from him forever.

How strange that at the same place where success smiled failure frowned. At the same place where his star rose so brightly, at Gilgal, it sank forever. We might pause, if you will, to recall that the place of good news is often the place also of bad news. The making of a friendship is joy; the sundering of that same friendship in death or misunderstanding is grief. Many of our fine traits can be reason, also, for our failures. Every human good can become a perversion whose evil is doubled by fact that it grows out of a great good. Friendship can become a tool of self-advantage, love can become a selfish possessiveness, learning can become a proud arrogance, religious devotion can become pharisaic pride, patriotism can become excuse for violence and bigotry by hardhats with soft heads. For us, our Gilgal, where a bright beginning is made, may be the place also where terrible failure is experienced, as with Saul.

I hear a familiar but terrible word upon the lips of Saul as Samuel confronts him after the king's battle with the Amalekites and their king, Agag. Israel has prevailed, and Samuel, God's man in Israel, has come out to meet a returning victor, Saul. Samuel believed that the command of God was that the Amalekites and all their possessions, their sheep and oxen, were to be wiped out. Saul failed to do this, and, if for reasons of mercy and humanity, he had so failed, Israel's first king would have would have introduced so early in history a great forward moral step. This was not, however, the reason that Saul spared Agag and the best of the sheep and oxen. Saul spared the king that he might have a trophy of his victory to parade before the admiring throngs of Israel upon his return. Likewise, Saul spared the sheep and oxen that he might have larger possessions and holdings.

When Samuel confronts him Saul first tries to excuse himself by saying that he has spared the sheep and oxen in order that he might make a sacrifice unto God. At that moment, Samuel speaks to Saul those words which have become so familiar, "to obey is better than sacrifice." With all defenses down and removed, Saul finally cries out words which might be on all our lips, the saddest words of human utterance, "I have sinned." At that moment Samuel tells him that God has rejected him, and we see a once proud king, broken by his own willfulness and rebellion against God.

Now Saul is kin to all of us. Our lives in Jesus Christ start out so brightly. There are such immeasurable resources available to us in God's word and among God's people when sin gets in the road and blocks our pathway. We must cry, "I have sinned." If you want to know what is wrong in your life, it is because you have been disloyal to the Lord. Now there is nothing to do but to set about by your own repentance and confession and promise to repair the broken altar. First we must cry:

> O for a closer walk with God,
> A calm and heavenly frame,
> A light to shine upon the road
> That leads me to the Lamb!

> Where is the blessedness I knew
> When first I saw the Lord?
> Where is the soul-refreshing view
> Of Jesus and his Word?

> Return, O Holy Dove, return,
> Sweet messenger of rest,
> I hate the sins that made thee mourn
> And drove thee from my breast.

Saul shows in his shame and in his rejection a touch of greatness. He knows that he must pay for his wrongdoing, for there is no other way. He remembers, not hypocritically, I think, his position before the people. He is the king, the Lord's anointed. Under the great load of his rejection, bowed down with the grief of what Samuel has just said to him, "the Lord has rejected you," Saul remembers that he has an obligation to his people. He turns to Samuel as if to say: "I know I have made a grievous mistake. I know that my opportunity is passed and gone. What I was is gone. But, please, don't shame me before the people. Honor me by standing at my side before the elders and the congregation as we have done in days past and gone. Don't let my shame and rejection become a display" (1 Samuel 15:30, paraphrased).

I think there is something divinely great about us when we re-member that there are those who trust us and those who believe in us. I do not suppose that anybody is good enough in mind, word, and deed to be a parent. We all make mistakes, but do you not sometimes ask the Lord to please let you walk with honor before your children? Don't let the children see how short I am of what I ought to be. Could I say that I am so anxious to make it on in without dishonoring my office? Oh, I know that I must pay for mistakes I have made, but I pray to the Lord that I might not be held up to public shame before the people of God who believe in me.

God does rebuke, but if our hearts are tender and right, he will forgive us. If we will not heed, he will bring us to open shame. Did I ever tell you about a preacher in my earliest years whose name was O'Mitchell? I think he has been gone long enough for me to use his name without a breach of ethics. In my teen years he attracted great throngs of people. It was said in our town that people were so anxious to hear him, they would crowd the windows around the church. His manner was attractive, his preaching persuasive and eloquent, and his voice golden and appealing. There was one glaring weakness in his life. He could not control his appetite for drink. He could not handle it; it handled him. This was the description I heard my father give as to whether a person should drink or not.

I saw this preacher, O'Mitchell, of whom I speak, in illness. He had been my father's friend, and I called on him in New Orleans. I was in the morning of my ministry and he in the evening of his, and the memory of looking at him burns and haunts me across all of these thirty years. His once piercing voice was hoarse and strained, and his stooped frame bowed over an open fireplace in a little rented room where he rubbed his hands together and talked, oh so sadly, of the days of glory snatched from him because the Lord had rejected him. We might all pray that we might stop short of that place where the Lord will bring us down for all to see. Lord, rebuke me but make me not a public disgrace.

There was one final word which Saul, broken and rejected, spoke to Israel's greatest judge, Samuel. It would be the last time he would see his old sponsor, for this same chapter says that "Samuel came no more to see Saul until the day of his death" (1 Samuel 15:35). How sad! Those words ring ominously like a bell tolling for some departing soul from some far-off belfry. For that last time, Saul said to Samuel, "Turn with me, that I may worship the Lord thy God." His kingdom was gone, his popularity on the wane, his career broken and in ruins, but Saul — and bless him for this touch of greatness — knew that he still ought to turn to God and bow down before the Lord his Maker. All was lost, but his power to call on God was not lost. The storm was raging around his head, but he could still bow down before the Lord.

Now what is wrong in many of our lives is that we do not take time to worship God. I know, how well I know, that sometimes headwinds blow and we feel so weak and so all alone, no friends to plead our cause, no shoulders on which to weep. No matter

how bad things might be, you can still call on God. When the
enemy rages, ask God to be in front and to fight your battle. We
all feel so weak sometimes, but the Lord says, "I will be your
strength and shield; lean, weary one, on me." I have heard the
Lord say in the language of events this week, and I have come
to tell you that "he giveth power to the faint; and to them that
have no might he increaseth strength. Even the youths shall faint
and be weary, and the young men shall utterly fall. But they that
wait upon the Lord shall renew their strength; they shall mount
up with wing as eagles; they shall run and not be weary; and they
shall walk, and not faint" (Isaiah 40:29–31).

THE CONSEQUENCE OF A WARMED HEART

April 30, 1972

And they said one to another, Did not our heart burn within us, while he talked with us by the way, and while he opened to us the scriptures? And they rose up the same hour, and returned to Jerusalem, and found the eleven gathered together, and them that were with them, saying, the Lord is risen indeed, and hath appeared to Simon. And they told what things were done in the way, and how he was known of them in breaking of bread. (Luke 24:32–35)

The authorities at Louisville Presbyterian Seminary asked that I have a clinic on preaching during the Caldwell Lectures on Preaching this past week. I soon discovered that the most chafing problem which these young men have as they go out to the churches is how they will be able to tell the truth of the gospel about things that are wrong in the society, like racism, war, and poverty. During the course of the discussion, one man who has been pastoring a number of years was talking about how one might be able to preach about these sensitive things to a conservative congregation and what one must avoid. Said he, "People don't like a preacher with a chip on his shoulder."

Well, I am sure that people do not like anybody with a chip on his shoulder. I know I don't. And too many of us are too unpleasant and nasty. Now everybody gets down in the doldrums sometimes, and everybody gets up on the wrong side of the bed sometimes, as we say. That is not the same thing as being perpetually half-mad and grumpy. Some of us even smile as if we have eaten green fruit, and our faces are drawn and stiff. Others of us are always sad and downcast. We do not radiate sunshine and the

Note: I am indebted to an old dear friend, the Reverend K. L. Moore, of Frankfort, Kentucky, for the kernel and seed of this sermon, for he gave the germ to me on the campus of Louisville Presbyterian Seminary. —GCT

joy of living. We are often gloomy, sad-eyed, sorrow-faced people. How to be delivered from these distempers into a glorious and authentic joy is what I am talking about this morning.

I am talking, then, about two people who were sad and depressed. One was named Cleopas, and they were on their way from Jerusalem to Emmaus, a journey of seven miles. There are times when only an imbecile can laugh, for things do go wrong and it does look sometimes as if all is lost and nothing at all is left to give light and laughter to these little lives of ours.

These were disciples of Jesus, and their leader and friend had come to a bitter and an unthinkable end. He had been broken on a rough, rude cross, and the splendid enterprise to which he had called them was obviously all over. There, there, I think, is the word which described this sad journey to Emmaus. It was all *over.* Once years ago I wandered into a great convention hall in Chicago where a major national election had been held in one of our sister denominations. The hall was empty which so recently had been packed with people; there was only silence when the hall had so recently had been filled with human voices and ringing with excitement. In one of the campaign booths sat a man on a trunk, looking dejected. Around him were the placards and banners of his candidacy, and he had lost. It was all over!

So in life sometimes it seems that it is all over. We march toward what we think is our city of desire, our shrine of fulfillment and success. Alas, after the long trek we discover that what at a distance looked like the sparkling minarets of a fair city have been but a mirage and an illusion. We have paced off the last mile, there is nothing ahead, and it is all over. Yonder a broken marriage, and it is all over. Here a terminal pink employment slip, and it is all over; there a grave and the end of a bright romance, and it is all over. The bauble breaks, the dream collapses, the vision fades, the hope perishes, and the grand purpose has become ashes and dust.

What then? What then, you ask, and I take my cue from what these two disciples were doing as they walked from Jerusalem to

Emmaus, from hope to despair, from joy to sorrow. "And they talked together of all these things which had happened" (Luke 24:14). They were talking about the Lord; they were trying to organize their thoughts and shape their lives in terms of what had happened to God's cause.

Now, I suggest that there comes a time in every single, solitary life when we have no choice except to hold on to the fragments and particles which we have left of what was once, or so it seemed, a full and bright blessing. Our faith can get awfully stripped down sometimes. We look around and there are so many things in our life which are quite obviously rich and undeserved blessings, largesse lavishly flung at us from God's open, loving and outstretched hands. Sometimes suddenly, more often bit by bit, we are stripped down until we scarcely seem to have anything left. It is hard going, but God's child has to hold on anyhow. We need more "anyhow" religion. More of us need to determine that we are going to serve God anyhow. If storm clouds rise, I am going to serve the Lord anyhow. If my pathway grows rocky and long, I am going on anyhow. If friends get few and praise turns to blame, I am going to serve the Lord anyhow. I may be wounded and I may be bruised, but I am going to try anyhow. I do the best I can and my friends misunderstand; I must still try to do my best anyhow. We must reach for this.

As these disciples talked, suddenly there was someone else there with them. Is there always someone else with us, uphill, down, around dangerous curves? This other one listened and politely inquired as to what the gravity of the conversation was all about. "What manner of communications are these that ye have...as ye walk, and are so sad?" (Luke 24:17). How often does the good Master, my Lord and my Savior, draw nigh, or, better still, remind us that he is very close, someone sang, "closer than hands and feet." Does he not still come close to burdened souls, and with a smile on his face and a promise in his presence bid us tell him all that is in our hearts? It is as if he says, "I am a good friend, and I have authority and power to settle things, if you will but tell me about your troubles. I will not laugh at you or put you down. I will not censure you, though sometimes I will lovingly rebuke you. I will not put your business in the street, but I will put it on my heart. What is it? I want to help."

And they told Jesus what was troubling them. They told him how their Master had been done to death when they had thought that he was to be their way out, their Savior, and now he was slain like a common criminal on a cross of shame. "We had thought," they said, but the conclusion had been different from what the data looked like. "We had thought."

There is much reason for doubt and, I guess, some room for despair. Last Monday evening at Louisville Presbyterian Seminary students chained the front door of the chapel to symbolize their hatred of this war. At Harvard last Sunday, I talked to black students who were protesting that great university's complicity in oppression and war by way of investments.

One understands the horror felt by the sensitive and the young at the calloused, blind stubbornness which makes us pursue this war in Indochina. War has never been a pretty picture. It is a savage and ugly business. At the same time, there is something solemn and in a way noble about men confronting each other and in the name of something they count very dear, being willing to die, even as they kill. The Nixon war, however, is death from the sky, from a largely uncontested sky. It is murder by anonymous killers; if we are willing to kill but not to die, as the *New Yorker* magazine pointed out, this takes from this war whatever heroic aspects war may have.

Yes, there is much reason for doubt and despair, but Christ is alive, and out of all our blundering and destructiveness, Christ is victor. This is what our Lord said to these despairing people on the Emmaus road. "Ought not Christ to have suffered," said he (Luke 24:26). This suffering of Christ, this cross thing was not some emergency brake desperately pulled to halt a hurtling train gone clean out of control. No, sir! This agony at Golgotha was not a lunge of God to try to right something that had gone terribly wrong and for which he had never made any allowance. Somehow or other, this death of Jesus fits into the pattern of a fabric which God wove and which contained from the beginning a crimson thread, attested to and described as a "Lamb slain from the foundation of the world" (Revelation 13:8). Ought not Christ to have suffered until all was all right which had been all wrong?

Then they saw it all and saw him. That is, indeed, a great discovery and a great mind-blower, if I may say so. To see what God means and to see him, ah! This is it; so they talked to Jesus and he to them, and he came home with them, for it is never enough until he is in our homes. When they had seen him for the Christ he was, they cried, when his ineffable and immediate revealed presence had withdrawn to the edge of their awareness. "Did not our hearts burn within us while he talked with us by the way, and while he made us understand himself in the Scriptures?" Did not our hearts burn when we found out we are not alone? Did not our hearts burn when we learned that the Lord lives and all is well? Did not our hearts burn when we found we have a Friend and that death and hell cannot destroy his sovereign and blessed purpose? Did not our hearts burn when he made it all so plain?

We dare not stop here. "We do not well: this day is a day of good tidings, and we hold our peace" (2 Kings 7:9). The Lord has done great things for us, and we must tell somebody. Let us go back to Jerusalem and tell them the good news, "The Lord is risen indeed." And they went to tell what their eyes had seen and what their hearts had felt.

Is it that way with you? The Lord has done great things for you, and you want to tell somebody that you do, indeed, know a great Savior. The Lord has been light and life, and must we not proclaim to somebody somewhere that he has blessed our needy souls? I must find somebody, to tell him or her that the Lord is good, that his mercy endureth forever.

✺ 10 ✺

A SINGER SINGS OF LIFE AND DEATH

January 7, 1973

Behold, thou hast made my days as an handbreadth; and mine age is even as nothing, before thee: verily man at his best state is altogether vanity. Surely every man walketh in a vain shew: surely they are disquieted in vain: he heapeth up riches, and knoweth not who shall gather them. And, now, LORD, what wait I for? My hope is in thee. (Psalm 39:5–7)

A year is gone! A year has come! We might well learn some spiritual lessons from the passing of the year and the march of the seasons. God, as Frederick Robertson had it, walks his appointed rounds through the year, and every season and every sound has a special voice and a specific lesson for the various phases of our existence. There is spring, when all is green and the birds sing and life is on the wing. Anthems of gratitude and praise seem to rise and swell from every created thing. Spring is unavoidably associated with youth. Beyond spring, there is summer with its steady heat and long days. It is the sure and unmistakable symbol of ripe manhood and mature womanhood. The interests of youth are gone, the prospect of an early grave lies beyond view and concern, though in the midst of life we are in death. It is a time of work and sweat, the steady beaming and beating of the sun upon the workman's head. The autumn, so wistful, so melancholy, touched and tinged with an unutterable sadness, heralds fading powers, lengthening shadows, and declining strength. And now winter, when the earth lies as in the grip of death, for does not everyone pass these seasons and come down to the end of mortal days? The damp mist, the slanting shadows, the dimmer skies, the winter sun with half its luster gone, the limp, falling leaves all tell of end time and death.

62

So, on this New Year's morning we cannot help thinking very seriously and very solemnly about life and death, their meaning and the purpose and intent of the God of us all who is before and beyond our human journey, from "everlasting to everlasting," mused a man in the long ago:

> Tomorrow, and tomorrow, and tomorrow
> Creeps in this petty pace from day to day,
> To the last syllable of recorded time.

So! As an old year passes and a new year arrives, the giddiest among us feel at least a strange tinge, a shadow, the leaping of a hope, a funny feeling, as we say. A long, long time ago a singer in Israel thought and pondered and sang his song of life and death. Read the thirty-ninth psalm, and you know right off that whoever wrote it as one of Israel's hymns was dealing below the surface, at the depths of human circumstances. Some long and tense and heavy and brooding silence has belonged to the author. Sickness and death in his family? Public shame? He does not say, but he does lift the veil which lies behind the melancholy music of this psalm and tells us that "I was dumb with silence, I held my peace, even from good; and my sorrow was stirred. My heart was hot within me, while I was musing the fire burned" (Psalm 39:2–3). We enter where the psalmist concludes his preface, his reason for the psalm by saying, "Then spake I with my tongue" (Psalm 39:3).

Right there the curtain rises on the first scene of this psalm, which is one of those cases where one man has become spokesman for all of us, for he has touched that universal river which flows in all humankind. The writer is talking here first about the brevity and smallness of human life. It is half a prayer, half a complaint about the fleetingness, the shortness of this mortal journey. Yet how reluctant we are to think on the quick passing of our days. Maybe, maybe we refuse to consider that we are so very temporary in the earth because most of us do not have a faith deep enough to give meaning and light to the shadow of death in which we sit.

Because we lack the courage and the "God vision" to look at how quickly we leave this life, we have invented a lot of defense phrases, smart-alecky evasions to avoid looking at the facts, though we say, of all things, that we are a realistic generation. If a preacher mentions death, we sneer, or attempt to, with a dismissal of what he says by calling him a "graveyard preacher," as if the graveyard is not the end yard toward which we are moving right now. If a friend dares to bring up the subject, we shut off that consideration with the abrupt word, "Can't you talk about something more pleasant," as if this life is a picnic with pink tea and all kinds of goodies. Not on your life! Not with a cross smack at the center of it all.

A great and deep reliance on God enables us to face the real facts of life. The psalmist did here. He is talking about the swiftness with which human life passes across our brief stage of action. Cries the man, "LORD, make me to know mine end, and the measure of my days, what it is" (Psalm 39:4). This writer is not wanting to wallow in a trough of self-pity or to fling his defiance in the face of the weakness and the shortness of his life. He merely wants to recognize his creatureliness and his smallness and his feebleness. He goes on, "That I may know how frail I am."

There is no use in our making believe. There is no use living in an illusion, comforting though it may be. Every pulse beat preaches of our passing and our impermanence. Every heartbeat pounds us toward our departure. The tramp of time goes on like some relentless army on the march which will not be stopped and will not be stayed. And for us, the psalmist puts it in an unforgettable figure of speech, "Thou hast made my days as an handbreadth," the width of four fingers.

Humanity "walks in a vain shadow," not in substance and reality, but in a shadow, a seeming, an unreal notion of permanence. We, says the psalmist, disquiet ourselves in vain, thinking so much of what really is so little, thinking so little of what really is so much. We sell our souls for houses and cars and clothes when those things must lie limp and empty in our helpless hands when we are gone and have nothing left but what we have tried to do and to be, under God, in other words, our souls.

Go to any museum and look around. You will see the ancient spear and the jeweled sword of an African warrior and a European knight. You will see the ceremonial mask of an African worshiper from an age which lies behind the first glimmer of European civilization, and these things will seem little the worse for wear. Yes, they will be almost as they were when first fashioned and first used, but what has become of the bright eyes which once flashed behind the eyeholes of the mask, what has become of the strong hands and flexing muscles that once gripped the hilt of the sword? "The knights are dust and their good swords are but rust." Material things last after their owners are long gone. "Man walketh in a vain shew and disquiets himself in vain. He heapeth up riches and cannot tell who shall gather them." How wise were our fathers and mothers when they spoke with age's strange wisdom and reordering of priorities. They said, "I'm wearing this world as a loose garment."

I think this leads us head-on into what must be not only on this New Year's Sunday but throughout our lives the central consideration of thoughtful and serious-minded and truly realistic people. The psalmist, having looked at life's grim reality and brief span, turns with consummate logic and judgment to ask, "Well, where can I put my hope and trust?" "Lord, what is my hope?" I think every man, woman, boy, and girl within the feeble sound of my voice might well ask that question, "Lord, what is my hope?" What is the bedrock upon which my hope is founded; what is the central confidence in which I am living my days?

The answers of so many of us are almost too obvious to be repeated by any thoughtful preacher. Someone says, "I am young, I've got a lot of living to do." Right, but do you know how quickly the blush of youth will pass from your brow, how rapidly your youthful beauty will fade before the blast of the rushing years? So soon you will say of things which seem now of paramount importance, "I thought this or that meant so much. I've found there was absolutely nothing to it." Another says, "My job, I'm needed where I am." Maybe, but what of your job when your hands are palsied and your mind falters and wanders? It will not be your job, but another's. What then? Someone else says, "My children, they are my hope, I live for them and they will see about me." I hope so, but are you sure they will not make you weep bitter tears? And I declare I have seen as undershepherd of God's people over and over again the evidence that often those we figure in the family to be the ones who will really see about us won't, and often those in whom we place the least trust prove truest and steadiest.

"Lord," says the psalmist, "what is my hope?" And having surveyed the alternate and futile possibilities, he looks toward God, whose throne time cannot shake and whose rule the years cannot weaken and cannot touch. The man sweeps away all false hopes and treacherous ground upon which to build his life and claims the Rock of Ages as his footing and his foundation. "Lord, . . . my hope is in thee" (Psalm 39:7). This man removes himself from all earthly and failing arms, which time paralyzes and age weakens, and rests himself in the everlasting arms and the eternal God who is the refuge of us all.

If this poor psalmist, living in the shadowy mist of faith which was before Christ, could cry out to God, "My hope is in thee," how much more so should we who live in the noonday brightness of the Light of the world and the Savior of humanity. If the psalmist could believe that God could lift the burden of life and the blight of death, then how much more should we, who have seen God's own Son and heard him say, "Come unto me, all ye that labor and are heavy laden, and I will give you rest" (Matthew 11:28).

God before Christ says, "When thou passest through the waters, I will be with thee; and through the rivers, they shall not overflow thee; when thou walkest through the fire, thou shalt not be burned; neither shall the flame kindle upon thee. For I am the LORD thy God" (Isaiah 43:2–3). In Christ that same God says, "I am the resurrection and the life:...whosoever believeth in me shall never die" (John 11:25,26).

I put my hope — do you? — in him and him alone who is able to stem the tide and to steady the soul, able to shelter us in the storm until the winds are still and the thunder is silent and the lightning is gone, able to hold us in the hollow of his hand and to lead us in green pastures and by still waters. I put my hope in him who never leaves or forsakes his own. I put my hope in him who is able to be the shadow of a great rock in a weary land and rivers of water in dry places. I put my hope in him who was able to be my purchase price at the gates and shall be my hope at the gates of death. Do you?

ᔕ 11 ᔐ

A BITTER QUESTION IN A HARD TIME

May 6, 1973

My tears have been my meat day and night, while they continually say unto me, Where is thy God? . . . Why art thou cast down, O my soul? and why art thou disquieted within me? hope thou in God: for I shall yet praise him for the help of my countenance. (Psalm 42:3,5)

A noted preacher once dealt in a series of sermons with some of the greatest questions of the Bible. Among the questions asked in the Bible which the preacher considered was that asked by God in the cool of the evening in Eden, "Adam, where art thou?" Another was the question which Jesus asked all of us, "What shall it profit a man, if he shall gain the whole world and lose his own soul?" (Mark 8:36). It is a question of frightening immediacy and importance in the United States of America right now. This famous preacher dealt with Pilate's question about our Savior on the night of the Lord's trial. "What shall I do then with Jesus?" (Matthew 27:22). The widely acclaimed preacher to whom I have referred might have included one or both of the questions raised in our text. "Where now is thy God? Why art thou cast down, O my soul?" There is the ring of reality in these questions. One of these questions is asked by malicious onlookers and the other by a man who is having a hard time. In Eric Goldman's touching biography of President Lyndon B. Johnson, a greater president than history has yet recognized, he mentions that one of the president's senior officers, Jack Valenti, urged the speechwriters to put a little heart in the message the president was to deliver. "Put some tears in it," said this senior officer.

The forty-second psalm does not need to have any tears or weeping put into it. The psalm itself reads like the sob of a wounded heart. Something in the man's life has gone wrong.

68

Whatever the affliction, the poor soul over whom the waters have passed has not found the trouble to be easy or light or swiftly passing. Whatever the pain of the psalmist's spirit might be, it is not a light and easy matter blown all out of proportion, as we do sometimes. There is reality here, and there is agony. Listen to the sob in the statement, "My tears have been my meat day and night." Now this is trouble at its worst. I used to hear my father say that a person in daily life can stand almost any buffeting out in the world into which he or she must go day after day, if there is relief and if there is understanding and sanctuary and rest and understanding when the day is done. If, however, when one limps home in the evening, wounded and cut and tired, he or she meets more of the same, then life is practically unbearable. It is too much when "there is trouble on the outside and trouble on the inside."

Husbands, remember that if your wives are out working just like you. Wives, remember that if you are at home and shielded from the cuts and bruises of the workaday world. Children, think of your parents in that way. They have a right to peace and love and, yes, you have the same right. This psalmist says that his diet, his meat, has been tears by day and night.

I suppose there are those here who feel that what this man is talking about is far removed from their own situation. Some of us have so narrowed our area of love, so tightened our affection circle that it is hard for us to get hurt. There are some, I suppose, who think of nobody and nothing but themselves. "I" and "my" define the full field which they claim and cultivate and care about. Someone said of a man he knew, "His conversation is one long parade of himself." I heard two women, two mothers, talking about their children one evening here in this church. Each was so busy talking about her child, I don't think she ever heard a single word about the other child. Well, many of our interests are even narrower than that.

But is that living? Walt Whitman once envied, so it runs, a cow grazing in a pasture because the cow did not have all of Walt

Whitman's loves and hazards and problems. Well, who wants to be a cow, to miss laughing and weeping, to miss praying, and, yes, sometimes cursing, to miss hope and to miss despair? Who would trade for that?

Martin Marty, the Chicago church historian, quotes recently from a book by a Colorado psychiatrist who writes about the death of his greatly loved wife in the book *Only a Little Time: A Memoir of My Wife*. The psychiatrist, Dr. Sidney Werkman, tells of a gift he made to his wife on their wedding day. Is it not so that the memory of that day is so precious for some of you that you can hardly bear to think about it? Dr. Werkman said, "On the day we were married I gave Sandy a silver mirror with this quotation from Dante, 'For thou art an angelic creature.'" Then far on in the book, Dr. Werkman is talking about his wife's last valiant but vain fight with leukemia. He said, "This angelic creature was beyond help. Yes, it comes to that, but who would forego the joy of a great love, or a bright and shining romance, of deep devotion to a blessed cause because there is danger of getting cut and wounded. The hazard of being human is being hurt."

There will be people here, some of whom I know, who can share deeply with the plight of the psalmist, "My tears have been my meat day and night." In the troubles we face and the loads we carry and the tears we weep and the sorrows we bear, we can give help to others. Now I know that this is no reason, at least no satisfying one, for the things we have to encounter and engage and endure. At the same time, you will never know, when you are bravely battling your way through a terrible storm, who is watching and who will be in his own storm and stress tomorrow and who will find strength and hope in the way you are waging your fight. The other day, if I may say so, I felt overwhelmed by problems and responsibilities which seemed quite literally more than I could bear. Twice God sent, or allowed me to see, people who are so bravely battling their way. One was a person I passed in one of the halls of this church of whose family problems I have known. As I passed her and remembered her plight, my strength seemed greater and my burden lighter. The other event was in a bare hospital room in Kings County Hospital at about twilight. The other two patients in the large and half-empty room in which our sister lay seemed in a coma. In that drab and deathly still room that woman battling the most dreadful disease we know lifted her hallelujah to God. Said she, "If I get back to the church and if I do not it's all right. I've got somewhere to go." And my burden rolled away. Well, we can help each other by the way we carry our condition.

You will know that I have not yet got in full sight of the gospel. I have not argued the case of him who has called me and blessed me to be his advocate and his lawyer. I want to state now my Master's case, his offer to bless, the sure promise of his presence and his power which cannot fail.

The psalmist says that in this life we are faced with a double struggle. We must fight life's fight, and we must contend with doubt and unbelief. We must stand the storm while being pelted with stones and rocks by those enemies within us and outside of us. Always there are those who look on while we struggle and who do not encourage us but who throw stumbling blocks in our way. The psalmist said that they did this to him while his tears ran down in salty streams by day and by night. Listen to the man again: "My tears have been my meat day and night, while they continually say unto me, Where is thy God?"

If friends or enemies have taunted you while your soul was struggling, then you are in good company, for so did they to your Lord before you. We shall never know how dark was the night nor how deep and cold the waters the Lord passed through at Calvary, but I think I know something that cut through the Master more sharply than the nails which tore his hands and the spike which passed through his feet. We can never know how dark was the night nor how deep and cold were the waters the Lord passed through, but I think I know a spear which drove to his heart more cruelly than the spear which pierced his side. See the Savior hang in the heat and pain of an awful Friday. Now listen to the conversation which runs sometimes aimlessly, sometimes bitterly beneath that cross. Here in God's most solemn moment, the heavens would not speak. The perfect music of the spheres rolling in their distant courses must have become mute and un-heard in the heavenly places. But men talked on and sneered on and scorned on! "If thou be the Son of God, come down and save us and yourself." That must have hurt as no steel and no blade could ever hurt. The Lord might have said, "Man, I am here for you," but he never said a mumbling word; not a word, no, not a mumbling word. Matthew said, "They that passed by railed on him, wagging their heads and saying, 'Thou that destroyest the temple, and buildest it in three days, save thyself' " (Matthew 27:40). The priests of religion, as Williams McKee was reminding us Holy Week, mocked him, saying, "Save thyself and come down from the cross." They were asking, "Where now is thy God?"

There are those who stand by and mock. You've been going to church, where now is thy God? You talk about being a Christian, where now is thy God? Sometimes the only answer we've got is the psalmist's answer. "Why art thou cast down, O my soul? And why art thou disquieted in me?" I've got something the world does not have. I've got a hope in God. "I shall yet praise him" (Psalm 42:5). There is a hope. It is hid now, but I will yet praise him; on ahead things grow better. We are a "yet" people made so by hope. I shall yet praise him. Our slave forebears had that. How can you sing in a strange land with your songs punctuated by the cruel whip? They would answer, "We are a 'yet' people." "There is a bright side somewhere." When my father died, I asked my mother what we would do. She said, "The Lord will make a way." She was a "yet" person. O pilgrim, keep on marching, O soldier, fight on, today the battle cry, tomorrow the victor's song. We who sorrow and weep shall yet laugh and rejoice. There never was a night so dark it did not have a dawn hitched to it. We shall yet see the morning.

⌐ 12 ⌐

THE WORD MOSES COULD NOT SAY

November 4, 1973

Yet now, if thou wilt forgive their sin — ; and if not, blot me, I pray thee, out of thy book which thou hast written. (Exodus 32:32)

This verse has a missing word! I think of nowhere else in the sixty-six books of the Bible in which there is a word missing and a dash drawn to show that some unknown word or words ought to be where now this blank occurs. The man upon whose lips were found the words of the text was Moses, not a trifling figure given to half-thoughts and flighty speech. The sainted Dr. Walter Horton, who at Oberlin led us so gently into the great deeps of the mind of God, used to say that in Israel's history three figures represent the highest peaks of godly reflection, and all three of them were named Moses. Dr. Horton used to say that classical Judaism could be summarized from Moses to Moses Maimonides to Moses Mendelssohn. Of the three Moses, this one, the law-giver, must be accorded the supreme place in Israel's long, grim history, the most recent scenes of which are being enacted even now in the hot desert of Sinai and in the Golan Heights.

A word is left out in the sentence in which Moses addresses God on behalf of Israel. We have in the background of this text a great confluence, a mighty coming together of mammoth events and vast and weighty considerations. Look back a bit, and you will see the people of God caught in the act of coarse and brazen idolatry. There was no prohibition placed by Jehovah on the em-bryo nation so strong as the one against idols, manmade gods, later documented at Sinai. A part of this strong prohibition rested in the danger that Israel might be contaminated in its worship of the one true and living God as it touched and was influenced by heathen nations along whose borders it passed and among

73

whose peoples it mingled in the long and roundabout journey from Egypt to Canaan.

Moses, the lawgiver and liberator of Israel, is summoned by God to go up into Mt. Sinai, beyond the view of the whole people. In the mountain solitude, alone with God, Moses was to be given by God the commandments, the laws, ten of them, by which the nation was to be guided and judged. The leader of Israel's journey did not come quickly down from the mount, for he was unlike those of us who have little time and less patience for the company of the Lord and the worship of his household. The people in the valley beneath became skittish and impatient. They prevailed upon Aaron, their priest, to give them something they could see and to which they might anchor their faith and love and hope. Moses, spokesman for the invisible Jehovah and their rallying point, was not to be seen. They needed something in which they might place their ultimate trust and hope. This is what a god is — the object of our trust and confidence. The cry, the yearning for such a god which is visible to this eye and touchable by these hands is idolatry. If your trust is in anything or anybody you can see with the natural eye and touch with the natural finger, you are guilty of the crassest and most primitive idolatry known to the heart of humanity. "God is a Spirit: and they that worship him must worship him in spirit and in truth" (John 4:24).

Aaron capitulated and bowed to the people's clamor. He became part of the long procession of men and women who have tried to be leaders not by challenging and luring the people to something higher but by becoming a reflection, a willing instrument, a reproduction of what is lowest and basest in those whose leaders they call themselves. You ought not want anyone in any role of leadership who has nothing better or more uplifting to say to you than to congratulate you. People are saved not by being flattered but by being faced and, in love, being opposed.

In the Mount of Sinai the word came from God to Moses that something was wrong in the valley below, where the assembled hosts of Israel had pitched their camp. Hurriedly, like a diplomat moving speedily from one arranged conference to face some sudden and deadly crisis, Moses rushes down the mountain and back toward whatever it was that caused God to break off negotiations in Sinai, so to speak. While still far off from the encampment, Moses heard shouts and cries. Canvassing his mind as to what was the reason for the sounds which rang through the hills from the camp, Moses could tell that it was not the cry of an army charging to meet an enemy in mortal combat. Nor yet were the sounds he heard the wailings of people who had been defeated in battle; rather it was the singing of pagan ballads of worship which fell on the ear of their leader.

As he came in sight, Moses could see stretched before him the shameful scene of a people who had forgotten the God of their fathers, who had surrendered to the heathen ways of immoral and idolatrous nations around them. There it stood in the midst of the dancing, singing, reveling crowd — a calf of gold. It was Israel's lapse into terrible idolatry. The senses were satisfied, for the golden calf glistened in the desert sun. The golden calf excited the emotions of the crowd, it was visible, it was bright and shining, it could be touched, it looked like some of the gods of Egypt and of their neighbors, it satisfied base passions. Whirling around the shameful idol, God's people dishonored the name of him who had brought them out of a bitter slavery. With eyes shining, bewitched by their new sensuous deity, the people chosen by God dishonored him who had fed them when they hungered between Elim and Sinai. They had forgotten the God of their fathers and who in not far-off days had quenched their parching thirst when they cried for water at Horeb. Look at them! God's people disgracing themselves before a golden idol! Look at them! God's own people whirling in sensuous circles, working themselves into frenzy by quick motions and shrill and frantic shouts. Shame! A thousand times shame! I will not stop to inquire if this depraved and debased condition of old Israel has not been reproduced by you and me who are the new Israel, the commonwealth of faith. On second thought, I will ask: How many have been the occasions and events when you and I have found something else dearer to us than Jesus Christ, some bewitching way of the world more fascinating than the worship of almighty God, some earthly pleasure, some worldly ambition more enticing than Jesus, who was our purchase price at the gates of hell? Shame! Shame! I hang my head when I think of times when something else or someone else has seemed more precious to me than my Lord who has lifted me when I was sinking deep in sin, who snatched me as a "brand out of the fire" (Psalm 40:2) and plucked my feet "out of the miry clay" (Zechariah 3:2).

Let me turn my text backwards and listen to Moses in a sublime moment when the fate of the people of God is more precious to him than his own life. How the nation cries and bleeds internally for men and woman who will put the public interest above their own welfare. How programs in our ghetto areas cry out for people who will put the lifting of their brothers and sisters above their own greed. Moses is willing to die for Israel. Our young and martyred prince and prophet, Dr. Martin King, used to say, and sealed his saying with his own blood, "If there is nothing for which a man is ready to die, then his life is not worth living." Listen to a true leader, a true lover of his people as he wrestles with God's righteous and holy anger. The man's fiery earnestness makes him willing to be lost forever if Israel can be saved. "Lord, if thou will not forget their sin, blot me out of the book which thou has written." If these whom I love cannot be saved, then let me be lost. What sublime heights of loyalty and devotion. We might well pray: Lord, give us such love as this.

Now to the heart and essence of what I am about this morning. Moses is dealing here with the profoundest question which can engage the mind and heart of humanity. He is talking here about sin and guilt and forgiveness. He is dealing with something gone wrong between the creature and the Creator. Moses is dealing with broken fellowship between Maker and made and which produced in Eden's garden a hiding tenant and a searching Landlord crying, "Adam, where art thou?" Moses is dealing with the offended majesty of God and the treason of a disloyal subject. No! No! closer yet, Moses is dealing with a loving parent and a disobedient child. He is dealing with that circumstance which makes us all cry out: "I hate the sin that made thee mourn and drove thee from my breast."

Moses is dealing with the final problem of our existence and God's eternal love. How can justice and mercy shake hands with each other? How can unrighteousness and goodness find a place to stand together in God's heart and in our forgiven lives? Moses knew there had to be a way. God must be able to forgive sin. There must be some antidote for the poison, some serum for the dread disease. There must be some way to be rid of the stain, but what will cleanse it all away? There must be some way back to Eden or some way on ahead to an older place than Eden where God and God's child are reconciled one more time.

Moses says, "If thou wilt forgive them," but now we see a blank. I thank God we can fill the blank which Moses left. We can speak the word poor Moses could not speak. I know One who broke the evil spell and while we were yet sinners, died for us. I know the missing word. It is "Jesus" — for he shall save his people from their sins. The word Moses could not speak is Jesus, for Moses lived too early, though he sensed there must be some such way. I know the name Moses could not call. I know a name that can change the leper's spots and melt a heart of stone. I know a name that can set cold lands on fire. I know a name Moses could not speak. I used to hear my mother just call his name sometimes, "Jesus." The angel told us to call his name "Jesus, for he shall save his people from their sins" (Matthew 1:21). I like to call his name. Sometimes when the world is tossing me like a ship upon the sea, I call that name, "Jesus," and he steadies me. "Jesus my God, I know his name, ... His name is all my trust, He will not put my soul to shame Nor let my hope be lost."

∽ 13 ∾

GOD AS A TROUBLEMAKER

March 17, 1974

He stirreth up the people. (Luke 23:5)

Calvary! How that name sounds and echoes, quietly thunders and reverberates through the caverns and halls of the human mind and memory. Calvary! That name almost sends shivers through the soul, all mingled with sorrow and joy. John Jowett, of princely pulpit gift, said that when a preacher begins to deal with Calvary he can sense a change, a shift of mood, a hush steal over his hearers as they sense that they are on enchanted ground. James Stewart tells us of Ralph Waldo Emerson's visits to England and Scotland. During such a journey, Emerson and Thomas Carlyle met and talked. As they walked on a Scottish moor, Carlyle suddenly stopped, gripped Emerson's arm, pointed to a church in the distance, and exclaimed, "Christ died on a tree, that built Dunscore Church yonder. That brought you and me together." Calvary! Yes, that built Dunscore Church, Concord Church, St. Patrick's Cathedral, Cornerstone Church. How many other churches?

What was it that brought Jesus to his cross? Those who delve into the study of God's Word and seek to systematize our faith, the theologians, say that Calvary, the cross of Christ, was the working out in event, the unfolding act in history, of God's love and interest in us. Calvary then, they say, was God's plan for our salvation. Something deeper than reason, more basic in us than anything we can ever explain says "Amen" to that. How else could a man, no matter how good, dying on a criminal's gallows two thousand years ago, build Concord Church, Westminster Abbey, a thousand years or more later?

78

All right, granted that the whole event has the background of the everlasting God in it — what about the foreground? What about what we can see, get hold of on the level of human happenings? What did they have against Jesus that brought him to Calvary? More fitting to our own time and moment in history, what did they have on Jesus which would have ended in his conviction and execution?

The charge against Jesus by his enemies changed according to where the charges were being made and before whom they were being made. Almost always in any situation when we are called on to explain our position, we have reasons we give which sound noble and high-principled. Along with those noble reasons, there are usually more selfish, less attractive reasons we have which we do not like to exhibit, maybe not even to ourselves. Often the reasons we give depend on to whom we are giving our reasons.

The charge against Jesus changed from forum to forum. When the hearing against him was in the Jewish court, the Sanhedrin, the charge was a religious one, blasphemy. "Art thou the Christ, the anointed one, the Messiah?" "Art thou the Son of God?" He claims, you see, to be divine, and therefore on a religious basis he ought to die.

Well and good for a religious court, but the Romans, who were really in charge, could not care less about all of these religious fine points, what they considered silly bickering about the minutiae of whether one claimed to be divine. Most of the emperors of Rome claimed to be divine. So! when the accusers got to the Roman court, they changed the charge from blasphemy to treason, from a religious charge to a political one. "He claims to be king."

There was more to it than that! They gave another reason, which is my text, "He stirreth up the people." This fellow upsets the order of things, he throws out of line the arrangements we have made, he introduces restlessness among the people. He is a troublemaker! That's it! I am glad to say that they were right in this charge. Jesus Christ, God's Son, we have seen was and is a troublemaker. He upsets friends and enemies, those who accept him and those who reject him. Christ upsets the social order and troubles the individual conscience. Christ annoys, troubles us, antagonizes us, if you please, by telling intelligent, supposedly well-adjusted, reasonable, respectable people that they are lost without God. We who preach either soft-pedal that or twist it with a lot of bellowing into nothing but polite evasion. The fact remains that nobody is ready to do business with the Lord until that person recognizes that he or she is lost (see Luke 19:10).

Without Christ, I am lost, you are lost. "I know what I am doing," my pride is likely to answer. "Don't hand me all of that tripe about being lost. I live on the corner of Brooklyn Avenue and President Street, Brooklyn, New York, postal zone 11213, U.S.A., thank you. I am not lost. Peddle your wares somewhere else." The Lord comes back in an irritating, troublesome, annoying way. "If you are not lost, why do you feel lonely, forsaken, unfulfilled, sad, discouraged, afraid? You are out of touch with the ground of your being, the source of your strength. You are lost now. And, oh yes, you live at Brooklyn Avenue and President Street. How long will you live there? Suppose you can't live there anymore. Where will you live then? Another house? Suppose there are no houses of brick or lumber or stone anywhere. Where will you live then? Do you have another house?"

All of this kind of thing troubles us, but this is the way God deals with us. If the question the Lord puts to us troubles us, if the moods the Lord provokes in us disturb us, then the cure he offers us troubles us also. He says we must repent, become sorry, humble ourselves. That goes against the grain. It is hard for us to say that we have been wrong, that we have made a mistake.

Now I think that one of the hardest things in the world for us to do is to say, sincerely mind you, "I am wrong." John is responsible, it is due to the way I was reared, I misunderstood, I did not intend to, "the devil made me do it." How hard it is to say, "I am wrong," to humble oneself, to repent, to be sorry. How many friendships are there represented here which now lie in ruins and which were once strong and stately edifices, and all because we could not say "I am wrong"? Is your family falling to pieces because you cannot say "I am wrong"? Our nation might have been spared much of the anguish we are passing through right now if, instead of trying to hide, to defend, to gloss over conditions, those responsible had said, "I am wrong, I am sorry."

God says to us in so many places and in so many ways that we cannot deal with him until we humble ourselves. God will guide us, but only when humbly we confess, "I cannot find my way and I am far from home." God will strengthen us, but only when humbly we confess "I am weak, but thou art mighty. Hold me with thy powerful hand." God will feed us, with heavenly food, but only when we humbly plead "Bread of Heaven, Bread of Heaven, feed me till I want no more." Do you think I speak only to those who are not Christians? Not on your life! There is a sense in which we all have to be saved each day. God confronts us all with our pride and our high-mindedness. I long for the day of worship, that return of Pentecost when in word and deed all of us who gather here for worship will say, "O come, let up worship and bow down: let us kneel before the LORD our maker, for he is our God; and we are the people of his pasture and the sheep of his hand. Today if ye will hear his voice, harden not your heart" (Psalm 95:6–8).

It is troubling to many of us that we should have to turn to a church and humbly take our place among people, some of whom are not as smart as we are, not as learned as we are, not so good as we are. Yet there is this troubling word which we cannot escape, "Yet the Lord added to the church daily such as should be saved" (Acts 1:47). Added to the church such as should be saved! Nonsense! I can serve the Lord on the highway, on the golf course, at the beach. I do not need a church, we are likely to say. This is troublesome, since our churches are such frightfully imperfect representatives of Jesus Christ. At the same time there is something strange and powerful about the assembled company of God's people. This difference may, will very likely, trouble those who are outside of the covenant of grace. This peculiar quality of the church will call forth sneers, anger, antagonism, attack. Of this one or that one serving in the church someone will say, "That's only old Joe. Pay no attention to him. He ain't nothing." No, nothing but someone upon whom the light of the knowledge of the glory of God has blazed in the face of Christ. "That ain't nobody sitting up there," the detractor will sneer, "except old Rosa, and there's nothing to her." No, nothing but a redeemed soul called out of darkness into the marvelous light of God's amazing grace. The church troubles the world because it looks like just another crowd of people. It is that, but so much more. There lives in the midst of the lives of God's people Another who is the Giver and Sustainer of life. It is the presence of Christ, animating, energizing, renewing, restoring, guiding. The Lord of the church spoke the promise whose fulfillment angers the world and must ever anger it until blazing suns have chilled and rolling planets have halted. "I will send the Comforter unto you," said Jesus.

Above all, that cross troubles and shakes the world. It troubles the believer unto life and troubles the unbeliever unto death. Like the ancient cloud which attended Israel, the cross of Christ gives light to those who believe but is darkness to those who do not believe. What a paradox! What a contradiction. That cross is history's darkest crime; it is history's brightest hope. One man died that all other men and women might live forever.

When that ugliest but loveliest of Fridays was past, there must have been people who helped to bring Jesus to his death who went home quite satisfied. They must have shaken their heads, cleared their throats of the dust, rubbed their hands together, and muttered to themselves between clenched teeth, "We've finished with that troublemaker forever." I must say to those men and to all like them that no one will ever be through with a troubled conscience and a restless soul caused by the Lord until he or she bows at his feet. Jesus died in the shadow of eclipse, when darkness lay over the whole land for three hours. Out of that darkness his glory shines with noontide splendor and will shine until every enemy of Calvary has surrendered. Humankind meant that this man's death would be his shame, but his cross has become the brightest jewel in his victor's crown. Many may fight against my Savior, but at last every enemy must stack arms and kneel humbly before him and confess that Jesus Christ is the Lord. Some may try to dodge him, but all things will betray them who betray him. One day, may God bring it quickly,

> Jesus shall reign where'er the sun
> Does his successive journeys run
> His kingdom stretch from shore to shore
> Till moons shall wax and wane no more.

His name shall be honored, his saving power shall be praised, nation and races shall ponder the sweetness of his name, kings shall come to the brightness of his rising, "every valley will be exalted, every hill and mountain brought low, and the glory of the Lord shall be revealed."

⌒ 14 ⌒

FAITH BEYOND FEAR

April 14, 1974

And when I saw him, I fell at his feet as dead. And he laid his right hand upon me, saying unto me, Fear not; I am the first and the last: I am he that liveth, and was dead; and, behold, I am alive for evermore, Amen; and have the keys of hell and of death. (Revelation 1:17–18)

Birth and death! The great brackets around our human span. Birth and death, the solemn issues of our existence. Birth and death, point of origin and final port of this voyage. No human being has thought deeply or honestly who has not pondered and considered these matters, which engage our attention this morning. Someone says, "I don't want to think about these things now, they are so serious and momentous." Ah my friend, but everyone born into the world is born into serious business. The mystery of birth speaks of the mystery of life. Life and death! These have been among the supreme considerations of poets and philosophers and makers of great music. Life and death are the grand and august themes of Easter. It is these thoughts, half-thoughts, feelings, half-feelings, whatever you want to call them, which have brought you here this morning and which fill churches from one end of the world to another on Resurrection Sunday.

We are all in this thing together. Now there are ailments and situations of which we hear and about which we say, "Well, that does not apply to me." A tornado strikes Xenia, Ohio, and we read of it. We are touched with sympathy, but we do not live in Xenia and we do not have kinspeople or friends who live in Xenia, Ohio. So! We say to ourselves that, thank God, we are not directly involved. There is a description of some newly found sickness in the papers. We think of our own aches and complaints and so read the article intensely to see if it describes our feelings and complaints. When the symptoms of the disease are described and we discover that they are far different from anything we have felt or experienced, we put the article aside and say, "Well, that does not apply to me." In the case of life and death and the considerations they draw forth, we are all in this together.

I think we have two distinct stakes in the matter of death and life, of Resurrection Sunday, or Easter. First, there is an objective kind of philosophical interest. Each of us thinks from time to time as to what is his or her view on this subject. There are some sound reasons why we lean toward belief in the life after death. Fifty or sixty or seventy or eighty or ninety years seem so short a time for all that goes into the making of a woman or man, the slow physical development, the mystery of intellectual growth and of spiritual expansion. Those of us who are getting along in years are aware that we are just beginning to understand, or so we think, what life is all about. So many of us are cut down in the midst of our strength and work. Jean Paul Richter, the nineteenth-century German humorist and poetic writer, began a book on immortality following the death of his young son. Richter's unfinished book was carried on his own casket. We read that Mozart's requiem was never finished by that master, for his musical inspiration was interrupted and terminated by the hand of death. We reason along this path that there ought to be a life beyond this, for we scarcely get to round out and to complete what we begin here. In "In Memoriam," Tennyson addressed the God-Person in this frame of mind, saying that

> Thou wilt not leave us in the dust,
> Thou madest man, he knows not why,
> He thinks he was not made to die
> And thou hast made him, thou art just.

It is to say that God would not give to us, nor let us have, the notion of endless life without giving us the answer to our desiring. I do not know if Tennyson is sufficient here.

We long for life beyond this life because we love deeply in this life. Here is a happy and healthy family. They share many joys and sorrows. Let us photograph them for a moment around the family dinner table. They are all together now: mother and father, sisters and brothers. There is a oneness and a wholeness, a gladness in their family closeness. They stand by each other, they love each other. Their faces are bright. Laughter rings through that house. Alas, one day there will be an empty chair around that table, never to be filled by the one who will sit there no more. And then another empty chair, and another. Is all that love to be poured down the drain, so to speak, by death? Is the ache when my mother goes never to be eased by reunion? Must the emptiness of father's absence be forever a loneliness? Something in us cries out against that. Oh, surely, our love makes us say, somewhere beyond the dying and sorrowing, we shall meet again where families never part and our spirits shall sorrow no more.

'Tis a lovely faith, only we fear that it may not be so. This is one of those things, this hope of an endless life, to which we cannot really reason our way. Our minds play tricks on us. This is one of those things, this hope of an endless life, on which we cannot totally base our feelings, as tender and precious to us as they are. There lurks the fear that it may all be an illusion. We are not sufficiently sure that there is any word to be said finally, beyond or better than "earth to earth, ashes to ashes, dust to dust." Thus, we fear, will fall this noble temple of our bodies. Thus will crumble the splendid pillars of our strength. Thus will darken these eyes of light and fire, thus will still forever these nimble fingers, thus will crack forever that noble heart, thus will hush eternally the music of each voice, and thus will die for always the dreams and hopes of our minds and spirits. It is a terrifying fear!

Those who believe in Jesus Christ have a surer, a more certain faith beyond their fear of extinction. We shall rest our final confidence upon the word and work of One who says to us, "Because I live, ye shall live also" (John 14:19). We stake our claim to resurrection and the power of an endless life upon One, even Jesus Christ, who says to us, "I am the resurrection and the life:

he that believeth in me, though he were dead, yet shall he live" (John 11:25).

We hold the old and holy hope of people out of the long ago who believed that God can and will bring to pass the power of life over death. As I write this, I listen to the lovely and haunting solo form Handel's *Messiah*, "I know that my Redeemer liveth and that he shall stand at the latter day upon the earth. And though worms destroy this body, yet in my flesh shall I see God." We have the word of men and women who lived and experienced in their own beings the resurrection of Jesus Christ. One of them speaks of "our Savior Jesus Christ, who hath abolished death, and hath brought life and immortality to light through the gospel" (2 Timothy 1:10).

Ah, but we have something infinitely more precious. As I have said, we have the word of Jesus upon which to base our Easter faith beyond the fear that it may not be so. It is such a scene which meets us in the first chapter of the Book of Revelation. We have a Christian who is in trouble because of his faith. John, by name, is a prisoner on the isle of Patmos. The man who writes and is commanded to write is not in prison because he is a criminal but because he is a confessing Christian. Now that phrase "confessing Christian" takes on importance because it denotes these men and women, our spiritual forebears in New Testament faith, who sealed their confession of faith in Christ with their blood in the days when the Roman Empire made it a crime to be a believer in Jesus. Perhaps in the time of the emperor Domitian, one John, a believer of Jesus, would not deny his Lord. For confessing Jesus, John was found guilty of being a believer in Jesus Christ. Because he would not recognize Domitian as divine, he was an "atheist." Of how many of us can it be truthfully said that we are found guilty of being believers in Jesus? I want to be guilty of that, do you not, also?

As punishment for his crimes, John is sentenced to hard labor on the isle of Patmos. Sore and weary after a week of backbreaking labor, John comes to Sunday morning, and his mind races back to where at home far away, the believers in Jesus would be getting ready to gather to praise God in worship. Some of you who are very lax in your regularity of worship do not know what a privilege it is to be able to come here on Sunday morning. One day you are not going to be able, some of us have experienced that, and you are going to find out what it means to long to be able to join your brothers and sisters in worship of almighty God.

John could not go to his church, but the Lord of the church opened before the confessing, believing prisoner excerpts from the worship of the new Jerusalem. This man heard the great, perfect praise of those who serve forever before the throne of God. He heard the stirring call to worship, "Unto him that loved us, and washed us from our sins in his own blood, and hath made us kings and priests unto God and his Father" (Revelation 1:5–6). There was a preacher that day, and the subject was resurrection. The preacher John heard was not stained with sin as we are who preach here. That preacher's voice would never be smothered by the grip of death. The preacher that day on Patmos dealt with resurrection faith. That preacher did not speak of things he had heard or read or believed!

Yonder on Patmos another preacher came. John described him, saying that he wore a flowing garment, I suppose the vestment of his priestly authority. A girdle bright like gold surrounded his vestment. John says that preacher's voice was like the sound of many waters. His eyes blazed like sunlight, and the words which leapt from his mouth were sharp and quick and cutting like a two-edged sword. John said that before the majesty of that presence, he fell as dead. This strange and awesome figure, John said, put his right hand upon John and said, "Fear not" (Revelation 1:17). Oh my soul, hear that! Where Jesus is, "Fear not." The night may be dark and we may be far from home, but if Jesus be there, "Fear not."

And then the glad announcement, the resurrection word to be uttered again and again, "I am the first and the last," I was before and I will be after, "I am he that liveth" (Revelation 1:18). Liveth!

He lives now! Christ is alive now! "I am he that liveth." "I was dead." He, the Lord is saying, has gone down where death reigns, or reigned, and has met and conquered the king of terrors. On an awesome field, our Champion has met the rider of the pale horse and has unseated the rider. I "was dead; and, behold, I am alive for evermore." Beyond that he says for our faith, "I have the keys of hell and of death" (Revelation 1:18).

I do not know how to die, but I have a Friend who died one time and "turned to flight the armies of the aliens." I cannot unlock the door, but I have a Friend who has keys and will unlock the door. Praise God, we shall enter there by his grace who leads us all the way from earth to bright glory.

ᔰ 15 ᔭ

WHY MURDER IN CHURCH

July 7, 1974

And again he sent unto them another servant; and at him they cast stones, and wounded him in the head, and sent him away shamefully handled. And again he sent another; and him they killed, and many others; beating some, and killing some. Having yet therefore one son, his wellbeloved, he sent him also last unto them, saying, They will reverence my son. But those husbandmen said among themselves, This is the heir; come, let us kill him, and the inheritance shall be ours. And they took him, and killed him, and cast him out of the vineyard. What shall therefore the lord of the vineyard do? He will come and destroy the husbandmen, and will give the vineyard unto others. (Mark 12:4–9)

I do not relish preaching which is joined too closely to current events, since it can become merely the preacher's comment on the passing scene. On the other hand, I shudder at the thought of preaching which never comes within sight of human affairs and happenings. This is the Sunday following the tragic murder by shooting of Mrs. Martin Luther King Sr. while she sat at the organ of Ebenezer Church in Atlanta, playing *The Lord's Prayer.* For the sake of those who listen, to say nothing of the need of the preacher to be delivered of how this relates to his gospel, a word must be spoken. Let all remember, at least, that the timeless gospel is timely.

The car had been sent to the Atlanta airport to get three of us who were arriving for the funeral of Mrs. Alberta King. One of the two ladies I learned later was born in Berlin, Germany, and lived there until the awful days of Adolf Hitler. She has served as literary agent for almost all of the books written by members of the Martin Luther King family. The other lady holds elective office in the city of Detroit. It was a blazing, hot day in Atlanta, and the two ladies sat on the rear seat of the limousine. I occupied the jump seat and sat looking out at the Atlanta countryside as the car sped on the expressway toward the city. During the drive into the city the Detroit officeholder asked the literary agent, "What meaning do you make of the murder of Mrs. King?" The other lady said, "My mind has not been able to get that far. I am still in shock."

We all passed that way when the news raced through the nation, as if on the angry wings of tragedy, that Mrs. Alberta Williams King had been slain while sitting at the console of the organ in Ebenezer Church playing *The Lord's Prayer*. "Our Father, which art in heaven, hallowed be thy name, thy kingdom come, thy will be done on earth as it is in heaven. Deliver us from evil. . . . " And somewhere, midst the music of that prayer, bullets ring out through the sanctuary, the house of God, and the organist, a gentle lady, a lover of the Lord's music, daughter of a distinguished preacher and his family, wife of another, mother of two sons and a fine daughter, slumped over, reaching for her face, someone who was there said to me, where she was shot and from which she would quickly die.

This event shocked us all. Sooner or later the mind moves beyond the answer that literary agent gave on the drive into Atlanta. Last Sunday, all unknowing as to what was happening right then, there was a sentence in the sermon here which spoke of a question on the lips of the ages about tragic, painful events, and which was on the lips and in the mind of Jesus on Calvary, "Why?" Well, why murder in church? Let us move along here as on a runway before we take off toward the everlasting hills and the eternal stars. Why murder at all?

A part of the answer is in the greed of our country, in us all. Again and again, attempts to pass gun control laws in this country have failed. Everybody knows that guns can be bought too easily in this country. A president of the United States was slain, but the Congress of the United States would not outlaw guns. A senator of the United States was killed, but his colleagues would not pass a gun control law. The nation's moral leader and apostle of nonviolence was slain, but the Congress would not pass a gun control law. The lame excuse is given that "if guns are outlawed, only outlaws will have guns." How many law-abiding people carry guns now? Political people are among the most jittery people I have ever known and react, usually overreact, to the most modest pressure. American people, white American people and black American people who will not register and vote, have shown no interest in outlawing guns, Have you? Have I? Why murder? Well there is no one reason. Greed! Profit! Selfishness! Indifference!

Why murder in church? Why murder in a black church! Why murder in a black church committed by a black man? Why murder in a black church, committed by a black man and aimed at a black organist? Insanity? What lies behind insanity taking this particular direction?

There is a poisoned atmosphere in our black communities. It is made up of more elements and particles than I know or could describe. It is composed of poverty, anger, drugs, bitter talk, sincere violence-prone revolutionaries, grim merchants of fiery speech who traffic in people's squalor and misery and whose angry rhetoric fans flames of violence in people whose kindling point is understandably low.

Jesse Jackson and I sat next to each other at the funeral, and in the wait before it began we talked about what has happened in the last ten years. In all of these things, we who preach and we who profess Christ have contributed to this bitterness on the part of many black people toward the church. We preachers, I do not claim exception or exemption, have not been as dedicated as we ought to be. We have paraded conspicuous display of prosperity before people trapped in the prison house of poverty and squalor and crime. We who preach have taken too much from people and given too little to them of ourselves. God must be asked to forgive us this morning. Also, black people have encouraged their pastors to exploit them because we do not adequately require from them fealty to the gospel.

All of us, or most of us, who profess faith in Christ and who are members of churches have helped to create the climate of poison which hovers over black America in regard to black churches. We have not been serious Christians. We have welcomed and laughed at every crude joke, every vulgar caricature of our black churches. We have thought funny the Rev. Leroy skits and the other coarse comedy about the most precious institution we have. We have forgotten, or chosen to forget, that the foundation of black education at the elementary level was in the academies of struggling black churches all over the South and North. We have not laughed the tender laugh of love at our one institution, but the laugh of self-contempt. How few are the black people who reach places of supposed honor and who turn to our mother church which suckled and sustained their growth? Count the black doctors, the black lawyers, the black people in industry and commerce who love their church and find honor in being a part of it. Yes, we who are the children of the church are guilty of helping create a climate of contempt which can turn to hatred and violence.

I shall not dwell on the bitter, blazing rhetoric of the sincere revolutionaries and the merchants of hate who have trafficked in our misery. Look at the black hero figures of the last ten years in our newspapers, magazines, on the blackboards of our classrooms, and you will see the answer. Yet when all is said or done we have no other institution which owes its life and strength to no earthly circle of power.

Let me take off toward the hills and stars. There is more to "Why murder" than I have said. There is powerful kingdom of evil. The Western world, the European person, black or white, became so intoxicated with our mechanical and scientific achievements, so drunk with counterfeit confidence that we could not believe that there was anything, even evil, strong enough to confuse us and frustrate us and defeat us.

We could manage anything, even evil; the answer is all within our own power. Jesus said again and again that the power of evil is mightier than we think. I must sound that note here again that we cannot deliver ourselves from evil. It is so powerful that only God, and at the uttermost of his "Godness," can match it.

Jesus told of a man who owned a vineyard. This man owned this vineyard because he planted it and built a hedge around it and arranged for its care and its prosperity. He let it out to some keepers, sharecroppers really, but the arrangement was honorable. He sent a servant to get his portion, his rightful due. Evil is a twisted and powerful thing. The keepers would not send the man his due but beat the servant and sent him away empty. I do not know the servant's name. Somebody said his name was Elijah or Jeremiah, or something like that. Again he sent another servant saying, "Give me what belongs to me from my vineyard." The men who had agreed to share profits were not impressed. They took that servant and stoned him and wounded him in the head. I do not know the name of that servant. Somebody said he was named Hosea or Isaiah, or something like that. The owner sent others; they were beaten and killed. Evil is an ugly, determined thing; it never reaches saturation in its outrages and ugliness.

The man who owned the vineyard had one son. He said, "Surely these evil people who have brutalized my servants, stoned them, and killed them will receive my Son." Those keepers of the vineyard said when the Son came, "This is our chance. This is the heir. Let us destroy him, and all of this will be ours." Evil is a powerful thing reaching to own all. They took the owner's son and killed him.

The man who owned the vineyard watched all of this. I will not call the owner's name, but I know the Man. I will not mention his name, for he has been called by many names. Moses called him "I Am." Some have called him El Shaddai, others said he is the Everlasting Father, still others the Daysman, the Umpire. Somebody said, "I call him my Rock."

What will he do? His servants are stoned and dead. His son is attacked and slaughtered. What will he do? He will not give up. He has a plan. He will pull down those evil men, and he will put other tenants in their place. He will have other servants and will raise up that Son whom wicked men slew.

God will not be defeated; his people will not be defeated. Twice last week I heard the Ebenezer choir. I talked with some people who had been in the church only two or three days before and who had seen the blazing flash of revolver fire and heard the staccato thunder of the gun. In a crowded church, they had seen innocent blood on the black-and-white organ keyboard. Frightened? Hiding? They filled the choir loft Tuesday and Wednesday, singing, "O God, our help in ages past / Our hope for years to come!" They sang "On Christ the Solid Rock I stand." They sang, "Surely goodness and mercy shall follow me." They sang, "Guide me, O thou great Jehovah / Pilgrim through this barren land, / I am weak, but thou art mighty / Hold me with thy powerful hand." Twice they sang, "All the way my Savior leads me / What have I to ask beside?"

Midst the tall Georgia pine trees, in the King family home, touched with the strange stillness of death, I sat with Martin King Sr. on Tuesday evening. He bit his lips and said, "They killed Martin, A. D. is dead, and now they've killed Bunch." He stopped awhile. Then he said, clutching my hand, "A. D.'s third son came to me the other day, and he is going to preach." Then he looked at me and said, "They won't be able to kill us off."

That's my word. We are surrounded by poison and evil in this life; they can destroy our bodies, but "they won't be able to kill us off." God has others. Christians tell the world, "They won't be able to kill us off."

᧞ 16 ᧞

HEARTS WAITING FOR WHAT?

September 29, 1974

And it shall be said in that day, Lo, this is our God; we have waited
for him, and he will save us: this is the LORD; we have waited for
him, we will be glad and rejoice in his salvation. (Isaiah 25:9)

In *Lines Composed Above Tintern Abbey*, William Wordsworth,
in words among the sweetest in the English language, speaks
of the haunting sense of high destiny that belongs to us. He
speaks for all of us when he describes an inward yearning toward
something worthy which he has not yet reached, a persisting,
poignant compulsion toward a fulfillment not yet achieved. In
heartbreakingly touching language, Wordsworth says:

> And I have felt
> A presence that disturbs me with the joy
> Of elevated thought; a sense sublime
> Of something far more deeply interfused,
> Whose dwelling is the light of setting suns,
> And the round ocean and the living air,
> And the blue sky, and in the mind of man....

There hangs over each of us the awareness of moving toward
something, of becoming something far finer than we have ever
been. Ah, we may wince, but we are never for long free of that
yearning to become better, that instinctive squirming to be let
loose from some imprisoning and crippling web in which we are
caught. This sense of inward struggle toward something, the dim
awareness of some huge, approaching wonder forms the basis
for the earth's finest literature, informs and indwells the world's
worthiest crusades, and fashions the splendor, the most glorious
splendor of our humanity. We speak of this characteristic in us
in many ways, as "getting ahead," or "bettering our condition,"

or "our ship coming in," or "the pot of gold at the end of the rainbow." Whatever the term, we are aware of something about to happen — big, wonderful.

In all the sweep of the Bible there is this constantly recurring note. Hearts waiting — for what? The Bible pulls the tinsel from around this awareness and says quite honestly that we are waiting for God. This is our contract with life. For the coming of the Lord God into our arena of action, into our theater of operation, the righting of wrong by the aid of the divine arm — for these things our world waits.

So it was with the ancient prophet, this strangely haunting poet whom we call Isaiah. In a day of darkness for his people, as black as midnight, the man speaks of the coming of God's feast: pride and arrogance shall disappear and the fortresses of evil shall be leveled with the dust. Beneath the events that fill the Bible there is this continuing theme of God in the act of bringing something unspeakably wonderful to pass. This is the evangel.

"And it shall be said in that day, Lo, this is our God; we have waited for him, and he will save us: this is the LORD; we have waited for him, we will be glad and rejoice in his salvation." We need a God who can get in it with us, and we need a God whose power and might are set against evil. In that day shall we say, "Lo! this is our God."

It has been repeatedly pointed out that a fatal flaw in Greek religious faith as it is represented in Greek mythology is the distance of the gods on Olympus from the heat and fray of life in Athens and the other Greek city-states. Almost all of the Greek tragedies end in the death and disgrace of all of the principals. No one survives, the good die with the bad, and there is no vindication for either right or wrong. The gods of Greece were too far from the needs of humanity, and so the cause of righteousness never knows a certain and worthy end.

Anyone who would bless the lives of people must somehow "sit where they sit." Wilfred Grenfell became the angel of Labrador because he went and lived with the people of that needy place. If

Christians are going to bless their community, it must be because they have entered the same sorrows, felt the same temptations, known the same heartbreaks as those to whom they would speak. As you know more about life you speak less easily about it, but what you have to say carries more weight. Arthur Gossip, so long the prince of the Scottish pulpit, said that shortly after his wife's bewildering and sudden death, when he had finished preaching in a church of a certain Sunday, he heard a woman say to another as he passed, "If I could only believe that man knows what he is talking about, I would start all over again." Another replied to her, "He does. His wife died but the other day." The world does wait for men and women who speak with spiritual authority because they have walked slippery ways and have found and can report that "underneath are the everlasting arms, and the eternal God is our refuge" (Deuteronomy 33:27, slightly paraphrased).

God, to be our God, must enter the arena of our troubles, the theater of our operation. This is at the heart of the good news we call the gospel: We have a God who comes where we are. I hear in the distance the cry of one who has stood over a fallen and wounded race and has watched the God of all the earth feel their loneliness, participate in their heartbreak. He cries, "In all their affliction he was afflicted" (Isaiah 63:9). We have no less a gospel than that God is kin to us. One hears the words of the brave old Book and takes hope, for our hearts wait for a God who can feel our sorrow and share our heart's desires.

Dare we hope that God throws his strength in on the side of truth and justice? Or is raw power forever on the throne and the heartbroken disinherited forever on the scaffold? Are we to fight these battles for peace, for a land of equal opportunity by ourselves? Granted the brilliant dedication of those who labor in the cause of true freedom in this land, is this all the strength we have? Is our last court of appeal our own Supreme Court, or is God going it with us? Is he near enough to know the hard fight of downtrodden people? Can he hear the groan of the slave?

A man in the South, a Negro handyman, was asked by his white employer, a bank president, "John, why are the colored people spending all of their money going to court to get equal rights? All of the money and power and government in the South are on our side. How do you hope to get the things you want if we fight you?" The Negro thought a moment and answered, "S'pose God say so?" Does he?

There is great sorrow these days in the hearts of many Americans who love this land and who believe that God has for it some worthier destiny than our bitter divisions of race and region. Of course, we must in sorrow and shame confess that we are reaping the bitter harvest after a long season of sowing expediency and sub-American ideas and attitudes. For the foreseeable future we shall doubtless find ourselves in a painful period of being purged and cleansed of our great national sins.

We can all take comfort and courage in the awareness that there is Another who throws in his strength on the side of justice and a fairer, juster world. Our problems are huge, the road we must travel in this nation and in our world toward peace and harmony may be a long and arduous one, but God travels it with us, or better still, leads us along the road we must journey. Our land, America, has a better day on ahead. We shall yet stand together in this land with all races and regions united in liberty's holy cause to the glory of God and in the vindication of our democratic assumptions. For God is in it with us.

There are signs almost beyond number of God's presence in the struggle of our nation toward its democratic fulfillment. Our history seems to say that God has presented all of us in this nation with the holy possibility of bringing to pass on these shores a society of unity and mutuality in the midst of all our diversities of color and creed and national origin. Step by step, sometimes in a way that we could not comprehend, we have been led toward the fulfillment of that destiny. To the glory of this nation, no matter how dim the vision of the better society has become betimes, it has never died in the hearts of millions of Americans. And at times, once in the great national sorrow of civil conflict, the vision has been the paramount concern of our American people.

Take our lives one by one, and there is a long chronicle of failure and mediocre living. Is God close enough to sense our broken dreams and our blasted hopes, our failures and our yearnings? How does he look upon our cemeteries of wasted years? The old Book puts it bravely: "Like as a father pitieth his children, so the LORD pitieth them that fear him" (Psalm 103:13). In this we can take hope.

James Stewart reminds us of a poem of Coventry Patmore. "The Boy," it is called, and it tells of how one day Patmore's little son, having been disobedient, was sent to bed without supper and unkissed. The poem goes on to tell how the father, his anger cooling, crept up later that night into the room where the child lay asleep, his face still damp with tears, and around him to comfort his sad little heart, the sleeping child had gathered some of his favorite toys. The father leaned over and kissed those childish tears away and left some of his own. As he did it occurred to him that God might feel the same way toward his children. He wrote:

> When Thou rememberest of what toys
> We made our joys
> How weakly understood
> Thy great commanded good
> Then, Fatherly not less
> Than I whom thou hast moulded from the clay,
> Thou'lt leave Thy wrath, and say
> I will be sorry for their childishness.

"Like as a father pitieth his children, so the LORD pitieth those that fear him."

Always the gospel proclaims God's nearness to our need. Always in our poor, stained humanity there is an anguished cry from broken generations, "Is there no balm in Gilead; is there no physician there? Why then is not the health of the daughter of my people recovered? O that my head were waters, and mine eyes a fountain of tears, that I might weep day and night for the slain of the daughter of my people!" (Jeremiah 8:22 — 9:1). And there is the answer of God, the tramp of his foot far off — thundering down the road of the centuries toward our relief and redemption, the cry on his lips, "O Israel, Fear not: for I have redeemed thee, I have called thee by thy name; thou art mine. When thou passest through the waters, I will be with thee; and through the rivers, they shall not overflow thee: when thou walkest through the fire, thou shalt not be burned, neither shall the flame kindle upon thee. For I am the LORD thy God..." (Isaiah 43:1–3).

God close to my crying heart, God close to our broken society — that is the gospel of the New Testament!

∼ 17 ∽

A Sound Word for a New Year

January 5, 1975

And from the time that the daily sacrifice shall be taken away, and the abomination that maketh desolate set up, there shall be a thousand two hundred and ninety days. Blessed is he that waiteth, and cometh to the thousand three hundred and five and thirty days. But go thou thy way till the end be: for thou shalt rest, and stand in thy lot at the end of the days. (Daniel 12:11–13)

Following watch meeting services last Tuesday evening, I talked with two other pastors. Both of them had noticed in their congregations what I thought I detected here on watch meeting night. That is, an unusually grave and serious and even apprehensive mood. I felt that here very strongly on New Year's Eve, as if people felt a more than ordinary uncertainty about what 1975 may hold for all of us, and all of this beyond the natural human perils to which we are all liable in any year and at any time.

Almost everyone will agree that as the year 1975 dawns, we in this country are far from the bright religious enthusiasm of 1955, when churches were reporting record attendance and record giving while many spoke of spiritual rebirth which they believed was about to break loose in the country like the clear, fresh winds of God scrubbing the sky clean of all smog of doubt and unbelief. Well, it hardly happened that way, but the mood of the country was bright and hopeful, if you remember.

I wish as we come into the midyear of the seventh decade of the twentieth century that we could greet one another in the bright hopefulness of 1965. Aroused by the death of John Kennedy, excited by the vision of Martin King's "Let Freedom Ring" eloquence at the March on Washington, the nation seemed poised for a new and exciting adventure along the skyways of liberty and freedom. A president, Lyndon B. Johnson, whose name will one day have a brighter luster among us than it does now, stood before the Congress, the Supreme Court of the United States, the diplomatic corps, and took up the cry of the civil rights movement back in those years of the 1960s. President Johnson's voice rang through the land with a lifted and eloquent vision of a nation of equals and thundered at the end of his grand peroration and climax, "We shall overcome." We had hardly begun to overcome before the nation became frightened, angry, defensive, vengeful toward those who disturbed its complacency.

We are now in 1975, the last quarter, the final twenty-five years of the twentieth century, and the mood is grim, fearful, apprehensive, uncertain. The cloud of unemployment seems to hang lower and lower over us as the days come and go. We seem in the grip of worldwide forces which we do not understand and with which we seem powerless to deal. The center of the world's wealth may be changing in this year and decade after fifteen hundred years residence in the Western world. One hears this week of the secretary of state and the president of the United States mentioning the possibility of war while the nightmare of Vietnam still lingers over the country. The bastion of liberty, the cradle of our democracy, Boston, is showing a resistance to a unitary, integrated public educational system scarcely matched in what we once called the most backward parts of America. We listen in vain for some voice in which there sounds loud and clear to American people a call to noble purpose and high aim. Bluntly, the present president of the United States is an appointee of a pardoned president whose deeds of criminality are preserved forever electronically. Former high officials of the government are now convicted felons, uncommon criminals. Even the case of the elderly seems to be used as a means of satisfying human greed and corruption. People turn to all kinds of religions and spiritualist movements because our churches do not communicate the reality of power and deliverance.

No wonder one detects wherever one turns a mood of anxiety and tension and gloominess. Even our pleasures seem too determined, too intense and joyous. Well, at a time like this the Christian person wants to know and the Christian preacher wants to search to find if there is any word from the Lord for such a time as this. When we turn to the Book of Daniel, we discover that ours is surely not the first unhappy time when the prospects seemed dim and unpromising. My text occurs at the last verses of the book. Listen to these words and see if you do not hear in them something anguished and stern and even painful, "And from the time that the daily sacrifice shall be taken away, and the abomination that maketh desolate set up, there shall be a thousand two hundred and ninety days. Blessed is he that waiteth, and cometh to the thousand three hundred and five and thirty days. But go thou thy way till the end be: for thou shalt rest, and stand in thy lot at the end of the days."

Do you not catch something ominous and tense in those words? I need not dwell upon the literal time span mentioned here. A thousand two hundred and ninety days, that would be forty-three months of thirty days. These days are not important; what is important is that something hurtful and painful which was going on would not go on forever.

Things were bad, grim, ugly, threatening. A heathen and arrogant overlord and his proud and powerful army were in control of the land of God's people. Men were buying the highest and holiest office, the high priesthood, of God's people. Some, the Hasidim, "the pious ones," named like some of our Jewish neighbors in Williamsburgh and Crown Heights, tried to be faithful. One thing led to another. The wicked and pagan king Antiochus turned his soldiers loose to pillage and plunder the city of God, Jerusalem. The people were forbidden to practice their faith, which held them inwardly inviolate and united. Women who had their children circumcised were put to death, with their children hanging about their necks. The ungodly king did not stop there but defiled the inmost shrine, the Holy of Holies, and set up in the most sacred place a heathen symbol, a pagan altar, "the abomination of desolation," said the Jews vainly trying to describe the horrors of it.

With the world gone mad, an author inspired of God dipped his pen in the ink of God's eternal purposes of vindication and wrote what our own Old Testament scholar and member, Dr. James Sanders, calls a parable. It was intended to rally the faithful to God and to God's ways. As Dr. Sanders says in *Torah and Canon*, the writer of Daniel "warns that one does not brave the future by deciding to be a nobody, by surrendering one's identity to enslavement to whatever force happens to be overwhelmingly powerful at the moment. One braves the future by deciding, even in the stark aloneness of a dungeon of lions or blazing furnace, to meet the appointment made at creation to live in the image of God, who gives man freedom from and hence delivery over very passing tyranny."

I suppose that is what my sermon is all about this New Year's morning. Daniel talks to those who are in the grip of a terrible 2,290 days of trouble, when the daily sacrifice is taken away and something ugly and ungodly is set up in the most sacred place of life. We can bear almost anything if there is some hallowed point in our lives to which we can repair and find solace and comfort. It may be bad when things go against us, but the worst that can happen is when what we believe and what we believe in is shaken, when we can no longer, it seems, hold on to what was our central preciousness. When the screaming hurricanes of evil blow down the temples of our faith, then we have come to true crisis. When those on whom our souls depended draw away or are taken away, then we have come to the dark night of the soul. When people standing around us and seeing our spirits shivering, naked and cold to the harsh winds of bitter circumstance or writhing and convulsing in pain, say to us in sarcasm, "Where now is thy God?" then do we face the soul's most severe trial. That is the abomination of desolation, when all around my soul gives way, when no anchor seems to hold in the whelming flood.

That is the abomination of desolation, when there is no star in the sky and no sign of the morning and one longs for the day while crying in the night and God seems far off or an old myth.

Says the writer, and I pass it on to you this New Year's Sunday morning, "Blessed is he that waiteth." Wait on the Lord; be of good courage. This is hard business, not cut out for weaklings and cowards. It means holding on when there seems nothing to hold on to. It means standing when there seems no ground on which to stand. "Blessed is he that waiteth." This means trying when you've given and given of yourself until you feel empty and numb and there seems nothing left, "Blessed is he that waiteth."

"Go thou thy way until the end." Do not stop halfway. If you can't go forward, don't go back, stand right still and oh! mark time, until you can move forward. Then press along. If we fall, we must rise and try again. It is our job to try on and pray on. You and I want to be able to say to him each day, "Lord, I've tried, Lord, I've really tried. I have never reached perfection, but I've tried. Sometimes I've lost connection, but I've tried. Sometimes right and sometimes wrong, hoping someday to be strong, then I'll rise and sing this song, Lord, I've tried, I've really tried."

"Go thou thy way until the end be: for thou shalt rest." God knows we get tired on this way, tired of trying, tired of failing, tired of being criticized, tired of being talked about, tired of being misunderstood, tired of being ignored, ill-used, ill-thought of . . . tired!

"Thou shalt rest, and stand in thy lot at the end of the days." God has a place for each of us; we shall stand in our lot. "We shall. . . . " I like the confidence of that. God's great hour is sure to strike. The earth is the Lord's, and even if the world seems as if it is run by the devil, God still holds the reins of the world in his hands. He rules, and as our fathers said, "superrules." The fist of evil may seem to hold the world in a remorseless grip, but God is still on the throne.

God's great hour is sure to strike for each of us. You weary one, try on, pray on, work on, believe on, serve on; God's great hour for you is bound to come. "Weeping may endure for a night, but joy cometh in the morning" (Psalm 30:5). Right now, you who are tired and weary may find it hard to so believe, "but they that wait upon the LORD shall renew their strength; they shall mount up with wings as eagles; they shall run, and not be weary; they shall walk, and not faint" (Isaiah 40:31).

And we have Christ to go with us to the end. He says, "I will be with you." In trials and tears, the promise stands. In sorrows and sighings, the promise stands. In partings and perils, the promise stands. I know the night is dark, but Christ says, "I will give you the morning star." I know the land is dry and barren where your spirit stands, but your Lord says, "I will lead you to living fountains of waters." I know we weep now bitter tears, but the promise stands, "God shall wipe away all tears from their eyes; and there shall be no more death, neither sorrow, nor crying, neither shall there be any more pain" (Revelation 21:4).

"Surely I come quickly: Amen. Even so come, Lord Jesus" (Revelation 22:20). Come and have mercy on us. Come, Lord Jesus, and deliver us. Come, Lord Jesus, and save us else we perish. Come, Lord Jesus, and renew us on our toilsome way. Come, Lord Jesus, the road is long, and we are far from home. Come, Lord Jesus, we are pilgrims in the night, children crying for the light.

∽ 18 ∾

THE GREAT "IF" IN OUR LIVES

November 9, 1975

Behold, I stand at the door, and knock; if any man hear my voice, and open the door, I will come in to him, and will sup with him, and he with me. (Revelation 3:20)

There it stands, who can doubt that it is one of the supreme texts of all the Bible! Here in this congregation it begins Sunday after Sunday the old journey, the grand pilgrimage of our worship together of almighty God. Here those words have been invitation to so many, no longer in this life, to open their hearts to the praise of God in this great assembly; one of the most splendid of that number being William Clapp, who entered this week the gates of paradise. I wonder if we have allowed frequent repetition here as worship begins to dull the cutting edge of these words, to dim their luster by familiarity and that half-attention which we give too often to things that are absolutely matters of life and death.

This morning will not be the first time I have tried to hold up this text before your hearts and minds — mark those last words, "hearts and minds," for this preacher has no desire to speak to either of these worthies without the other. You will be, I hope, in the wrong church this morning if you want the preacher to get at your feelings while you mind is excused; likewise, I pray, if you want to think without feeling.

This will not be the first time, then, that I have faced you with this text, nor, please God, will it be the last. If any preacher believes that he has finished with a text because he has used it once or twice, then he vastly overestimates his powers or almost unforgivably underestimates "the unsearchable riches of Christ" (Ephesians 3:8) and that love of God which "passeth knowledge" (Ephesians 3:19). I daresay the most gifted and thoughtful of

108

preachers could spend a lifetime preaching on this text and never exhaust it, for does it not tell of a patient God, the importance of men and women to his heart, their freedom, his yearning to be near them, and the rich reward of communion with God? Ah, the winds of all eternity blow through this text, and it vibrates with the endless love of the everlasting Father.

Today I would have our emphasis to fall on this great *if*, set forth in this text. "If any man hear my voice and open the door, I will come in to him, and will sup with him, and he with me."

There will not be many of you who have not seen reproductions of William Holman Hunt's fine and memorable painting, "The Light of the World." The Lord Jesus stands in the painting at the door of a neglected cottage which shows signs of falling into ruin. In front of the cottage, tall weeds grow and long grass waves on the pathway leading to the door. In front of the tightly closed door stands a tall and stately figure with the lovelight of Calvary in his eyes and the sadness of a seeking love upon his countenance. In his left hand he holds a lantern whose light shines softly on both the lone figure who stands at the door and on the cottage entrance. The figure wears a robe which seems to be the cloak of royalty. The right hand is knocking. It is the picture of a wanting and waiting Lord, the thorn-crowned King knocking at the tightly closed door of the human heart and listening intently to hear if there is any answer from within. The picture touches and moves the heart. G. Campbell Morgan told of how the artist showed the picture when it was first painted to his best friend. The friend looked at the kingly figure and studying the detail of the door suddenly said, "Hunt, you have made a terrible mistake here." "What mistake have I made?" said the artist. "Why, you have painted a door without a handle!" "That is not a mistake," replied Hunt, "that door has no handle on the outside. It opens only from within."

There is a great "if" in our lives. It is a mighty risk. You cannot take that element of risk or choice out of life. Well, you say you get tired of the "if" in life. You want things clear, unmistakable, open and shut, beyond question. Well, you do not know it, but you are asking for a dull and boring life. It is the element of risk, of choice, the "if" which gives excitement and splendor and heroism and character and glory to life. Let me illustrate. The principal sin of governments which have no elections is that choice, risk is taken away. The harm in the claims of astrology, fortune telling, the like, is that they, if they could be successful, would take the risk out of the future and its decisions. You sit and look at a television drama. In order for it to have compelling power it must show someone, a child, a woman, an elderly person, a character who has gained your favor in danger, risk. And almost always there is an "if," a choice. Will he turn this way or that?

"If any man hear my voice." There is a knock at the heart of each of us over and over, time after time. I cannot detail or catalogue the forms which that knocking takes and the tones in which that tender voice calls to us. It calls on days when the world is sweet to us and yes, when the world is bitter like gall. That knock sounds and that voice calls in times when sickness lays us low and when we experience the miracle of recovery. That knock sounds and that voice calls on days when we are surrounded by many friends and yes, when lonely paths are appointed in which for us to walk, on days when God gives us so much, yes, and on days when he takes so much away. On days when we shake with deep and hearty laughter and on days when we shiver and tremble in nameless grief and chilling trouble. In all our days and years, in all our comings and goings, in all our risings and fallings,

> Hush, somebody is calling my name.
> Hush, somebody is calling my name,
> O my Lord, what shall I do?

Now the awesome risk, the terrible option, the fateful choice! "If any man hear my voice." This element of risk, this power of choice which is in your grasp ought to make you tremble in those pews. How sad if we let anything or anybody shut out the sound of that knock and the calling of that voice. How often do we miss the signals in life. Children cry out for love that is not mere softness, and we often fail to hear. Parents sound out their love and care, and sons and daughters fail to hear. Great sadness ensues and the families are turned into scenes for grief and sadness. A husband calls out for encouragement, but the wife does not hear; a wife pleads for understanding and care, but the husband is too busy. The signal is missed, the knock is not heard, the voice does not reach the ear.

Above all, Christ knocks. I cannot detail the ways in which he knocks. "Be not forgetful to entertain strangers: for thereby some have entertained angels unawares" (Hebrews 13:2). Watch out for need; do not shrug it off too quickly. Never forget those words of our Lord about the joys of the redeemed and the awful departure of those whom he at last will know not. "I was hungry, and you gave me food. I was thirsty, and you gave me water. I was a stranger, and you took me home. I was naked, and you clothed me. I was sick, and you came to see me. I was in prison, and you visited me." "Lord, when saw we thee in such a fix?" Look out, all of you, about the opportunity of that nursing home next door. Don't dismiss with some smart-aleck remark this breakfast program for children each morning. Don't snicker at this clothing exchange across the street. Don't turn up your nose at community efforts for improvement. Hear your Lord, if he is your Lord, say, "Inasmuch as you did it unto one of the least of these my brethren, you did it unto me."

> Somebody's knocking at your door.
> Knocks like Jesus.

"If any man hear my voice — if you are tuned to hear me, if your listening faculties are opened to spiritual matters, if the noises of selfish striving and bargaining for more possessions do not drown out my voice, if you have the spiritual sensitivity to hear and the energy, the will to open the door, I will come in." It is not enough to hear the Lord calling, though God knows our faculties ought to be trained by prayer and meditation and study of the Scriptures to hear God. Happy is the soul who can say:

> I heard the voice of Jesus say
> Come unto me and rest.
>
> I heard the voice of Jesus say
> Behold, I freely give.
>
> I heard the voice of Jesus say
> I am this dark world's light.

'Tis not enough. If any man hear my voice and has the faith, the will, the energy, the determination to open the door, I will come in. It is good to be able to say:

> I heard the voice of Jesus say
> Come unto me and rest.
> Lay down, thy weary one, lay down
> Thy head upon my breast

One other thing is needful:

> I came to Jesus as I was,
> Weary and worn and sad.
> I found in him a resting place
> And he has made me glad.

What a grand promise the Lord makes at the end of this text. "I will come into him, and will sup with him, and he with me." Ah, here is what we need, all of us, every one of us, daily communion with God. We do need in this bruising life a closer walk, daily walking close to him. The Lord promised it here, gives his word that if we will but open the door, bid him enter, make him welcome, he will come in. Never mind what the house is like; he will see about that.

"I will sup with him, and he with me." Do you hear that? The Lord is saying that he will take of what we have and he will give us what he has. Did you ever think that you can gladden the heart of Christ, of the eternal God? "I will sup with you. I will be pleased to receive what you have. You will sup with me. I will give you what I have."

There is a knock! I hear a voice! I will open the door! "Come in, Lord Jesus. I have so little to give." "Never mind," he says, "I will take what you have, and I will give you what I have." "I have but a sinful heart." "Give me that," he says, "and I will give you my holiness and my righteousness. That you might not be found having your own righteousness which is of the law, but that which is through the faith of Christ, the righteousness which is of God by faith." You say, "I have only weariness." He says, "Good, bring that. I am the shadow of a great rock in a weary land." You say, "Lord, I have only a broken heart and a wounded spirit." "Good," he says, "bring that. I am that balm in Gilead to cure a sinsick soul. You say, "Lord, I have nothing to give but a weary burden." He says, "Good, give me that. Come unto me, all you that labor and are heavy laden, and I will give you rest." You say, "Lord, I have only the soul's hunger to offer." He says, "Good, give me that. I am that bread of life. I am the living bread which came down from heaven." You say, "Lord, I have only my weakness." He says, "Good, give me that. That's just what I need. My strength is made perfect in your weakness."

∽ 19 ∾

OUR CHRISTIAN DANGER
AND PROTECTION

November 7, 1976

And the Lord said, Simon, Simon, behold, Satan hath desired to have you, that he may sift you as wheat: But I have prayed for thee, that thy faith fail not: and when thou art converted, strengthen thy brethren. (Luke 22:31–32)

We are allowed in this text to peek a little ways into the mystery of evil and to glimpse its formula for getting things done. We catch a little view of the strategy of Satan. It would help us to understand the danger of playing with evil if we realized that we are up against a cunning adversary whose resources of mind and plot are endless.

Twentieth-century people do not take favorably to this old biblical idea of a shrewd devil who is out to get us in order to do the Lord in. Modern people are willing to see a plan in everything else except evil. In fact, the idea of a plan is one of the trademarks of people living in our time. In our recent election, you can be sure that the strategists for both sides devised a plan of victory. For one candidate, it was quite obviously to get a solid Southern vote plus several industrial states on the eastern margin of the nation or the Midwest. For the other candidate, the plan was to take the normally conservative Western states, plus one of two decisive industrial states in the Midwest or East. Yes, "plan" is the watchword of our time. Nor is it a bad way of going about things. I can still hear the sainted Dr. J. A. Bacoats, my college president, saying to us boys and girls in the long ago, "It is better to fail with a plan than to succeed without one." Now that may be open to question, but there is a germ of unarguable truth in the saying.

114

Is it not interesting that people such as we are, so friendly and even slavish toward the idea of a plan, would be so unwilling to accept the evidence that Satan, evil, the tempter, the devil, our adversary, call him or it what you will, has a plan also? In our high-spoken way we say that the bad things that go on, the ugly acts, the violent deeds, the mean and petty tricks we see and do are due to some accident, not a plan. It is cultural lag, we say — and when the slack is taken up, everybody will act better. Then murders spring out in highly cultured Westchester and among well-trained people in Oyster Bay and the like.

Jesus said bluntly that there is somebody out to get us. You remember our Lord's parable about the wheat and the tares reported to us in Matthew 13:24–30. A householder, a farmer, said Jesus, carefully sowed good seed in his field and waited for the harvest. Alas! when the green sprouts showed themselves, there was an added something in the field which was different from what the farmer planted. There were tares, weeds, unwanted plants. The servants of the farmer express shock and surprise. "Sir," they say, "didst not thou sow good seed in thy field? From whence then hath it tares?" The reply of the farmer was that these weeds are not accidental, they did not just appear. "An enemy hath done this."

In our text, the Lord is saying the same thing to Simon Peter, the natural leader of the little disciples' band and to us, also. I think Christian people can never approach consideration of that upper room without a strange and terrible hush passing over the spirit almost like a silent shudder. There is the tense sense of a gathering storm. Deep, moving emotions held in check by the greatest effort. The flickering candlelight. The brooding, pensive face of the Master. The broken bread. The poured wine. The words from his lips so loaded with farewell and finality. How simply, almost starkly, does Luke speak of it all. "And he took bread, and gave thanks, and brake it, and gave unto them, saying, This is my body which is given for you: this do in remembrance of me.

Likewise also the cup after supper, saying, This cup is the New
Testament in my blood, which is shed for you" (Luke 22:19–20).

The Master looks around the table and speaks an awful word
about the friend, the trusted ally, who is to betray him, "Truly
the Son of man goeth as it is written of him: but woe unto that
man by whom the Son of man is betrayed!" (Matthew 26:24).
Also, in that solemn and dreadful hour the disciples begin arguing about place and prominence, which one will be the greatest.
I think maybe we ought to remember when we come to the table
of the Lord today that even at that first table there were many
questionable and unworthy thoughts which passed among those
who gathered there. I knew a church once where the table of the
Lord's Supper was almost deserted because people in that church
had misread, or misunderstood, the words of the New Testament
about how we should come to the Lord's Table. They believed
that no one who is unworthy should take the bread and wine.
That would mean that few would dare approach the table. The
passage they misunderstood in Corinthians says, "For he that
eateth and drinketh unworthily, eateth and drinketh damnation
to himself" (1 Corinthians 11:29). "Unworthy" means "not of
sufficient merit." "Unworthily" means "without due reverence
and regard, indifferently, casually." The disciples surely were not
worthy, nor are we, but we may come with deep and becoming
reverence for the holy act of taking the elements.

Nevertheless our Lord, in that large and spacious way of his,
spoke of these men in such lofty and gracious terms. He puts a
badge of merit on them, so to speak, unworthy though they were.
I am always overborne and shattered within when I think of how
the good Lord of us all takes our poor, clumsy efforts and ac-
cepts them so warmly and gladly, almost as if we had done our
best. I cannot stifle the urge to say to you that few things move
me in my ministry so much as thinking of how much God has
done with what little I have given to him. How he has taken
the half-hearted loyalty, the mixed motives, the shabby service,
the halting loyalty, the erratic, spasmodic devotion and made so

much of it all. I shall wonder and praise him for that straight to the gates of everlasting day and on beyond until silenced by the signal that all of the redeemed are to blend their voices in the great coronation anthem to Calvary's hero, "Blessing, and honor, and glory and power, be unto him that sitteth upon the throne, and unto the Lamb for ever and ever" (Revelation 5:13). And in that blessed shout I shall still praise him. So! our Lord spoke to these sluggish, half-hearted, slow-witted men, saying to them, "Ye are they which have continued with me in my temptations, and I appoint unto you a kingdom, as the Father hath appointed to me" (Luke 22:29).

Then looking at the leader of the band, Jesus lifts the veil but a little and lets us peek into the dim, murky region where evil does its work! Satan plies his awful trade. "Simon, Simon," he calls Peter by his old name. It is as if Jesus is calling Peter back to his poorest, lowest self, "Simon, Simon, Satan has asked for you." He wants to shake you as in a sieve to sift you as wheat. Satan has desired to shake you violently until all the protective husks, the veneer, the shell is shaken loose.

Oh, my people, be not fooled. We are up against an awful enemy. The trials that vex our souls, the adversaries that plague our days, the stumbling blocks that line our pathways are not accidental. We are up against a mighty enemy. If you are not careful, the devil will get hold of you. If you are not careful, you will turn back. This is a crafty enemy. He strikes us where we are most vulnerable, and he strikes at the best.

We have elected a new president this week. As for me, and I have said it before, I feel that the nation is in for a new spirit of hope and promise. At the same time, I feel an enormous compassion for the new president. First, he is a Southerner and white. Southerners have felt themselves stepchildren of privilege in this country, never mind all of their ugly racist attacks and claims of superiority. Second, blacks and others in the fragile coalition which elected Mr. Carter will be wanting their rewards and spoils, nor do I say that this is bad. Above all, the new president has said openly that he is a Bible-believing, God-fearing, Christ-serving, Spirit-led Christian, and anything he does out of line will be pounced upon in a way some of the adventurers and operators we have had in the White House never would have suffered.

It is ever the way of Satan to shake the best God has. We who are in this fight of faith need to brace ourselves. It is a hard fight. Try to do right, and the fight gets harder. Try to love everybody, and the fight gets harder. Try to serve the Lord, and the fight gets harder. Try to be honest and truthful, and the fight gets harder.

It is the way of Satan to strike at God's best. The evil one knew that if he could pull Simon Peter, the spokesman, the natural leader, down he could bring the whole Jesus movement crashing to earth. It is a hard fight against the powers of evil all around us, and we must ever be on the alert. Do not settle back and loll around. Miss church one Sunday and you feel less guilty, until it is easy to miss and hard to go. Do not drowse or settle back.

The Scriptures are very clear on this point: "Watch ye, stand fast in the faith, quit you like men, be strong" (1 Corinthians 16:13). Who can ever forget Paul's great word about the nature and seriousness, the awful danger of this Christian fight in which we are engaged? To the Ephesians he said,

> Put on the whole armor of God, that ye may be able to stand against the wiles of the devil. For we wrestle not against flesh and blood, but against principalities, against powers, against the rulers of darkness of this world, against spiritual wickedness in high places. Wherefore take unto you the whole armor of God, that ye may be able to withstand in the evil day, and having done all, to stand. Stand therefore having your loins girt about with truth, and having on the breastplate of righteousness, and your feet shod with the preparation of the gospel of peace; above all, taking the shield of faith wherewith ye shall be able to quench the fiery darts of the wicked. And take the helmet of salvation, and the sword of the Spirit, which is the word of God: praying always. (Ephesians 6:11–18)

It is a hard fight, but I have come today armed with the authority to say to you that you are not in this fight by yourself. Jesus said to his disciples, "Simon, Satan hath desired you, Satan has asked permission to sift you." I take that to mean that as powerful as evil is, it is not supreme. The power of Satan is under the jurisdiction of our God. The dominion of Satan is encircled by the rule of our heavenly Father. The decisions of Satan are appealable to a higher court. Satan may sift, but God reigns.

Jesus right here throws in heaven's mighty answer to hell's mighty strength. "Satan has desired," and Jesus does not say that Satan will not sift Peter. He says rather that he puts himself ever against Satan in our defense and interest. Satan has desired to sift you, "but I have prayed for you." You may be shaken, but you will come out all right. I like that "when" which my Lord speaks. He does not say Simon will not be tried, and God knows he was that night when he denied his Lord. "But I have prayed for you, and when you are delivered help your brethren." Satan desires, but Jesus prays. Yes, and when we are delivered, we shall be conquerors. Jesus is right now pleading our cause. Hard may be the fight, but there is a "when" of deliverance, and sweet will be the victory. Heavy may be the cross, bright will be the crown. Steep may be the hill, clear will be the view of Beulah land. The tide may bear us far, but we may well hope to see our Pilot face to face. The storm clouds may rise, the sun will still shine on our pathway.

~ 20 ~

Jesus Christ

March 20, 1977

For the law was given by Moses, but grace and truth came by Jesus Christ. (John 1:17)

To announce the dear name Jesus Christ as a sermon subject is to realize that no one sermon, no, nor one million sermons can exhaust this title. Two thousand years of preaching and Bible study and Bible teaching have not been able to do more than touch the hem of the garment of this subject: Jesus Christ.

There are themes too grand, too broad in their sweep, too vast to be treated even in a passable manner. Did I ever tell you of an incident which happened near the end of my first preaching mission in Australia? Our Baptist people in that country appointed one of their number to carry Mrs. Taylor and me to the studio of an outstanding Australian landscape artist. The artist was Sir Hans Heysen, knighted by the then ruling English king. The painting they gave to me hangs now in my office just beyond this sanctuary. During our visit to Sir Hans's studio, with its great skylight overhead, my eyes caught sight of a rather massive canvas only half-finished. I asked the artist about this partially painted picture. Sir Hans shook his head, a little sadly I thought, and said that it was to have been a painting of sky touching the landscape in the strange beauty of the Australian northern territory, but having seen the view, he could not paint it. The scene was too much for the artist.

This is the glory and pain of my work as preacher, never more so than today. There is much that I see and know about Jesus Christ, but I cannot say it. One feels sometimes, with Robertson Nicoll, that "the desire to explain [the atonement] Christ may go too far. The reality of Jesus Christ is much more readily under-stood than many explanations. Its onlyness is the main thing." Every preacher must feel sometimes like the woman who said, "I understand who Jesus Christ is and what he does for me. I understand it well until some one asks me to explain it." Well, the preacher's job is to explain and proclaim Jesus Christ, and it is too big a subject for any human mind to grasp and any human heart to take in and any human lips to speak. So! This sermon will be a failure, but may it be a godly failure and give honor to the Lord who calls it forth.

Jesus Christ! That was the name the first missionaries carried up through Asia Minor. You and I ought to think now and then on what all of this is which we have inherited. We ought to ap-preciate how the name Jesus Christ spread from a mere handful of people to become the light and life of millions. Our chapel next door is named the Chapel of the Churches, a gesture of thankful-ness to many of the churches who helped us following our fire and whose names are carried on the pews. You notice on the walls some small rocks and pebbles with the names of the seven churches of Asia Minor which were the first Christian congrega-tions outside of Palestine. I brought them back from the original sites. Once Mrs. Taylor and I followed the route these preachers took, and I told you about that — they went to highly cultivated cities. Take only one for example, Pergamos. Here was a city of culture and pagan power. It was said to be the most spectacular city of Asia Minor, due to an imaginative feat of city planning. One can see still the ancient health spa and hospital center famous through all of that cultivated portion of the earth. The physician Galen did his work there in the first century after Christ, and his medical methods reigned supreme for sixteen hundred years. At the summit of a hill a thousand feet above the city stood the Temple of Zeus. The Book of Revelation spoke of Pergamos as the city where Satan's seat is. To this sophisticated and cultured city came the New Testament people calling a name then little known, Jesus Christ. That name at last charmed Pergamos and all of the rest of the seven cities of Asia Minor. That name, Jesus Christ, can still save and bless each of us. This community, this borough and city and state and country and world.

Our text in John speaks of the name which is the center of all we do here as the people of the Lord. "The law came by Moses." And so the writer, glorifying and rhapsodizing on the greatest and grandest mystery of our Christian faith, pays full compliment to the whole dispensation of the Old Testament. Nor do we seek to minimize it, for law is the basis of all community and order. Moses and the old dispensation stand at or near the fountainhead of all law and regulation.

Our writer of the Gospel of John, having saluted the majesty of the law and Moses, the lawgiver, turns to another and speaks of the Magna Charta of our faith, the letters patent of our royal connection, the seal and sign of our salvation. Listen, "Grace and truth came by Jesus Christ."

Now I would want to fasten this morning upon those two titles joined together: Jesus Christ. Here is what all of our preaching is about: Jesus Christ. Here is what all of our believing is all about: Jesus Christ. Here is what all of our community work is about: Jesus Christ. What we do in the projects and enterprises we have undertaken here, unmatched in scope and versatility by any voluntary group of black people in the history of this city, is all done not as something aside from, separate from, but as a result of Jesus Christ and our relationship to him. I want to talk about him this morning and see how in him we are blessed. "Thou shalt call his name Jesus" (Matthew 1:21). That was the signal at the birth of our Lord that we have in him a reality. A man, a person.

Now it is impossible to overestimate the importance of Jesus as man, person, one of us, "a man for others," as Dietrich Bonhoeffer called him. The Heidelberg New Testament Professor, Gunther Bornkamm, stresses that in the Gospels we have an emphasis upon the person of Jesus. The writers stress the authority of his words, what he said, and the authority of his deeds, what he did. Ours is not a misty, thin, airy faith, no pious fantasy without living reality. I wish that people would some day understand that. Ours is an earthy faith, not something way out somewhere from the reality we know. If people understood that they might see Christian people in a different light rather than the muddle-headed, thick-witted notion passing for shrewdness which assumes that when you see a Christian you see a dunce, that to be tender-hearted one must be soft-headed. Stupid!

Our Lord lived here. His name was called Jesus, an earthly name which many mothers in Israel gave to their little boy babies. He sanctified the name as he hallowed everything he touched. My soul and mind take great comfort that Jesus was one of us. I read thankfully that he became thirsty and cried in the extremity of his suffering, "I thirst." It was one of his great identifying cries with me. He must have known hunger and the want of food, for he said to his disciples about the hungry multitude, "I will not send them away fasting, lest they faint in the way" (Matthew 15:32). Hear that from your Lord, you materialists, you sight and sense worshipers. He felt the dread tug and pull of temptation to do wrong. The second chapter of Hebrews says, "He took not on him the nature of angels but of our humanity." "Wherefore in all things it behooved him," "it was necessary," says Ms. Montgomery, "it was imperative," translates Dr. Phillips, "to be made like unto his brethren, that he might be a merciful and faithful high priest... for in that he himself hath suffered being tempted" (Hebrews 2:16–18). Again the writer strikes that note in Hebrews 4:15, "for we have not an high priest which cannot be touched with the feeling of our infirmities; but was in all points tempted like as we are." Tempted by pride? Yes, Jesus! Tempted by money? Yes, Jesus. Tempted by sex? Yes, Jesus. Tempted by praise? Yes, Jesus. He is my brother. Let my imagination have free play a moment. Where he sits at the right hand of God, he can interpret how we feel. When I cry, he says, "Father, it is like this," and explains. When I am hungry, get angry, forget to think of others, he knows, though he was without sin. The tempter reached at him, at even Jesus. Never give that up, Christian. He is our Brother, our fellow human!

Matthew, anxious to establish the Lord's Jewish earthiness, traces him back to Abraham, the father of the Israelite nation, and so certifies Jesus as the Son of David. Luke, interested in his universality, traces his genealogy, his roots, if you please, back to Adam, and so he is the Son of Man bound to all climes and clans and colors.

John in my text traces him back to eternity, "In the beginning was the Word, and the Word was with God, and the Word was God" (John 1:1). So he is Jesus, yes, but he is Jesus Christ. He is the anointed of God, the express image of the Father, God encapsulated in time and space. "He is that Bread which came down from heaven." He combines the three great offices of the Israelite covenant: prophet, priest, and king. As Prophet, he speaks God's will. As Priest, he makes sacrifice, in this case himself. As King, he is raised in majesty and shall one day return in glory to judge the world.

Jesus is the Christ, the Lord. Put that in its Gentile sense of divinity. Behold, I show you a mystery, but it is a mystery upon which Christianity stands or falls. It is a mystery upon which the church of Jesus lives or dies. He is a man, and he is God. I cannot explain it, but my soul, my life resonates and exults upon that faith. Born of a woman, but the only begotten Son of God. William Holmes Borders said, "On his mother's side born of a woman, Mary, but on his Father's side, Son of God."

Always by the lowliness of his humanity, we must place the lordliness of his divinity as the Scriptures do. Dr. Maclaren pointed it out.

> He is born a weak infant, but angels herald his birth; he lies in a manger, but a trembling star hangs bright above his cradle, and leads sages to bring their tribute to his infant presence. He sits wearied and thirsty on the stone coping of a well and asks water from a peasant woman; but he gives her the "Water of life." He sleeps as a man exhausted in the stern of a little fishing boat, he

awakes and as God bids his creatures, winds and waves, to lie down like pet dogs at his feet. As a man he weeps beside Lazarus's grave, but as God be flings his voice into the dark recesses of the tomb and the sheeted dead came forth.

The old preachers said that he called Lazarus by name: "Lazarus, come forth." If he had not called Lazarus's name, they said, and had spoken only the words "come forth," the dead from Adam would have come out of their graves in a premature resurrection. Jesus, yes, a man! But Christ, also, my Savior and my God!

He is the fulfillment of what men did not know they were describing. Jesus Christ. They wrote, I believe, in ways and with exalted praise beyond their own awareness, but Jesus Christ is to many the Shiloh, in Genesis, who is to come. He is the Umpire, the "days-man," of whom Job spoke unknowingly. He is that Shadow of a great rock in a weary land, talked about by Isaiah. Jesus Christ is the Horn of salvation the psalmist sang about. He is Immanuel of whom Isaiah wrote. He is the great "I am that I am" in Exodus. Christ Jesus is the Ancient of Days Daniel talked about. He is Haggai's Desire of all nations, Zechariah's Fountain opened in the house of David, Malachi's Messenger of the covenant." He is the Stone the builders rejected in Matthew. He is Paul's second Adam and Revelation's Bright Morning Star.

Jesus Christ. Can you not say it, too? He is our peace and pardon. He is our light and life. He is our lawyer and leader. He is our hope and help. He is our way and way maker. He is our strength and stay, our deliverer and delight. He is my substitute and Savior, my Jesus, my God.

↜ 21 ↝

The Sinner's Friend

October 30, 1977

The Son of man came eating and drinking; and they say, Behold a man gluttonous, and a winebibber, a friend of publicans and sinners. (Matthew 11:19)

Many of us grew up on household sayings, almost all of which have some truth in them. You can think of a dozen such sayings, one of which is often true but not always true. It is, "A person is known by the company he or she keeps." Ordinarily it is a fair measurement of who we are, what we are, and where we are headed. You young people particularly need to be careful not to fall in with the wrong crowd for, to use another of those old sayings, "One bad apple can spoil a barrel." Your parents have a particularly hard problem at this point in dealing with you because, as you know, the more they warn you against people whose company does you no good, the more glamorous and exciting and attractive such people become. We have had saddening incidents of fine young people who have faced problems not because of what they were doing but because of the people they were around. Flee people who have no aim as a plague! Shun young people who are forever talking everything down and who are not looking up.

With this ground clearing, it is now necessary to go on to say that this saying, "A person is known by the company he or she keeps," is not always true. A doctor is likely to spend most of his time among the ill, but this does not mean that he is ill. On the other hand, a minister is likely to spend most of his time among religious people, but this does not make him religious. The lawyer

126

does not necessarily have legal troubles, the cook is not necessarily hungry, and the policeman who spends most of his time among law breakers may well not be a criminal.

Well, that old saying, "A person is known by the company he or she keeps," may or may not have been used during the time of Jesus Christ in the earth, but his critics applied its principle to him. The rumor began being whispered about that there was something not right about the new prophet from Nazareth. It may surprise some of you who have felt or some of you who have peddled gossip to know that your Lord was the victim of such underhanded slander. Ah, the finger pointers wagged their heads and almost behind their hand spread the rumor that the man from Galilee was not all that he made believe he was. These dinners and feasts lasting late into the night where good-timers and other suspicious people gathered and talked and told jokes were not the place for someone to be who was palming himself off as a holy man. It wasn't a matter either, the ugly, poisoned whisper went on, of whether he knew what he was doing. If he was a prophet, as he gave the impression of being, he would know the kind of riff-raff he was always hanging out with. If you wanted to find him, the venomed word ran on, you'd better go where these dinner parties were being held and where there was more than a little wine being poured and consumed.

Jesus had the opportunity to deal with this gossip designed to undermine his influence, even as this text gives me the opportunity to warn against harmful and unfounded tale bearing which rarely reports the truth or even a lie as it was first heard. Each idle tongue, each wicked heart, each twisted brain adds its own stinging twist to the original slander. John's disciples come to Jesus to represent that grand figure now languishing in Herod's jail. The emissaries of John ask of Jesus if he is indeed the Messiah as John had said when Jesus came to be baptized in Jordan River. Jesus sends word back to John, based not on any claims which Jesus makes about himself but solely founded upon what he was doing.

Tell John what things ye have seen and heard, how the blind see, the lame walk, and so on.

Jesus then reflects upon the greatness of John the Baptist, the austere righteousness which he represented and with which he sought to confront the people of God. Quickly he passes on to deal with the poisoned tongue which takes something and twists it into an ugly and damaging report. John, said Jesus, came among the people neither eating bread nor drinking wine. Seeing this stern dedication and the sweeping consecration, the gainsayers and the faultfinders twisted what they saw into something unwholesome and ugly. "He hath a devil," the critics said.

Now Jesus, shedding the unbending asceticism of John, came in quite the opposite way, entering the regular ways of people, attending dinners and, yes, drinking wine in that moderate way Jews have almost always used alcohol, not in the sick way other cultures have debauched and drowned themselves in whiskey and cocktails. Now, having said that John, who would neither "eat nor drink," was a devil, what would they say of Jesus, who came eating and drinking? Was this bright and friendly way what the critics wanted? Not on your life! Having said John was a devil because he neither ate nor drank, they said that Jesus, who came eating and drinking, was "a man gluttonous and a winebibber." They, as they thought, shot the dagger home with what was meant to be the death stroke, saying that Jesus was "a friend of publicans and sinners."

Jesus accepted the label, the slander, and turned it into the brightest jewel in the dear Savior's crown. He made the libel his label! He took his stand among the outcasts, the broken, the rejects of his society, the bruised, the abused, the second class, and the sickened class. Never before in history and never since has anyone come among us actually throwing in his lot with such dump-heap, garbage-pile, dime-a-dozen folk. Others have claimed for their own selfish ends that they were for the disinherited, the scorned segments of society, all of the while holding such in contempt, never choosing such for friends and turning abruptly from them at the first opportunity. Jesus stayed among such lowly people, announced himself for them from the beginning to the very end.

He, the Son of God, was born of a peasant woman in an outcast's manger. He began his public life with a declaration embracing the needy. "The Spirit of the Lord is upon me, because he hath anointed me to preach the gospel to the poor; he hath sent me to heal the brokenhearted, to preach deliverance to the captives, and recovering of sight to the blind, to set at liberty them that are bruised, to preach the acceptable year of the Lord" (Luke 4:18–19). He stated his intention again and again, saying once, "They that are whole need not a physician; but they that are sick. I came not to call the righteous, but sinners to repentance" (Luke 5:31). He spoke pardon to a man palsied and sick with sin, "Son, be of good cheer, thy sins be forgiven thee" (Matthew 9:5). To a poor woman held up in public shame he said, "Go, and sin no more" (John 8:11). Guilty and sorrowing people felt welcome to bow and weep at his feet; they sensed and then saw that he would not turn them away.

As he came near the end of his earthly day, he was heard calling this motley crowd, this ragtag circle friends. "Henceforth I call you not servants... but I have called you friends" (John 15:15). Looking on to Calvary and that dark night and wide river through which he would soon pass, Jesus connected his death with his care for us, his regard and affection for us. He said, "Greater love than this hath no man than this, that a man lay down his life for his friends" (John 15:13). At Calvary, where it happened, it is that which melts my heart and bathes my eyes in thankful tears — that he, the blessed Savior, would lay down his life for us sinners and for me!

I cannot understand how anybody, hearing and knowing that Christ laid down his life for such a sinner as you are or I am, can remain cold of heart and unmoved. Does the gospel read or sung or preached not touch you? What hardness of spirit some of us must have that we do not break down in tears and repentance and sorrow. I speak not of the persuasive powers of any preacher. Let this preacher be too limited in thought, that one too learned, one too emotional, the other too cold, one too sensational, the other too dull. I care for none of these excuses. Forget the preacher! Remember the gospel! Christ loved us and loves us still. The gospel! Christ died for us. The gospel! Christ died as the friend of sinners, such as you and I.

He did! No matter what you and I have done. No matter what we are doing. No matter what we will do. However shameful, however low, however loathsome, Christ died for us. I am a sinner and am glad, so glad that Christ died for me. Croesus once scornfully remarked to an early Christian about the no-good people who were attracted to the company of the people of Jesus. "Yes," replied the Christian, "we look for common people." And it was said of our Lord that "the common people heard him gladly" (Mark 12:37). The "common" then meant sinners. Rejoice, my sinful soul, that thy Savior took his place at your side and in your stead. He was numbered with the transgressors, enrolled himself by your sinful name, stood in your sinful place, suffered and died in your sinful stead, and made intercession and still does for sinners such as we.

He is a friend who all our sins does bear. We will never find a friend so faithful who will our sorrow share. He knows our every weakness, and we may take it to our friend in prayer. Our Friend he is by day and our Friend by night. Our Friend in bright days and in dark. Our Friend in health and in sickness. Our Friend in youth and old age. Our Friend while life shall last, and our Friend in death's trying hour.

He bids us come to him, never mind our condition. He is the Friend of sinners.

~ 22 ~

GOD'S THREE GREAT SABBATHS

February 12, 1978

Then cometh the end, when he shall have delivered up the kingdom to God, even the Father; when he shall have put down all rule and all authority and power. (1 Corinthians 15:24)

The Hebrew word *Shabbath*, from which comes our word *Sabbath*, means "rest." Now I care not whether someone observes Saturday as the Sabbath or Sunday. I am sure that the people we need to worry about are those who observe no day as the day of rest and worship. The passing from our society of a generally accepted day of rest and or worship is, I think, but another sign in the weakening and decline of our Western society.

As a citizen, I have problems about an official law as to the day of rest. I do not have problems about the day on which we worship, but I do have problems about an official day of national rest. This is so because we are not all Christians in this country, and Jews, for instance, observe Saturday. Even among us Christians some observe Sunday, others Saturday.

En route on a Sunday morning to a preaching engagement in South India, I asked young Rev. George if Sunday is generally the day of rest in India. He replied that Sunday is the day of rest. Hindus and other non-Christian people do not close their stores generally. He went on to say that Christians usually close their shops on Sunday, but some, according to my young friend, open the back door and do business anyhow. We know how that is.

Sabbath day means rest day, according to the original definition. Sabbath day suggests rest from labor — cessation, completion of effort. That was the original meaning. A man who

---

I am indebted for the structure of this sermon to W. Robertson Nicoll, one-time editor of the *British Weekly*. —GCT

should be better known than he is has suggested that the Bible speaks of three great Sabbaths — in the sense of rest, cessation, completion of a portion of work. And how often we have heard it said, or said it ourselves that "I want to finish this job before the weekend, or before Sunday."

The first Sabbath of which the Bible speaks occurs in the account we have in Genesis of how God created the heaven and the earth, the beasts of the field, the birds of the air, the fish of the sea, and then made man in his own image. This teaching instructs us that because God created the world, this old lopsided, out-of-shape, gone-wrong world has spiritual influences, and determining ones, at its center and core.

In years gone by, some supposedly smart people sought to scoff at the idea that God created the world. It came, they said, by natural evolution. They never explained what "natural" means, or what or who makes "natural" natural. You and I may be fools in believing that God actually created the world. I think it takes a bigger fool to believe that all of this just happened all by itself. They say that the earth just appeared, and flowers and fruit just blossomed out of the earth, and the rain just watered the plants and fruit, and the sun just warmed them, and so all of these things are just there. I think they are just fools who just say such things.

God made the world, and humanity cannot take it away from him. We saw that this week. We go along with all of our little machines and data sheets and slide rulers and laser beams and computers and weather charts with their radar screens and feel very comfortable in the notion that we are in charge of all of the world. Then God drops a hint, snow begins to fall, not all of his snow, just some of his flakes. What happens? Proud Boston stops, cultured Connecticut shuts down, and the Empire State discovers it is a colony of helplessness; sophisticated New York stalls. Christians suffer in it, too, at least a part of them, but the larger and truer part of Christians, seeing what we have seen of the blizzard and snowstorm of the last week, can say, "Ride on, King Jesus, ride on, conquering King, no man can hinder you."

When God had created all of this, the broad carpeted earth, the noble mountain ranges, the restless sea, the great dome of the sky, and the mind and heart of man and woman, the Scriptures say that he looked at what he had done and found it satisfying. Then occurred the first Sabbath of God, and we were a part of that as the crowning act of God's great creative impulse. "And on the seventh day God ended his work which he had made; and he rested on the seventh day from all the work which he had made" (Genesis 2:1).

The first Sabbath of God occurred after creation; the second completion of labor and cessation from effort occurred in our redemption. This is what Lent is all about. The centerpiece of our gospel is that God came among us in Jesus Christ and took up the work of bringing us back where we belonged. The bedrock, the cornerstone, the "without which nothing" of our Christian belief is that "God was in Christ, reconciling the world unto himself" (2 Corinthians 5:19). Hear that, every sinner! Hear that, every believer! The work of the Son, the life of Jesus Christ, represents the second great work of God. And what a worker he was!

Before he was born the angel commanded that "thou shalt call his name Jesus: for he shall save his people from their sins" (Matthew 1:21). Let every sinning heart hear those tidings like the sweet sound of silver bells. When he was a little baby gurgling in his mother's arms, an old man with his foot near Jordan's chill tides said, "Behold, this child is set for the fall and rising again of many in Israel" (Luke 2:34). When he was a young man, his mother said of him to a wedding host without wine one night, "Do whatever he says." It is still a good word to every believer. In the midst of the fury and storms of his ministry, enemy agents who heard him said, "Never a man spoke like this man." In the powers of his holy sonship and in the working out of his mighty acts of redemption, he spoke to his servants whom he had first known in the work of creation, the lashing winds and the raging sea. When they bowed quietly at his feet, those who watched exclaimed, "What manner of man is this, that even the winds and the sea obey him" (Mark 4:41). All of this was part of his work of showing himself, confronting evil and winning his people.

Yes, Christ represents God's second great work, the work of redemption. Said Jesus, "My Father worketh hitherto, and I work." And he did work, he healed the sick and he raised the dead, he drove out demons and restored sanity. He taught as one having authority. For us the Bread of Life became hungry and the fountain of Living Water became thirsty. For us the strength of God became weak and the Eternal bowed down to death.

When Christ died, he completed the work of redemption. Those who killed him lived to see him conquer. They would see that when he died with his pierced hand he seized the initiative and gave back to the sons of men another Eden with no tree in the midst of the garden from which we cannot eat. On the rugged mount with his own wounded hand he planted a vineyard and made of Calvary a very fruitful hill. When he died, there was nothing left undone. When his humiliation was passed, when his travail was over, when he dieth no more, when he passed clear through the winepress, with his garments rolled in blood and the power of sin and death broken, when his work was over, John says simply, "He bowed his head." "Jesus says "I have finished the work." At Calvary the word was "It is finished." Thus came the Sabbath of the Son. Then his work on earth was complete, and he need never again go into the Holy of Holies to offer another sacrifice. "He that is entered into his rest, he also hath ceased from his own works, as God did from his" (Hebrews 4:10). This is the second Sabbath of God, rest from the finished work of redemption.

There is the promise of a third Sabbath, a third completion, the consummation of the age. There is a struggle going on now. This is not to say that Christ has not done his work on earth. This is to say that some regions of the creation have not gotten the message. One of the celebrated victories of American military history is the battle of New Orleans in January 1815. Jackson's victory is memorialized in Jackson Square in the Vieux Carré of old New Orleans. This battle was fought, however, fifteen days after the treaty of peace was signed at Ghent ending the British-American war. Jackson and his army had not heard the news.

And so, though Christ has died and in so doing has taken the measure of all evil, corporate and massive, private and messy, the battle still rages. And yet we who love Jesus know how it must come out. The powers of hell have not received the communiqué, but the battle has been fought and won.

I do not say that the conflict is not hard, that the warfare does not rage furiously through the creation. It does, and many of you know much of life's hurts and its wounds and its bitter disappointments. We cannot help feeling discouragement and despondency sometimes. We move midst confounding sorrows and long and grim desolation. There are heavy afflictions and devastating disappointments. Hostile powers are arrayed against us, and formidable are their weapons. Sin and sickness and sorrow and pain and motives misread and, yes, death. Have you ever talked quietly with someone you know very well and who knows that six months are all that is left? Yes, it is a hard battle, and we must pass under the cloud.

It is a hard fight and heavy labor, but there is the promise of rest and fulfillment. It is the third Sabbath of God. Hear how Paul states the matter in that soaring and surging fifteenth chapter of 1 Corinthians, "then cometh the end, when he shall have delivered up the kingdom to God, even the Father; when he shall have put down all rule and all authority and power. For he must reign, till he hath put all enemies under his feet. The last enemy that shall be destroyed is death" (1 Corinthians 15:24–26).

Sometimes, it seems such a frail hope. Standing midst the graves of those we have lost and the thinning and weakening of those we are losing and very much aware that in the midst of life, we ourselves are in death, it seems such a far-off and dim pronouncement. Yet the Sabbath of which I speak is as true as the others. "Then cometh the end." The end of sin, the end of sorrow, the end of sickness, the end of separating, the end of stress, the end of slander, the end of suffering — death's end. The end of ends!

That will be the third Sabbath of God, and our own rest. The number of God's chosen shall be finished, and the kingdom will be fully come on earth as it is in heaven.

What a promise! How sweet to live life in its confidence. The Sentinel of our souls keeps his sleepless vigil over us, even here. But then God will be all in all. Never more a frown upon the brow. Never more can fear or sorrow or pain or sickness or death touch those we love. Never more can they fall or fail. Never more can our eyes grow wet with tears. Then cometh the end, when God will be all in all. God above, God below, God all around, God within, God ahead. Forever! "There remaineth therefore a rest to the people of God" (Hebrews 4:9).

⟅ 23 ⟆

THREE TESTING TIMES AND GOD

June 11, 1978

Thy shoes shall be iron and brass; and as thy days, so shall thy strength be. The eternal God is thy refuge, and underneath are the everlasting arms. (Deuteronomy 33:25,27)

Life is a forced march, and we must keep moving. Sometimes we wonder what it would be like if this life was not like a forced march. Suppose we could stop at this point or that and refuse to go on. Some people do in mind and in emotions refuse to step into the future at some time or other. We are hearing much of the new dieting disease in which young girls, particularly, diet themselves to a sickly and sometimes fatal illness because they do not want to become women with the new burdens and responsibilities and sexuality which adult womanhood brings.

All attempts to go on living and to quit the journey of growing older is a doomed effort, no matter whether it is attempted in childhood or at some point in adulthood. Think of the little girl playing cooking with her toy stove or the little boy with his toy automobile. This is cute, but parents have a right to feel alarm if at age fifteen or sixteen the now not-so-little girl is still playing with toy stoves and the boy aging toward manhood is still playing with a toy automobile.

In the town where I grew up, we had an example of that attempt to stop time in its tracks, to refuse to go on to the next stage in life. In fact, the woman was a teacher, and I suppose a good one, but she was a laughingstock because she insisted on wearing clothes which little girls wore. Her face was the face of a woman; her clothes were the clothes of a girl. How people talked about that, for in that far-off time and limited place we had not too much to talk about.

137

Maybe I ought to point out some examples of what I am talking about that are not so extreme and let us see where we fit into this matter. The fifteen-year-old who whimpers and whines like a little child is trying to stop time. The twenty- or twenty-five-year-old who has no more sense of responsibility than a fifteen-year-old and who is still fuzzy about what he or she ought to be doing in life fits what I am trying to describe. People who won't make wills or prepare their souls for death are such foolish people, acting as if they can stop time.

If we could stop time, we would miss so much. The earliest of our years hardly give to us our greatest moments. These belong to a time of maturity and understanding. If we could stop time, we would miss so much. Our friends would go on to life's mature and richer experiences and we would be left-backs, like children failing to pass on to the next grade. There is the story of the Greek character, Tithonus, the handsome prince of Troy, whose lover was Aurora, the goddess of the dawn in Greek mythology. She persuaded Zeus, according to the ancient Greek legend, to grant her dashing prince immortality but forgot to ask for the gift of youth. To her dismay, he aged but could not die. Finally, when he was old and toothless, she could bear his presence no longer and shut him up in his chamber from whence his feeble and piteous voice could be heard crying and pleading. That is hell. I cannot quite persuade myself, much less you, and yet it may be true that death is not a terror, surely not at a certain time. It may be our best friend, and J. M. Barrie may well have been right when he said that he thought death would be life's last and grandest adventure. At any rate, time will not stop and should not and we will understand better and better what Browning meant when he wrote:

> Grow old along with me, the best is yet to be
> The last for which the first was made.

Along that journey of living, there are some major testing times, and the text seems designed for such times. The words of the text are brave and inspiriting like mountain air. They have about them a noble and robust sound. "Thy shoes shall be iron and brass; and as thy days, so shall thy strength be." Skip a verse or two and we come upon another verse, or part of one, which is almost without equal in the kindly promise it brings from God to our poor, exposed, shivering years in the earth. "The eternal God is thy refuge, and underneath are the everlasting arms." It has been traditionally believed that Moses was the author of these words as he addressed the assembled nation of ancient Israel in his farewell discourse, his valedictory address to his people before God buried him in Mt. Nebo's craggy heights.

It is a fetching thought, and these words bear a grandeur worthy of the great and solitary nature of the life of Moses, and especially his death. Dr. James Sanders reminds us that what Moses did survived in a way unrivaled by all of Israel's kings, the matchless David not excluded. These words would be fitting for one shortly now to be buried in a mysterious grave which no human eyes are to behold. No traveler to the Holy Land has ever had pointed out to him the grave of Moses. Every tourist knows that Abraham's and Isaac's and Jacob's graves are still to be seen among the graves of Hebron, or their supposed graves. The bones of Joseph sleep, we are told, after many wanderings in Shechem, in the parcel of ground given to him by his father. Rachel's tomb stands on the road to Bethlehem, for there her strength failed her and she died giving birth to Benjamin. The sepulchre of David is by Jerusalem, the joy of his heart. But the last resting place of Moses is claimed by no city. God rocked him to sleep in the lonely fastness of Nebo. God closed his eyes in death, angels were his pallbearers, and God buried him up where the stars go to sleep, up where the meteors shoot and the lightning is loosed.

So these words would have been proper on the lips of Moses as farewell, but no matter who spoke them, they have the ring of experience and certainty and conviction and assurance. I want to address them to three major testing times in our living and pray

God that some of you passing through this one or that of these three experiences will lean heavily on them.

I think that there are three supreme times of testing in life. One occurs in adolescence as we turn from the rather formless pleasures of childhood to the more structured demands of life in adulthood. It is a time of passage, and it is very perilous. This is a time of embarrassment, of gawkiness and awkwardness. For one is no longer a child and is not yet an adult. Ah, you parents, how careful and prayerful you must be with those in this testing time.

Let those who are there and those who are responsible for them hear the promise of God, "As thy days, so shall thy strength be." How sad that so many of our young people turn from God and from the church at the most ill-advised and trying time of their lives, when they need the arms of God around them and the sweet fellowship of the church as never before. God has a large place for the young. Samuel was but a boy when God called him and David but a child when he became God's warrior. Mary, the mother of Jesus, was doubtless scarcely more than a girl when she became his mother. Our Lord was twelve when the house of God drew him like a magnet and he was found talking with the doctors of the law.

"As thy days, so shall thy strength be" and "the eternal God is thy refuge" are words that speak to us in the testing time of changing from boys and girls to men and women. God offers what we need at that stage, and what do we need, you ask? We need high ideals, and there is Jesus Christ saying, "I am your model." We need then great religious inspiration, and there is Jesus Christ saying, "Follow me, and I will make you...." What do we need as we move toward adulthood? We need a cause that will claim our fervor and our ardor. And there is Jesus Christ saying, "If any man will be my disciple, let him take up his cross and follow me." And, yes, we have a God who tells the young as they face life's fight, "The LORD is my light and my salvation; whom shall I fear? The LORD is the strength of my life; of whom shall I be afraid?... Though an host should encamp against me, my heart shall not fear.... For in the time of trouble he shall hide me in his pavilion: in the secret of his tabernacle shall he hide me; he shall set me upon a rock" (Psalm 27:1,3,5).

There is, I think, a second great testing time. It occurs when we have labored and striven and sacrificed and struggled our way to some measure of success. In the business of living and striving we doubtless make some enemies, and they may rise up when in weariness we lower our guard. We have spent in struggling much of our vital and nervous energy and are likely to show nervousness and irritability. The first fervor of our marriages has passed, and we are likely to start feeling apprehensive about our physical attractiveness. The children are about grown, and the end of that parental effort brings a letdown. If successful, we are likely to repeat the foolish words of a foolish man, "Soul, thou hast much goods laid up for many years; take thine ease, eat, drink, and be merry" (Luke 12:19). We see that in many who as success and security come, or seem to come, find less and less time for the hour of worship and the service of God. "Fool," said Jesus, "life's testing is upon you. Whose shall these things be?" Did you know that soon, very soon, every little prideful prize we clutch so determinedly in our hands today will fall from our lifeless grip? How tragic that our society with all of its wealth allows hunger and poverty to run rampant in the land. We are under God's judgment for our neglect of the poor, the vulnerable.

"As thy days, so shall they strength be...the eternal God is thy refuge, and underneath are the everlasting arms." And so in the days of middle age, of prosperity and position, God gives us strength. He promises renewal when the first fervor and the early passions have gone, when energy flags and our enthusiasms dull and our appetites are glutted and sated. I hear God say to such, "They that wait upon the LORD shall renew their strength; they shall mount up with wings as eagles; they shall run, and not be weary; and they shall walk, and not faint" (Isaiah 40:31). And there is the promise for what is old and tired, "Behold, I make all things new."

There is one other testing time which I will touch upon but for a moment. It comes to most of us before we die, and more so now that people are living longer. Our work is finished, but our departure is not yet at hand. Our friends are all gone, but we linger on. The children no longer need us; nobody seems to need us. Someone told me of a businessman in my community who daily struggles downstairs to the office for fear the work can go on without him. The sun has gone down, we are in twilight, but night has not come. The work is finished, but the time of sleep is not yet. I saw that once in a hospital sickroom at the bedside of a woman who served her church in one capacity perhaps longer than anyone in its history. She wants to leave here but still lingers. More and more that note crept into my mother's conversation toward the end. Our day is gone, and we must move among strange people and strange ways. We are no longer able to do for ourselves and must wait for others to do for us. No one admires us or seeks our company any longer. People at the end of their lives feel the indifference and hostility too often of government and community.

"As thy days, so shall thy strength be." The Lord raises up people to see about us, and it is true. Psalm 37:25: "I have been young, and am now old; yet I have never seen the righteous forsaken, nor his seed begging bread." God says in Isaiah 46:4, "Even to your old age I am he; and even to gray hairs will I carry you: I have made, and I will bear; even I will carry, and will deliver you." When the world turns its back on us, the Lord says, "The eternal God is thy refuge," and when the world has no outstretched arms for us, throws us on life's dump heap, repudiates us for somebody new, withdraws its hand of fellowship from us, God says, "Underneath" — you cannot fall — "Underneath" — with no more work that needs us, and no more strength to go and come, laid aside — "Underneath — are still the everlasting arms." God is our shelter and protection. "The eternal God is thy refuge, and underneath are the everlasting arms."

∾ 24 ∾

THE POWER OF HIS RESURRECTION

April 15, 1979

Yea doubtless, and I count all things but loss for the excellency of the knowledge of Christ Jesus my Lord: for whom I have suffered the loss of all things, and do count them but dung, that I may win Christ, and be found in him, not having mine own righteousness, which is of the law, but that which is through the faith of Christ, the righteousness which is of God by faith: that I may know him, and the power of his resurrection, and the fellowship of his sufferings, being made conformable unto his death; if by any means, I might attain unto the resurrection of the dead. (Philippians 3:8–11)

What we have in this passage is a kind of postscript, a glorious and wonderful afterthought, loaded with the fragrance of faith and hope that in Christ shall endless be. The language and pace of the closing verses of chapter two sound like those personal references which usually brought Paul's letters to their conclusion. This second chapter in its earlier passages has sounded the great and awesome depths to which Christ Jesus came from his glorious place as equal of God down to the humblest earthly station a poor human being could occupy. This is called the great *kenosis* doctrine, the self-emptying of the Lord of all of his divine majesty and honor to be one of us — and we know how frail and weak is that state.

The second chapter passes into what the musicians call *diminuendo*, lessening, lowering of tone and volume. Paul drops down, if I may put it this way, to some personal references and calls the names of Timothy and Epaphroditus. It is the way we refer to people by name in friendly letters toward the end. "George will be coming your way soon," or "Susan has been sick." The second chapter gathers up some strands. As the third chapter begins, Paul falls into a failing of many preachers to whom "finally" does

143

not mean finally. "Finally," he says and then goes on for what are now two more whole chapters. I know that some biblical investigators think that we have here a fragment of another letter which Paul sent to Philippi and which happened to be included in this letter. Some of us prefer to believe that what we have here are new thoughts which crowd in upon our author as he prepares to end his letter. You have done that and I have done that. "There is something else I want to say to you." That's what we have here.

In the early portion of the third chapter Paul deals with an annoying issue which confronts the church, and his language becomes robust, almost offensive as he speaks of some whom he considers to be enemies of the church, "Beware of dogs, beware of evil workers" (Philippians 3:2). Confessedly this is language of which the apostle might not be proud. It is to say that all of us sink sometimes to levels which do not become men and women who have been with Jesus and who know the great salvation which is in him. Paul does not remain at this low level of angry invective and bitter language and stinging epithet, mean talk. Nor can any Christian ever be content to wallow in mud. We may fall sometimes, but something within makes us struggle toward our feet even before we have finished falling. It is a Christian's part to be hopeful, not defeatist; confident, not hopeless; believing, not doubting; persevering, not giving up.

The mood shifts, and the apostle begins to prepare for takeoff. Watch him, for as the fourth verse begins he taxis toward the runway and the engines begin to roar as he prepares for flight. "We are the circumcision, which worship God in the spirit" (Philippians 3:3). Then Paul recites his own earthly credentials. "I might have confidence," he says, "in the flesh." I was born under the most approved conditions, on the right side of the tracks, so to speak. "Circumcised the eighth day, of the stock of Israel, of the tribe of Benjamin, a Hebrew of the Hebrews" (Philippians 3:5). "Look at my pedigree, behold my background," he is saying.

Paul says that all of these things, these certificates of respectability, these documents of earthly superiority are nothing but trash. He goes further, and in a daring figure of speech, trying to show how little they count, he says that he looks upon all these gilt-edged credentials as little more than rotten refuse of the body, the waste material from our digestive process, foul and putrid excrement, manure, feculence. I will not use the expressive word with which vulgarity describes what Paul is talking about. All earthly glory is that worthless, that pointless, that futile over against what his spiritual eyes had seen. Listen to the apostle's faith and hope as they take wings toward the sunrise of the Son of God. "But what things were gain to me, those I counted loss for Christ. Yea doubtless, and I count all things but loss for the excellency of the knowledge of Christ Jesus my Lord . . . and do count them but dung."

"That I may know him," and here my subject and text occur, "and the power of his resurrection." That word *power* used here, the *dunamis* is used at least seventy times in the New Testament. We may say that it is one of the characteristically Christian words. Here it means miraculous might, capacity and ability to do. Here is Paul's supreme ambition. Here is the writer's paramount purpose. Here is our author's primary passion. Here is his dominant motive, his chief aim, his first desire.

"That I may know him and the power of his resurrection." He speaks of a living Christ, not a dead relic. Hans Küng, the Tübingen scholar, reports that he asked the rather skeptical Rudolf Bultmann whether he felt that Christ lives because we believe in him. In other words, is Christ alive only because we remember him? This would mean that the church keeps Christ alive by its memory of him and its preaching of him as Lord and Savior. "No," said Bultmann, "he does not live because we believe in him; we believe in him because he lives." Believers do not keep Christ alive; Christ keeps believers alive.

The resurrection is the necessary conclusion to the crucifixion of Jesus. There is a great power in his death, yes. We are strangely moved when we stand at Calvary. A strange awe crosses us when we see the sun stop shining while his friends stand around crying.

We are moved when we hear the Savior groaning and his friends sadly moaning. Yes, sometimes it causes me to tremble. It was a saving, substituting, sufficing death. He saw the travail of his soul and was satisfied.

There needs to be something else, and I am so glad that Jesus rose from the dead. Paul was, too, saying, "He was delivered for our offences, and was raised again for our justification." He died one time and dieth no more forever. He was cut off from the land of the living, but God did not leave his soul in hell.

Evil must never think that it has the field to itself. Wrong must never think that it has won. Oppression must know forever that there is a God above who judges and rules the affairs of people. People who are out to crush and to degrade and to mistreat others must always know that there is a power that makes for righteousness. Because Jesus rose one day, bigotry will disappear from this country. I do not know how, I only know that Christ was raised from the dead and, therefore, truth crushed to earth will rise again. One day every evil character, whether in Uganda or Zimbabwe or Birmingham or Washington, no matter the supposed power, must go down. I do not know politics, but I know God raised Christ from the dead. "God is so high you can't get over him, so wide you can't get around him, so low you can't go under him." He is God; there is none other.

Paul stakes everything on the resurrection. He sounds this note again and again like a great symphonic theme in the music of his life and in the anthem of the universe. "If we have been planted together in the likeness of death, we shall be also in the likeness of his resurrection.... If we be dead with Christ, we believe that we shall also live with him" (Romans 6:5,8). "As in Adam all die, even so in Christ shall all be made alive" (1 Corinthians 15:22). Again and again he strikes that dominant chord: "the first man is of the earth, earthy: the second man is the Lord from heaven" (1 Corinthians 15:47). "Flesh and blood cannot inherit the kingdom of God" (1 Corinthians 15:50). It is not healthy enough. "Behold, I shew you a mystery.... This corruptible must put on incorruption, and this mortal must put on immortality. So when this corruptible shall have put on incorruption, and this mortal shall have put on immortality, then shall be brought to pass the saying that is written, Death is swallowed up in victory. O death, where is thy sting? O grave, where is thy victory?" (1 Corinthians 15:51,53–55).

The power of his resurrection means that he has ascended on high, that he has gone to prepare a place for us. And as we prepare for our place, our place is being prepared for us. He comes back to get his people. He came to carry my friend, Sandy Ray, home the other day. He comes back himself. We do not have to depend on any inferior escort to usher us into our place. "I will come again...myself." I will feel better if my escort home has nail marks in his feet. I know he knows the way, for he has traveled the road to and through death and into life before us.

I am not overly curious as to how and where and what. I only want to know that Christ is there and that he is in charge of the arrangements. We may rest everything on the faith that Jesus rose from the dead. I care not how he rose; I only want to know that up from the grave he arose, with a mighty shout over his foes. I care not with what body we are to be raised. We need only know that Jesus arose and he lives, lives among us here, lives on high, lives to save us, lives to bless us, lives to keep us, lives to guide us, lives to come back for us, lives to put his arm around us, lives to lead us through Jordan's cold, chill stream, lives to lead us to great reunion, lives to assign us a room in our Father's house, lives to give us back our dead forever, lives to be admired eternally by his people in a land where we never grow old and in a land that is fairer than day, in the house not made with hands, in the city that lieth foursquare, in the new Jerusalem from which death is forever expelled and where goodbyes are not known in the lexicon and language of the redeemed citizens who are to live there forever, serving and never growing tired.

✑ 25 ✑

GOD'S GREAT ABOUT-TO-BE

December 16, 1979

The glory of the LORD shall be revealed, and all flesh shall see it together: for the mouth of the LORD hath spoken it. (Isaiah 40:5)

Do you have a Christian outlook on life? I think that there is a test of whether you do or do not have such an understanding of events. I am convinced one may be a Christian, a true and earnest Christian, while still having something other than a Christian view of what life and its events are all about. You may test yourself on this Christian outlook on life — one does not want to be so fancy as to say "a Christian philosophy of life" — by putting to yourself several questions. Here are some of them: What do you think of events in your life? Are they just happenings, accidental or chance occurrences with no significance beyond what a man I used to know would call "one of those darn things"? Are the events of the world, the thunderous roar of public life, just so many incidents that take place without rhyme and without reason?

Many Christian people, one fears, would give one of several sub-Christian — non-Christian — answers to such a test. Some would likely reply that they are simply puzzled by the goings on in their lives and really do not know if there is any meaning to the lights and shadows which fall across their days in occurrences of joy and sorrow and whatever is in between. Not knowing, they have no particular belief about such matters but just take things as they come. If such is your answer, then score yourself as a Christian agnostic. Agnosticism means that we cannot know, we cannot affirm, and we cannot deny the existence of God. If we cannot affirm or deny the existence of God, then we have no way

148

of believing that meaning and purpose belong to events of daily existence — both the big events and the small ones.

Another answer, if many of us will be honest with ourselves, is that we see no meaning whatsoever in the occurrences of our lives and that we do not believe that they have any meaning. Things just happen, and when they have happened, no pattern emerges, no meaning arises out of the days and nights. This is close to atheism or the belief that there is no God and hence no meaning. And if there is a God, he does not care, takes little or no interest in our affairs, or he is a spectator, if not a prisoner, in this great world, without authority, without activity and, yes, with little claim on our loyalty or love.

There are still others who, if honest, would confess that they see whatever of meaning and worth in life as being located in the past. There was a time when God spoke to men and women, but that was in the long ago. In those days, once upon a time, God walked the earth and influenced human affairs, but no longer. Such notions are really ideas of a lost innocence of our human existence. Paradise belongs to the childhood of the race. The only Eden that ever was or ever will be was in the long ago.

The Bible has little to do with these notions. Never mind how bleak the outlook, never mind how dark the night, God is still active, God moves, God determines. And this is as true of the huge scenes where nations live out their role in history as it is true in the small snapshot photographs, so to speak, where ordinary men and women — whatever that word *ordinary* means here — live out the days of their years.

A search of Scriptures will reveal few times and places where emphasis on the presence and activity of God in human events is more pronounced than in the fortieth chapter of Isaiah. Almost all respectable biblical scholarship today recognizes that here in this chapter we have a different time, different circumstances, and a different mood from what we see in the first thirty-nine chapters. Beginning with this fortieth chapter, some feel we are face to face with another writer known now as the second Isaiah, Deutero-Isaiah. When George Adam Smith first presented the theory of the second Isaiah at Northfield in one of the Dwight Moody conferences, Mr. Moody is supposed to have said that it was a shame to tell people about a second Isaiah when they had not heard of the first Isaiah.

Still, we do have a different atmosphere beginning with the fortieth chapter. Here are mysterious voices, the first of which is God's: "Comfort ye, comfort ye my people, saith your God" (Isaiah 40:1). When we hear these words in the *Messiah*, be reminded that they come like a dawn song after a long and bitter night of exile and slavery. The proud nation of David was no more. In 588 B.C. the Babylonians under the rule of Nebuchadnezzar laid siege to the holy city of Jerusalem. After eighteen months of the most intense suffering, the great city of Hebrew religion fell, its buildings destroyed, its temple burned. The proud aristocrats, the artisans, the merchants, and the priests of Israel were carried into slavery by the low canals and among the weeping willows of Babylon. Zedekiah, their king, had his eyes put out after he was forced to watch the execution of his sons (2 Kings 25:7). The glory of Israel as a free nation passes forever, except for a short period of time, from the pages of ancient history. The people, scattered in a strange land, struggled to find meaning in their slavery. God, they believed, was active in human affairs. They traced his mercy and his purpose even in their heartbreak and national shame.

Desperately, with spirits bleeding and faith fighting a furious battle with doubt and defeat, these Israelite slaves held on to their faith that God was not dead and was not deaf. He had not forsaken the work of his own hands. He was not quitting on the good work which he had begun in them. They would come forth from the fire purged and purified. The morning would surely come though the night seemed so dark and so endless. They were still God's people; he was still their God. In the midst of the mighty march of great world empires in military pomp and power, Babylon, Persia — what is now Iran — God still moved, and in all the storm and fury of nations locked in mortal combat, God would keep his people, God would bless his people, and God would deliver them. Thus the cry of "the glory of the Lord shall be revealed, and all flesh shall see it together."

Strangely enough, like a rainbow in a cloud-filled sky, this is what happened. Israel went into captivity half heathen, with its idols and images mixing with and corrupting the true faith in one God. Israel came home seventy years later with no heathen elements in its faith. Israel came home, sure that God is the God of history. He acts and moves in and through human agents and affairs even when people think they are acting on their own and without any reference to God whatsoever.

"The glory of God shall be revealed," they said. It was revealed. Proud Babylon with its wonderful hanging gardens and mighty war machine perished in the desert sand; God's people lived, and God's purpose marched on. We see better than they how true was the word that the future belongs to God. The whole future is God's great about-to-be. Persia marched to the center stage of history, strutted a moment against a backdrop of God's eternity, and passed forever from world dominance into obscurity. God's people lived on, and God's purpose marched on. Syria, under Antiochus, lunged forward to seize the world's spotlight for just a little and then sank into comparable oblivion. God's people lived on, and God's purpose marched on. Think of Babylon, Persia, Syria, and Rome. What do they matter against the supreme tidings of history? "Unto us a child is born" (Isaiah 9:6) tells of an event far surpassing the little glory of nations. That figure, the true glory of God, will forever stand taller than any nation.

As with nations so will it be all our lives: "The glory of the LORD shall be revealed." Do you believe that about your life? Think of our little time in the earth, our faults and our failures, our little strivings and surrenders, and believe, won't you, that in the midst of it all, God's glory is yet to be seen in all of its fullness and all of its splendor. Whatever of the Lord's presence we have already known, we shall yet know far more. The glory of the LORD shall be revealed in us. So the best God has for us is yet to be. There are days when in worship God has seemed to descend with mighty power. We have not yet seen in any place the glory of God as we shall see it. One day — may God make it soon — these walls will seem in the glory of worship like jasper walls, shining like jewels; these doors in the glory of worship will one day seem like gates of pearl. Our music will take on the sound of the songs the angels sing. Our praying will be in perfect tune with heaven, and our preaching will lift Christ up so irresistibly that he will draw all people unto himself. The evils of racism, war, and poverty will be chained and banished. It will happen!

"The glory of the LORD shall be revealed." We have not yet seen the best of what God can do and what he will do. The best sermon has not yet been preached. The best song has not yet been sung. The best prayer has not yet been prayed. The best service has not yet been rendered.

"The glory of the LORD shall be revealed." Does the Lord God himself not say in the Revelation, "Behold, I make all things new" (Revelation 21:5)? So we have in Jesus the promise of something far more glorious than anything we have ever known. How dare any Christian sigh and yawn as if we enlisted in some dull and unexciting cause! We have not yet begun to know the full glory of God. We have scarcely begun to taste the fruit of Canaan land. We have come but to the outskirts of holiness. We have viewed only from afar those bright, extended plains where God "the Son forever reigns/And scatters night away." We have but heard the overtures of redemption's song.

"The glory of the LORD shall be revealed." Does not the Lord God himself say, "Behold, I will do a new thing" (Isaiah 43:19)? And in Christ we do have a new beginning. The babe in Bethlehem symbolized a new humanity. In Jesus, we have a new covenant, and in the church Jesus planted, we have become God's new Israel. In the death and resurrection of Jesus, we have a new and living Way to God's own heart. Thank God through Jesus for a new name, a new walk, a new talk, a new hope, a new song, a new commandment, new hands, new feet, a new mind, a new heart, and a new will.

I hear Peter cry, "We...look for new heavens and a new earth, wherein dwelleth righteousness" (2 Peter 3:13). I hear John answer,

> I saw a new heaven and a new earth: for the first heaven and the first earth were passed away; and there was no more sea. And I John saw the holy city, new Jerusalem, coming down from God out of heaven, prepared as a bride adorned for her husband. And I heard a great voice out of heaven saying, Behold, the tabernacle of God is with men, and he will dwell with them, and they shall be his people, and God himself shall be with them, and be their God. And God shall wipe away all tears from their eyes; and there shall be no more death, neither sorrow, nor crying, neither shall there be any more pain: for the former things are passed away. And he that sat upon the throne said, Behold, I make all things new. (Revelation 21:1–5)

✒ 26 ✒

TWO NAMES IN THE MORNING

March 16, 1980

Jesus saith unto her, Mary. She turned herself, and saith unto him, Rabboni; which is to say, Master. (John 20:16)

When our astronauts first reached the moon, an American president, in that excessive, excited way of speaking which many political people, and preaching ones, too, have, exclaimed that the trip to the moon was the greatest news story since the creation. The astonishing feat made the statement understandable, but the statement revealed, also, shallow understanding of biblical truth. Billy Graham reminded the president that the voyage to the moon, as stupendous as it was, was not the greatest news ever to break on earth. The resurrection of Jesus Christ is the greatest news story in the history of this planet — and I believe of all other planets.

When Job put the question to all centuries and to all religious faith, "If a man die, shall he live again?" he addressed himself to a concern which has engaged the mind of humanity since the dawn of creation. Vernon Johns has reported another part of this great problem of human existence contained in a question set in hieroglyphics, those early picture words, found in an ancient cave. Near what must have been a burial place and standing at the foot of a pile of human skulls, the question was propounded by some unknown philosopher of 3000 B.C., "What difference the virtuous and the foolish?" In other words, what is there that gives meaning to this crazy quilt we call life where all, the wise and the foolish, die alike? Well, if this be all, then we end in the equality of nothingness and what we do here has no lasting meaning — unless a yes can be given to Job's question, "If a man die, shall he live again?" If the answer to that question is yes, then it may make a world of difference as to how we conduct this life. A world? An eternity of difference.

It all has to do with Jesus and why congregations gather in the size and spirit they do on Easter Sunday. When Friday's death was over, all who knew and loved Jesus were dazed and numb with that cold, chill heaviness which death ever brings to our human hearts. The horror of it. The public shame! The nails and the spear. The life of Jesus was snuffed out in the heat of the day and in the midst of shadows when they fell strangely on the earth, making a midday midnight. The crowd, some curious, some angry and jeering, had stood around. Jesus' words on Calvary rose out of his pain, beginning and ending with a cry in the direction of God, "Father, forgive them," and then at the last, "Father, into thy hands I commit my spirit." And then silence! How final it must have appeared to all who loved him! The end! death! a grave!

The end, yes, but love is such a stubborn, determined thing propelling us in the direction of cemeteries, cities of the dead we call them, where we can neither speak nor be spoken to. Still, love bids us go, and it bade Mary Magdalene to go out to the cemetery. Nothing but love could do that. When are we going to stop confusing things? We call men tough, or steel, or government, or guns, but not one of them can make us voluntarily get up and go out where we know there is nothing but a memory and some scarred places in the earth which we call graves. Logic can't make us go to such places, but love can. Common sense can't make us go to such places, but love can. "The heart has its reasons which reason knows not of," said Blaise Pascal.

In the yet-dark morning hours, Mary Magdalene makes her quiet and reverent way to the sepulchre where the body of Jesus had been laid. She makes an astonishing discovery — and that is putting it mildly. The stone has been rolled away from the mouth of the grave! What an eerie shiver must have passed through this woman as she discovered that the body of Jesus is not where it had been placed. She has to tell someone, and so she runs and finds Simon Peter, on his way back in spirit and action from the terrible triple denial he had made of his Lord. Peter and John come to the tomb and, sure enough, it is empty. The disciples go back, doubtless with their minds a fever as to what has happened.

Mary's word to the disciples is, "They have taken away the Lord out of the sepulcher, and we know not where they have laid him" (John 20:2). In my student days in seminary, when new theories of the Bible were being tossed about almost recklessly, this was a favorite saying of students about the new ideas: "They have taken away my Lord, and we know not where they have laid him." How many ideas and discoveries have appeared, and, hearing their startling assertions, timid souls have predicted that the faith of Christ would fall, that it was all over for the church of Jesus. A sophomoric and presumptuous science once said that its findings meant the end of the faith. The doctrines of Karl Marx and the communist philosophy once claimed that they would wipe out Christian believing. There swept through black America ten years ago some new slogans and some new religions which ere supposed to wipe out our churches in what some called the black revolution. There was much talk of the white man's religion; the talk was in English. Timid people thought that they had taken away the Lord Jesus. Well, some few not well-adjusted people went off, but the church of Jesus Christ continues to march on. Still men and women are being saved, still communities are being blessed by churches, still salvation's story is being told. The dark glasses are gone; the church is still here. The dashikis are gone; the church is still here. The black-power people are living abroad or are in jail or are trying to stay out of jail; the church is going on. And yet Mary's fear is understandable: "They have taken away the Lord, and we know not where they have laid him."

Peter and John came to the grave, and indeed the body of the Lord was not in the tomb. There had been no violent action; the grave clothes were lying neatly folded. But the occupant of the tomb was not there. The disciples leave and return home, perhaps, to try to regroup their thoughts and to regain control of their emotions and fears. Ah, but Mary goes back to the grave. She has been once and fears that some evil has been done, but she must go back. There is a kind of love, and it is not to be disparaged, which goes as far as it can reasonably go, then faces facts and says, "Well, there is nothing else to do." Then, thank God, some of us have been the recipients of another kind of love which keeps going back when it looks as if failure is complete. There are people listening to me now who found a firm footing in life because a mother, a father kept coming back, would not give up. Someone here got through school because a teacher somewhere kept coming back to the empty tomb. Some of us know the Lord because preachers somewhere kept coming back to the gospel and in one way or another would not stop saying to us, "Look unto the Lord and be saved." Yes, and faithful deacons and deaconesses and members and choir singers kept on worshiping God and praying when it looked as if nothing was happening; out of that persistence came strong, vibrant congregations greatly honoring the name of Jesus.

Mary saw what she took to be two angels, one sitting at the head and one at the other end of the tomb. Someone pondered if these bright forms were the same who hovered over the manger in a stable and who stood near the shepherds on the hills near Bethlehem. If so, they bowed in a yet more awestruck reverence at the Savior's grave than they knew at his cradle, and in the cemetery they saw a deeper depth of the love and power of God than they saw in the stable at the birth of Christ Jesus.

Mary had one thing on her mind which was not to be turned aside even by the sight of angels. She turned from them. John of Antioch, old Golden Mouth, preaching at the turn of the fourth century in Constantinople, fancied that Mary Magdalene turned because the eyes of the angels alerted her that someone else was near. At any rate, she turned. In the early morning light, Mary took the figure she saw to be the garden keeper. She had not seen the hands, or they would have told her this was no mere gardener.

Her eyes had not beheld his feet, or she would have known right off that this was no mere attendant.

Hers was the request, the poor, pathetic request of love unmindful of practicality. "Sir, if thou have borne him hence, tell me where thou hast laid him, and I will take him away" (John 20:15). This is love talking, not common sense. How could she, poor woman, carry the weight of a man's body? And yet many a poor woman has in love carried the whole weight of a whole family, and now and then a man has carried a nation. Where could this poor, pardoned sinner carry her Savior? What place did she have? Ellen G. White, the prophetess of Seventh-Day Adventism, mused that Mary may have thought that someone decided that the grave of a rich man, for such was Joseph of Arimathaea, was too fine for the likes of Jesus and so had taken the body away. Well, her Lord had made one grave vacant, and she would get him somehow to the grave where Lazarus had lain. He could occupy the grave he had already, himself, emptied.

And then it happened. He called her name. Jesus called Mary Magdalene's name. She could not mistake that voice. He spoke to her there in the morning light as he had spoken when he cast seven devils out of her poor, storm-swept soul. "Mary!" She would know that voice anywhere. The voice which spoke in the cemetery was the same voice which taught the multitude, the same voice which healed the woman who touched the hem of his garment, the same voice which spoke and the blind saw. This was the same voice which talked with Moses and Elijah in the heaven-sent light of the mount of transfiguration. "Mary," he said, and she would have known that voice anywhere. It was the same voice which stilled the storm and made the winds be still and one day spoke peace into Mary's very soul. "Mary!" That voice must have sounded to Mary like the music of many waters, like countless violins in the moonlight, like some great celestial organ whispering its melodic harmony, like a mighty heavenly choir singing its Gloria, like cathedral bells far off and stealing across the hills. "Mary!" In the morning light, Mary answered, and the stone rolled away from her poor, sorrowing heart. "Rabboni, Master, it is you." She answered, "Master, it is you, all is well now, you are near. We are in a cemetery, but all is well. The heart hurts yet from Friday, but you are here, and all is well."

Jesus says that he knoweth his sheep by name, and "my sheep hear my voice, and I know them, and they follow me" (John 10:27). Our fathers sensed that and sang, "Hush, somebody's calling my name, O my Lord, what shall I do?" "My Lord calls me, he calls me by the thunder, the trumpet sounds within my soul, I ain't got long to stay here." "When he calls me, I will answer. I'll be somewhere listening for my name." The music here of the spiritual celebrates the supreme meeting and dialogue in all of the universe — that between the risen Lord and one who knows that life can be forever different only when the Lord's voice has spoken and the enraptured soul has heard it and replied. "Mary." "Master!"

ᵔᕋ 27 ᕋᵔ

Providence:
The Control and Care of God

April 25, 1980

And Joseph said unto his brethren, I am Joseph; doth my father yet live? And his brethren could not answer him; for they were troubled at his presence. And Joseph said unto his brethren, Come near to me, I pray you. And they came near. And he said, I am Joseph your brother, whom ye sold into Egypt. Now therefore be not grieved, nor angry with yourselves, that ye sold me hither: for God did send me before you to preserve life. (Genesis 45:3–5)

It had been my expectation to be dealing with some other Christian truth on this morning, but I got waylaid on Mother's Day with the death of Rachel giving birth to Benjamin, the only full brother Joseph had among the sons of Jacob. The Joseph part to which I referred but slightly got hold of me. And so here we are this morning talking about Providence: The Control and Care of God, as it shows forth in the life of Joseph.

That word *providence* was once used far more frequently among believing people than it is today. The word *providence* is an important part of the vocabulary, of the language of God's people and Christ's redeemed family. We can ill afford to lose it in the speech of the church of the Redeemer. We heard that word in our opening hymn:

> Judge not the Lord by feeble sense,
> But trust him for his grace;
> Behind a frowning providence
> He hides a smiling face.

Paul Tillich used to speak of God's providence, his control and care and the way he provides, as a "foreseeing" and a foreordering. Providence, he said, is a quality which "drives" or "lures" us

160

toward whatever it is that God has set out to do in our lives and beyond them. Providence as God's direction and control means that something is going on, so to speak, behind the backs of people in all their designs and plans. Joseph Parker spoke of providence as God working out his plan, and all our little schemes and aims are drawn into it as "the whirlpool sucks all streams and currents" — and I might add, all debris, gum wrappers, and driftwood — "into its mighty and terrible sweep."

The Bible uses the word *providence* only in Acts 24:2, where an orator accusing Paul is flattering a heathen ruler, Felix. The sense of the word as God foreseeing, foreordering, and, therefore, providing for his people underlies and characterizes the Bible on almost every page.

God's care and keeping come to bold clarity and to unmistakable view in the account of Joseph. Where shall we look for a drama more touching, a success story more thrilling, a revelation of God's providence more vivid than in the story of Joseph? The whole record of Joseph as we have it is worthy of a dramatic genius in its pathetic simplicity. Here in the literature of faith we have an account which touches the heights and depths of human experience and the motives and ways of people in a way and to an extent rarely attained by the most inspired novelists and playwrights.

We see Joseph as the eleventh of twelve children of Jacob and learn promptly that this son is the favorite of his father. One passes quickly over the questionable wisdom of Jacob in showing so openly his favoritism for Joseph, thus arousing resentment in the other brothers. There might be some excuse for such preference shown for a youngest child, a baby, but Dr. James Sanders, the distinguished Old Testament scholar and former member of the Concord Baptist Church of Christ, tells us that Joseph was seventeen years of age when his father showed his preference by giving him alone a strikingly colorful and beautiful coat, much to the resentment of the other children.

We look upon Joseph as a young dreamer with his thought-less, innocent, selfish reports to his brothers that he is to be over all of them. The brothers are naturally incensed. I think that the child psychologists now call this sibling rivalry. This week past a prominent man in the life of his state was telling me how his brother feels competitive toward him and wants to excel in every-thing. Thus Joseph, fancying and imagining his future greatness, sees himself over his brothers and father. He tells them of such a dream. I can still hear the almost hypnotic voice of Adam Clay-ton Powell Jr. as he quoted in reference to the death of Martin Luther King Jr. what the brothers said of Joseph and his visions, "Behold, this dreamer cometh. Come now therefore, and let us slay him" (Genesis 27:19–20). Instead they sell him into slavery.

We look again, and Joseph is a servant in the household of a captain of Egypt's army. Another scene shows Joseph in jail, vic-tim of the fury of a woman scorned. He meets there the chief baker and chief butler of Pharaoh himself, who have fallen into disfavor with the king and are fellow prisoners with Joseph. There Joseph explains to them dreams which the chief baker and chief butler had in jail. It turns out as Joseph has said, and the chief butler, restored to his place, remembers Joseph when Pharaoh has a puzzling dream. Joseph interprets Pharaoh's dream and tells him that after seven years of plenty in Egypt, there will be seven lean years and the nation must prepare in the years of abundance for the years of leanness. Pharaoh makes Joseph prime minister, next to himself and in charge of the whole agricultural economy of Egypt. Some would say that this is an interesting but disconnected series of events. Some of us would say differently. Some would say coincidence, others providence.

Joseph's father, Jacob, and his brethren and their families begin to feel the pinch of famine. The ground is parched; crop after crop fails. At last the cupboards and food closets of Canaan are bare. Jacob hears that only Egypt has food, but he has no notion who it is that is in charge of all the foodstuff of that strange, foreign land by the Nile. Jacob knows only that there is corn in Egypt and that there is no corn in Canaan. So trips are made by the sons of Jacob where they meet the prime minister. Joseph recognizes his brothers, but they do not know who he is. And so we come to our text.

The brothers of Joseph appear before the seemingly remote and severe prime minister and plead for food. He tests them in several ways. Joseph has forced them to bring his only full brother, the youngest of the family, Benjamin, with them to Egypt. Joseph knows these petitioners to be his own brothers. They do not know the identity of the puzzling, aloof, seemingly austere man who sits in the seat of prime minister of all Egypt. So the story builds.

We now reach the moment of truth. Joseph, looking upon his family from whom he has been separated so long and by their own envy and resentment, can scarcely control himself. He has inquired as discreetly as he could about the health of his father. All of his brothers, including his one full brother, Benjamin, stand before him. Great tides of pent-up emotion rush like volcanic lava in Joseph, demanding to be let loose. The prime minister motions all of his retinue to leave. Those who lingered beyond the door could hear passionate weeping within the room.

Joseph announces to his brothers between sobs, "I am Joseph." What flood tides of hope and fear and bitter memory must have stormed forth in the men before the prime minister when that announcement was made. "I am Joseph," and all of the long years came rolling back. Joseph's brothers had done wrong twenty-odd years before, and now it has all caught up with them. "I am Joseph." This revelation must have struck an awful terror, an indescribable shock, an almost paralyzing memory. We do not get away with anything in this world which God has created and which he has charged with moral accountability. Nobody gets away with anything. All in this drama were sinners, like each of us, and all had paid. Jacob's shrewdness gave him much when he was young, but in his old age and in the famine he had to plead for bread for his family. Joseph had been a vain and self-centered lad, and he paid in a long, lonely time separated from family. The brothers had done wrong in selling their brother, and now they paid in fear and shock and sorrow at the words "I am Joseph."

When will we recognize that we are all in rebellion against God and that there is a price to be paid? Riots continue to remind us that we are still a nation of sinners and we cannot escape the consequence. America keeps trying to forget what it is without changing from what it is. Race defines America underneath everything else. Two events have shaped this land. The Revolutionary War in the 1770s gave the nation a chance to reach for independence and freedom. The Civil War in the 1860s gave the nation a chance to rid itself of slavery and racism. The opportunity was not fully grasped in either case. Between these two polarities the nation has lived its life and enacted its history. Black people could have forestalled much that has happened to us, of course, by exercising the rights we do enjoy. If racism is the sin of white America, irresponsibility is the sin of black America. And so we pay and pay and pay.

In the account of Joseph, we see more than the guilt and fear of Joseph's brothers. God does something behind people's backs and before their faces. All that had happened had brought Joseph to the exalted position of prime minister of Egypt. Thus there are those who say that the brothers of Joseph needed feel no remorse since it all had turned out for good. They did not set out to do good, and we must be judged by our intention. There are others who would question why there needed to be the twenty-two years of sorrow and homelessness of Joseph if God really was in charge. Why do we have such trials if there really is a God and he is in control? These things I cannot explain, but I do know that people may propose and in proposing act and that God can dispose and so change evil intentions into blessings. I remember Dr. William Preston Hayes, once minister in this city's Mt. Olivet Church, preaching in the Concord pulpit on "all things work together for good to them that love God." He said that that passage may be likened to a pharmacist mixing drugs, either one of which may by itself be poison, but brought together the mixture is good in the healing of the body. And so of different events, some painful, God brings blessings.

Joseph greets his brothers as prime minister of Egypt and saves their lives. The way was not easy, and yet I seem to see a pattern. If Joseph had not been sold into Egypt, he would not have been servant in Potiphar's house. If he had not been servant in Potiphar's house, he would not have been thrown in prison on false charges of his master's wife. If Joseph had not been thrown in prison, he would not have met Pharaoh's butler and interpreted his dream. If Joseph had not met the king's butler, he would not have been summoned to interpret Pharaoh's dream and thus would not have become prime minister. It all started back as a boy when an ugly thing was done to Joseph by his own kin.

Joseph said it again to his brothers in the fiftieth chapter. "As for you, ye thought evil against me; but God meant it unto good" (Genesis 50:20). Something cynical in me does not want to believe that, but my experience says otherwise. There is a hand which guides our footsteps if we will but trust God, no matter what anybody may say or do. The world may try to hurt us, but God keeps our souls. Evil influences may try to block our way, but God tears down obstacles or makes us leap over them. The enemy may wound us, but God will heal our wounds. Strong winds may blow, but they speed us to port.

People may do what they will, but God is in charge. On a black Friday some men did Jesus my Lord to death. They then went to their weekends clucking their teeth and satisfied, but God acted and brought him from the dead. I rest upon that. Trouble may hinder me, but God opens the way. Circumstances may stand against us, but God leads his dear children along. God will provide. God will make a way. God will protect. God will defend. The Lord will make perfect that which concerneth his saints. I rest me upon that. One day we shall thank him for all that has happened in our lives — for every tear, every fear, every hurt, every opposition, every trial, every ache, every sorrow.

ᴕ 28 ᴖ

A Word We Must Never Forget

June 29, 1980

But Zion said, The Lord hath forsaken me, and my Lord hath forgotten me. Can a woman forget her sucking child, that she should not have compassion on the son of her womb? yea, they may forget, yet will I not forget thee. Behold, I have graven thee upon the palms of my hands; thy walls are continually before me. (Isaiah 49:14–16)

God is not something like us, only better. We are rather something like God, only infinitely less. This something like is what makes dealing between us and him possible. If there were, indeed, a great gulf fixed between us and God, an impossible chasm, an unbridgeable gap, we could never know contact with the divine mind nor be touched by the divine pity. It is this something like, this kinship, this similarity which puts us in touch with God and makes it possible for us to have dealings with our Creator. All and all I count this the most wonderful truth in the entire universe, allowing for the fact that Jesus Christ is the central evidence and supreme manifestation of that "something like."

Thus Jesus did not mind showing us the ways and character of God by using our human situation as a kind of measuring stick. It is a means of getting to the unknown by way of the known. Jesus once spoke of the thoughtfulness and goodness of God in terms of our human ways. Given their sense of the holiness of the Lord God and his greatness and majesty, those who listened must have seemed puzzled at the comparison, the step leading from earth's low motives and imperfect understanding up to the purity of purpose and the all-understanding mind of God, what formal theologians call the omniscience of the Almighty. Said Jesus, "If

166

ye then, being evil, know how to give good gifts unto your children, how much more shall your father which is in heaven give good things to them that ask him?" (Matthew 7:11).

Bearing that in mind, I cannot help wondering how God must look on our doubts and faithlessness. Of course, we are consoled in the word with which the psalmist comforted us when, speaking of our frailty and unbelieving, he said of God, "For he knoweth our frame; he remembereth that we are dust" (Psalm 103:14). Still, using our own little feelings and grasp of things, how it must sting the heart of God when we doubt him in the face of all he has done for us.

The lament which opens this chapter is not the wail of a people who never knew the God who is our Father. On the lips of some spiritually unvisited people, the words which open the text might, just might, be understandable, even justifiable. Listen to them: "But Zion said, the LORD hath forsaken me, and my LORD hath forgotten me." To be sure, Israel was in an awful plight when this bitter mood of desolation and forsakenness was given voice by the prophet. Jerusalem, and all that that dear name called to mind, lay in ruins, a desolate and dismantled city. The once-proud metropolis, symbol of all that was sacred in Israel's history, was almost a wilderness: for many years its altars, once ablaze with sacrifice, had been cold and untended. Wild animals cavorted openly in the city's once-proud streets and avenues. The children, once of royal houses, were slaves in a strange, heathen land. Thus the mood, bitter, sad, hopeless: "But Zion said, the LORD hath forsaken me, and my LORD hath forgotten me."

This mood, this wail, this lonely cry echoes in all of our hearts. You and I are now and then brought into circumstances in which we are likely to think that God has turned his back on us. We seem so overborne by obstacles and difficulties beyond our capacity to meet and to match. The good work we have tried to do seems to be seen by others as of little value and importance. Friends seem so few and far between, and those we have disappear in the fierce spray of Jordan. We cry, or we feel like crying bitterly and hopelessly, "The LORD has forsaken me, and my LORD has forgotten me."

Now the heart of God must be saddened at this, as I think I hear clearly in the surprise and astonishment of the passages which introduce the chapter. Old Israel, over whom this mood came, had known God in a thousand deliverances. We, his new Israel, have known him to deliver us every time we have stood in need. Yet we doubt. Though, indeed, God has rescued us every time we have stood in great peril, yet each new time we face a new peril the old doubt arises, and the old mood comes back with the deceiving lie that "the LORD hath forsaken me, and my LORD hath forgotten me." The Lord God, if we may use our own minds and hearts as clues, must wonder what does it take to get us to believe. "He keeps his promise a thousand times, and yet the next trial makes us doubt him. He never faileth; he is never a dry well; he is never as a setting sun, a fading meteor; he is never as a melting vapor, a disappearing phenomenon. And yet, we are vexed with anxieties, molested with suspicions, disturbed with fears as if our God was a mirage in the desert." So said C. H. Spurgeon when he looked at this passage.

We could be spared so much fear, so many anxious hours, so many sleepless nights, so many troubled days if we could only believe in God as David did when he faced the menacing hulk of the huge Philistine giant, Goliath. Saul said unto the little shepherd boy that one so small and so inexperienced in the martial arts as David was could not hope to cope with an experienced warrior like Goliath. David reached back into what God had done for him in the past to find evidence and support for the faith and confidence that he could master mighty Goliath. David said, "A lion and a bear came when I kept my father's sheep and took a lamb out of the flock. I went out after them and left both lying dead. 'The LORD that delivered me out of the paw of the lion, and out of the paw of the bear, he will deliver me out of the hand of this Philistine'" (1 Samuel 17:34–37, author's paraphrase).

The amazement of the divine mind at the unbelief which says, "The LORD hath forsaken me" shows forth in the reply stated in the form of a question. That question is meant to lead us up to something far beyond the natural answer we give to this question which scarcely needs an answer: "Can a woman forget her sucking child, that she should not have compassion on the son of her womb?" Thus we come again to the willingness of the Lord God to be likened to us in order that our poor human minds and comprehension might be drawn up, toward a better understanding of the God of heaven and earth. What amazing affection does a mother show toward her child! She seems to listen even in slumber for its slightest cry. In the child's sickness, others may grow weary of the long night's watch, but her eyes are wakeful; her ears are attentive.

Dr. Sandy Ray used to tell of an incident in his childhood which I could hardly bear to hear. He spoke of a night in the far-off years in Texas during his childhood when the sheriff knocked on their family's door. Small children huddled around their mother as the sheriff told the mother that he was arresting one of her sons on suspicion of what was in the South in those days a supreme crime. Dr. Ray said that his mother, half-dressed, ran alongside the buggy carrying her child to she knew not what. Finally, the sheriff let her ride on the buggy's rear platform. The suspicion proved to be groundless, but what could this poor black mother have done to protect her child from not only arrest but also lynching? In this country, particularly in the South in that far-off day, there was absolutely nothing Dr. Ray's mother could have done, but she could not abandon her child. Isaiah compared the care of God to such love as a mother's, but he quickly recognized that comparison did not go far enough. Now and again mothers do desert and forsake their children. "They may forget," said God, "yet will I not forget thee." How this passage reminds us of the words we read in the twenty-seventh psalm, "When my father and mother forsake me, then the LORD will take me up" (Psalm 27:10).

There is a still more daring figure employed here to declare the depth and extent of God's love and care. "Behold, I have graven thee upon the palms of my hands." Boys once wrote in ink in their palms the names of girls they liked. An extra mark of love was to do so with indelible ink. It soon wore off. We have all seen the durability of tattoos on arms and hands.

God says through Isaiah that he has graven us on the palms of his hands. That word *graven* suggests "deeply carved," "inerasably inscribed," "scored," "chiseled." Now, of course, this is figurative language. I trust that I have already established that our small, earthly symbols are used for divine meaning. God does not have hands as we do, but the text intends to let us know how close and how permanent we are in the divine consideration.

In that sense, I pursue the figure. God says here that he has focused his attention on us in such a way that we cannot be forgotten. Our image, our remembrance, is not set up in heaven, as Spurgeon put it, lest we feel, in our poor human way, that God might leave heaven and thus we would be forgotten. God's awareness of us is not carried on a signet ring upon God's finger. For — forgive this clumsy human figure — the ring might be taken off. If I may speak still after the manner of earth, our presence in the divine mind is not carried upon the Almighty's skirts, for he might disrobe, and thus we would be forgotten. God says, "I have graven thee upon the palms of my hands" — I have graven not just the name — "I have graven thee," thy person, thy image, thy case, thy circumstances, thy needs, thy weaknesses, thy wants, and thy works: "I have graven thee upon the palms of my hands." And so we are indeed held in the hollow of God's own hands. We are, therefore, wherever God is.

I visited Vernon Jordan, then the national Urban League executive director, shortly after the assassination attempt on his life. This gallant young leader of our national life was passing through the painful process of recovery from the bullet of a cowardly sniper who did his heinous work under the cover of darkness. We talked about many things. Vernon Jordan said that he saw himself die out on a dark road — in a strange city. His life, he said, in the fifteen minutes he lay there wounded, lying in his own blood, passed before him. When we know the nature and extent of his wounds, we cannot help feeling what I expressed to him — that he had been killed and did not die.

One thing kept coming back, Vernon Jordan said. When he was a student in school and away from home, his mother would write him every day. Some letters were short, and some were long. Some bore much news of home, and some said very little of the family. Always, at the end of each letter and after his mother would sign her name, she would write these words in the light of her own experience with her God: "Remember, son, if you trust him, he'll take care of you," every day for seven years. Vernon Jordan said that out there in the darkness lying in his blood, his mother's words came back to him, "Remember, son, if you trust him, he'll take care of you." When his mother came from Atlanta to Fort Wayne and stood at Jordan's bedside, he reached for her hand and spoke not as one of America's first citizens but as his mother's child. He said, "Mamma, you told me if I trust him, he'll take care of me. Mamma, thank you." Tears welled up in my eyes when Vernon Jordan told me this.

There is no better word to be passed along than that which a mother who knew once told her child, who found out, "If you trust him, he'll take care of you."

⌀ 29 ⌀

A NEEDFUL CHRISTIAN QUALITY

November 16, 1980

After this manner therefore pray ye: Our Father which art in heaven, hallowed be thy name. (Matthew 6:9)

The purpose of what we do here in this church is to help bring us each to our full growth in Jesus Christ. Anything said or done here which will help us in reaching our full development in Jesus Christ is in order. Anything done or said here which stunts our growth or impedes our way in rising to "the stature of the fullness of Christ" is out of place and counterproductive (Ephesians 4:13). The end purpose of our conversion and our membership in the body of Christ which we call the church is to help us on to God, to put on Christ fully in our words and in our work, by lip and by life.

In the life of a disciple of Christ, there are many aspects, qualities, features which go to make up a character which at last can be truly called Christian. We know some of these qualities, these portions of our Christian personality. Some, says the Book of Timothy, are "righteousness, godliness, faith, love, patience, meekness" (1 Timothy 6:11). I want to speak of another quality which I think must characterize and saturate all of these other traits. It is a quality of which, I fear, we are in embarrassingly short supply. I refer to reverence, due regard for what is holy, an appropriate attitude toward the sacred. I think I must ask myself, "Am I reverent toward whom and what ought to be held in sacred consideration?"

Reverence is a hard word to define. It is much like what my mother used to say about her relationship to her God. She would say sometimes to me, "I know what the Lord means in my life,

172

but I cannot explain it." Ah, dear sleeping dust, almost always the things that are dearest are the hardest to explain. Reverence falls in that category. Charles Jefferson, who preached in Broadway Tabernacle and which alas! is no more, tried once to define reverence, only to discover that this word is not easily explained. Reverence is respect, but it is more than that. One may respect a bulldog, but reverence for such an animal is unlikely. Reverence means esteem or honor, but it means more than that. We may esteem or honor a famous athlete or musician, but we, other than groupies and fanatics, are not likely to bow down to worship such people. Now, reverence suggests something like bowing down and worshiping. Jefferson finally declared that "reverence is respect and esteem flying at high altitudes." Reverence involves a deep movement of the soul, an emotion, an awareness which touches our minds and our hearts and makes us want to confess and to give thanks. Many of us learned that the final law for Boy Scouts is "A scout is reverent." Reverence means adoration, awe, affection. It is a mixture of terror and love. It speaks of God and what is of God!

I have to suggest that so much which approaches reverence, even respect, has passed from our lives, and we are not better off because of the loss, either. There are people in the Christian world with whom some of us disagree almost wholly but who are right when they say that we have become too loose in our attitudes and in what we tolerate. We too often reward spoken garbage with a smile. Public filth in our recorded material and in our movies and in our books is looked upon with too much acceptance, with not enough shock. We get taken by the charge that it is hypocrisy not to drag out in the open everything which has been secret. Honestly, realism became the excuse for all kinds of dirt to be put on public display.

It became stylish for people in the public eye to exhibit their secret habits, their sexual preferences, their most questionable thoughts before the world. Bit by bit there slipped into everyday talk language which was once heard only in locker rooms and among the coarsest people. Movies became more and more open in language and in scene. Now vulgarity is palmed off as art and gutter talk is described as honesty.

I say all of this to raise the question of whether the loss of a sense of God and church among so many brought this on, or whether all of this vulgarity and exhibition of our most secret acts brought on the loss of faith in church and in God. Whichever, there is among all of us, Christian people included, too little of a sense of the sacred. There is something wrong with people who are so hardened that nothing makes them gasp, nothing makes something of awe stir in them. I, for one, am sickened by flippant references to God, careless and casual use of the name of our Maker and our Father. No matter that one of our stupid, shallow movie actresses once spoke of the God of heaven and earth as "a living doll." God is not some "man upstairs," and to so refer to him is to admit a shocking irreverence and an almost unbelievable ignorance. The Bible tells us that rather than being some vague man upstairs, our God inhabits all creation, since he says in Isaiah 66:1, "The heaven is my throne, and the earth is my footstool." God is not a shadowy presence about whom we can speak airily, saying, "Somebody upstairs loves me." He is the God of Abraham, Isaac, and Jacob.

Jesus, our Lord, has told us how we ought to look upon the God who has made us and before whom we must each one day appear. In the prayer our Lord gave us as a model and a pattern and which the centuries have come to call the Lord's Prayer, the matter of reverence occurs near the beginning. It may well be that no other part of the Lord's Prayer has been so overlooked and so casually viewed and even ignored as those words which deal with reverence, a proper respect for the holiness of God. At the start, Jesus said to us, "When you pray, say, Our Father, hallowed be thy name." "Revered be thy name," "Let thy name be treated as holy." These words lie almost hidden, if I may put it that way, between the wonderful and tender address of God, "Our Father," and the mighty hopes and needs to follow. We brush past these

words in our eagerness to get on to mighty things, the coming of
the Lord's reign throughout the earth and our own physical and
spiritual needs. We had better go back and understand that Jesus
says we must come to a reverence for the great Creator who loves
us before we can approach the agenda of his reign or our hunger
or spiritual needs. "Hallowed be thy name."

There is much that is sacred in life, and we ought to recognize
what has the divine in it wherever we see it. Notice, please, that
I say the divine in this and that, not that all things are divine.
It is pantheism to say that everything is divine, and that is not
Christian. I speak rather of *pan-en-theism* — God in all. There
is a respect approaching reverence which I owe to you. I do not
owe that respect or reverence to you because of what your name
might be, for someone might give your name, or mine, to a dog
or a cat. The respect approaching reverence which I owe to you
is not due to your position, because tomorrow you and I might
not occupy whatever position it is we hold today. I look upon
you with a respect approaching reverence not because of your
physical appearance. The distinguished American, Vernon Jordan,
was saying to some of the leaders of this city the other evening
at dinner that in sickness, nurses and others see us in all kinds
of positions and conditions when we are not able to be carefully
groomed and all proper and upright in appearance.

I must look upon you with a certain respect approaching reverence because there is something of God in you. Just what it
is of God in you to which I refer I cannot define. As the Book
of Genesis tells us, God has put something of himself in us. We
are not all God, but something of God is in each of us. And
that I must respect. Bishop Azariah of the Church of South India
once spoke much to me of this as we traveled by motor launch in
South India's backwaters to a remote, water-surrounded community. He said that the Hindu puts his hands together in a gesture
of prayer whenever he meets another human being. In so doing,
he is saluting the divine, the God, in every other human.

You may hardly have noticed that in referring to our regard for other people, I have repeatedly spoken of a respect approaching reverence. When we look to our dealings and our relationship to God, reverence unmixed with anything else becomes us. The name of God is awesome and overpowering. Beginning in the third century before Christ, Jews stopped calling God's name. They did not stop calling on him, but they stopped using his name. It was too holy for human lips. So instead of speaking of their God as Yahweh, they began to use the word *Adonai*, the Lord. Later even that was too familiar, and so they shrank from ascribing human sound to God.

We need not follow this practice; indeed, we draw closer to our God upon the authority of Jesus Christ and so believe that we may come "boldly unto the throne of grace, that we may obtain mercy, and find grace to help in time of need" (Hebrews 4:16). Still, there ought to be in us a dreadful awe, a wonder, a reverence when we contemplate our great and mighty God. The sheer spectacle of nature, the immensity of space, the great cosmic highways where the planets move in stated precision ought to make us reverent and wondering and bowed down before God. Did I hear that Saturn is twelve billion miles away from us? What a God it must be who made all of that!

I am told that when we pray, some of you keep your eyes open and your heads upright. I will agree with anyone who says that outside form is of no spiritual standing with Christ. Yet there ought to rise up out of our hearts and minds at thought of dealing with God, a sense of worship, of obeisance, adoration, of humbling ourselves before him. How our fathers made language serve the cause of reverence when they would pray to God, "we come before thee in the humblest way that we know how, our hearts below our knees, and our knees in some lonesome valley."

Our God is as great as he is good and as good as he is great, and this is to say marvelous things about both his goodness and his greatness. The God we serve merits our reverence, bowed heads, bent knees and trembling spirits, the touch of a whisper in our voices and unstudied pauses of silence when we talk with him. Our God is different from us creatures. A creature almost by definition is someone that was not always. "Creatures are what they are made to be or what they grow to be. Creatures are what they one day will not be. They are what they were not, they are what they will not be." But God is as he ever was and was as he ever will be. I bow before him, because God is without start and without finish, is without increase and without decrease, never grows better because he is already, and ever was, perfect. God never grows worse because in him there is no changing. He is first and last. God demands and receives my unqualified reverence. He is underived from anything, un-dependent on anything, lifted above time and change, self-existing, self-determined, and self-continuing. I bow before him.

Ah, Christian, approach our God as we have known him in Christ with every reverence. Wherever we see him in the Bible and out, he is the same holy being, apart and yet drawing near to us who could not pull ourselves up to him. Whenever we see him or hear of him, let us now and always remember that he is holy. In Horeb Moses hears "put off thy shoes from off thy feet, for the place whereon thou standest is holy ground" (Exodus 3:5) — charged with the divine Presence. Looking at God, the twenty-second psalm declares, "Thou art holy, O thou that inhabitest the praises of Israel" (Psalm 22:3). In Isaiah, angels shout antiphonally across the celestial temple, "Holy, holy, holy, is the LORD of hosts" (Isaiah 6:3). They repeated "holy" three times because the Hebrew language has no way to express the superlative except by repetition. All through Isaiah, God is the Holy One of Israel. In Revelation 4:8, as the sacred record closes and we into glory peep, heavenly creatures are crying ceaselessly, "Holy, holy, holy, Lord God Almighty, which was, and is, and is to come." I bow before him in reverence, for all that he touches is holy. His name is holy, his Book is holy, his house is holy, his people are holy, his way is holy, his truth is holy, his love is holy.

⎯⌒ 30 ⌒⎯

THE PROMISE IN THE MANGER

December 21, 1980

They came with haste, and found Mary, and Joseph, and the babe lying in a manger. (Luke 2:16)

Christmas is the story of a manger, the story of a birth. Whether we look upon the scene and time of a manger and a birth as a promise or a threat depends greatly on how we view passing events and what is our faith about God and his story which we call history. Granted, and without argument, there is evidence, more than a little, that mangers, births, and the arrivals of new babies have represented a threat to the world, not a promise. It is hard to imagine that some of the most monstrous butchers of history were once babies, gurgling infants, lying in innocent cradles, thrashing their little feet in their mothers' arms, and hearing the sweet, calming strains of lullabies. Think of the Caesars marching through blood, contemplate the Napoleons leaving mountains of human skulls, reflect on the Hitlers wiping out millions of lives in gas chambers, wantonly and heartlessly. Remember the various white Southern sheriffs of a bygone day with their vicious dogs, cattle prods, and fire hoses; recall lynch mobs holding up children to watch the torture of another human being. How hard it is to think of these — I had almost said *fiends* — having once been babes, sleeping so peacefully and feeding so gently at their mothers' breasts. The threat of the manger, the curse of babies — yes, one might say that.

The promise of the manger? Indeed, one might speak rather of the hazard in the manger: the risk of birth. I held on my knee the other evening a little baby boy. In the natural order of things, that little life is scheduled to journey on into the twenty-first century and, with some likelihood, into the last half of the coming one

178

hundred years. This lad I held will likely be living in 2050. What hazards lie ahead in that journey now just beginning! How many days will it seem that all is against his life? For what prizes will he reach only to throw them away impatiently once they are in his hands? What loves, what disappointments, what hearty laughter, what silent weeping, what fears and trials will there be before the little life to which I refer has finished its mortal journey? Yes, one might speak of the hazards of the manger, the perils in birth, and the dangers in the cradle.

Speaking of hazards of birth, I marvel that we know of no time in our black history in this country when there was a movement among black people not to have children, particularly male children. I wonder sometimes if black mothers and fathers could ever look at a newly born, black male child in early generations without seeing the shadow of the lynch rope, a young body dangling by the neck, or the air sick with the odor of burning flesh. Did you know that between 1865 and 1940, more than four thousand people of color were lynched in this country without benefit of even the mockery of a trial? I say nothing of the thousands and thousands who were hustled through rigged courts with juries committed to the death sentence long before the routine of a trial ever began. And yet I know of no such movement.

Against all of these somber and repulsive colors, something hopeful and forward looking in the human spirit bids us think of The Promise in the Manger: not the threat, not the hazard, but the promise. Such is true even before we look at the birth of that baby who has made more difference in the story of humankind in this planet than any other child who has ever opened his or her eyes on this wild, wonderful world. We have mentioned some of the monstrous, cruel people of history, but the centuries have been blessed by other babies grown to adulthood. Louis Pasteur, who made milk safe for the world and whose name is incorporated in the term "pasteurized milk," was a baby in a cradle before he was a scientist with a microscope. Florence Nightingale, who gave the world the concept of trained nurses, those angels of mercy who have blessed so many of us in dark, lonely hospital nights, was a baby before she was swept along by her compassion onto the battlefields and into the military hospitals of the Crimean War. Walk the campus at Tuskegee Institute, and one almost feels the presence of Booker Washington and George Washington Carver, both babies before founder and chief scientist, respectively, in an institution which has blessed our land so bountifully. In Atlanta, they will point out to you the sturdy, simple home in which Martin Luther King Jr. was a baby before he rose so nobly to his destiny as one of the emancipators of America.

There is a promise in a manger and above and beyond all in the manger of Jesus at Bethlehem, where centuries before Rachel had died, where Ruth had been courted, and where David was likely born. The Savior of the world was a baby in a manger. Looking at the cradle in Bethlehem, we may see the most powerful force in all the earth. There are many lessons in the Bethlehem manger, and one is that the future direction of humankind is not determined by guns, buildings, swift automobiles, mighty jet airliners, great spacecraft, or classic language written by profound philosophers. The future of humankind is determined by mangers, and particularly by one manger where the Christ child lay and where the hopes and fears of all the years are met.

"For unto you is born this day in the city of David a Savior, which is Christ the Lord. And this shall be a sign unto you: Ye shall find the babe wrapped in swaddling clothes, lying in a manger" (Luke 2:11–12). It is pathetic truth that these words have fallen on our ears so often they have lost their ring and their startling force. What a contrast, "A Savior...the babe." How strange of God to provide what the world needs more than anything else by the way of a manger. No one will doubt that a Savior is what we all need more than anything else. Sometimes we are aware that this is our need, sometimes we are not so aware, and sometimes we make believe that we are not aware. We continue to delude ourselves with the notion that this earth's leader or that one will get us where we long to go.

It is not a leader we want most, for the truth of our plight is that we are not able of ourselves to follow the road upon which we are led, granted that we are being directed on the right course. It is not an advisor that we need, for we have not had the strength or the capacity to act upon the best advice we already possess. Forget reformers; we need to be remade, not reformed. Something in us needs to be taken out, and something we do not have needs to be given to us. This is far more than saying that everything necessary for a new life — our salvation — is in us and only needs to be rearranged. We need to have the stony heart taken out of our flesh and a new spirit put in us.

We need a Savior. A Savior is more than any earthly office; it is not a kingship, robed in purple and bedecked with a crown before whose majesty people bow down as slaves or captives. The word *Savior* speaks of one through whom other lives are snatched from the burning fire and saved. The word *Savior* speaks of one through whom other lives are snatched from cold, deadly waters — "saved." And this we need in the lostness of our poor, lonely human journey. This we need in the terror and fear of all the things that might befall us. This we need in our frailties and feebleness, our weaknesses and our wickedness, in our sicknesses and in our dying.

The good news of the New Testament, the saving word of biblical religion, is that in the babe at Bethlehem we have a Savior, one who can snatch us from the burning fire, pluck us from the roaring river, heal us from all our soul sicknesses, direct our wandering footsteps, and calm our stormy passions.

A babe can do all this? This babe can save us because his coming to Bethlehem represented the miracle of birth, but something more. The coming of Christ Jesus to Bethlehem represents the working out in time of what God planned in eternity. First Timothy 1:15 says it bluntly, "Christ Jesus came into the world to save sinners." He did not take up saviorhood; he came to save. Christ did not decide to be our Savior as he looked around on our needs: "Christ *came* to save sinners." This connects him with you and me, for we are sinners, and he came to save sinners.

A preacher I greatly admire once pondered what went on before Bethlehem, before Mary and Joseph, and before a manger and wise men and shepherds ever entered the picture. That preacher fancied, not altogether vainly, I think, that there must have been two sad days in heaven. One would have been when Satan fell, dragging down with him a third of the stars in heaven. The other time of grief, mused this preacher, was sadder still — when the Son of the Most High, the most-admired among angels, left the bosom of the Father to come to this ugly world in the interest of sinning, stubborn, sordid, sneering souls who will not turn to God though One comes from heaven and though One returns from the grave. The Son said to the Father, "A body hast thou prepared for me: . . . I come (in the volume of the book it is written of me), to do thy will, O God" (Hebrews 10:5–7). "Go," said the Father, "and thy Father's blessings be on thy head." Then the Son unrobed himself of garments of perpetual light as angels crowd around and watch with awestruck eyes. He laid aside his crown and said to the Father, "My Father, I am Lord over all, blessed forever, but I will lay it all aside." A diadem of thorns will pierce his brow. He strips himself of the bright vestments, lays aside his shining mantles embroidered with stars, to dress himself in a robe of flesh. Look at the picture, give rein to your imagination! Watch as the angels attend the Savior through the streets of the nightless city and sing, "Let the King of glory pass through" (see Psalm 24:7–10). The angels must have followed him down to earth and watched over him as he put on our humanity in a manger in Bethlehem. When the angelic deputation had seen him safely in his mother's arms, the Prince of glory now a child of earth, the angels, returning home to God, paused above Judean hills looking for somebody to tell that the Savior had come. These first Christmas preachers spied some shepherds, and the angels preached to these simple keepers of sheep. "Fear not: for, behold, I bring you good tidings of great joy, which shall be to all people.

For unto you is born this day in the city of David a Savior, which is Christ the Lord" (Luke 2:10–11).

Ah man, woman, hear my voice, the Savior has come. He lies in a cradle in birth and hangs on a cross in death to make it well for my soul and for your soul. His manger tells us how God came down to us. His cross tells us how we may get up to God. He was born once unto us that we might be born forever unto him. He came down that we might go up. He appeared among us that we might appear among angels. He descended that we might ascend. "Glory to God in the highest" (Luke 2:14). At Bethlehem the Savior came, and with those once-infant hands which at last were marked by nails, he passes to us our royal birthright, puts in our grasp papers of citizenship in the heavenly kingdom, and gives to us authority over all devils. This baby appoints unto us a kingdom of which there is no end, and, all praise be unto him, puts the seal of the Father in us and writes God's holy name on our foreheads that all people and angels might know that we are bought with a great price and that we are not our own, but we belong to him who was born in Bethlehem in order to die at Calvary, that he might rise from Joseph's tomb, that he might reign truly as "Wonderful, Counselor, The mighty God, The everlasting Father, The Prince of Peace" (Isaiah 9:6).

✍ 31 ✍

JUDGMENT AND MERCY AT PALM SUNDAY

[The date of this sermon is unknown but thought to be before 1981.]

And when he was come near, he beheld the city, and wept over it, saying, If thou hadst known, even thou, at least in this thy day, the things which belong unto thy peace! But now they are hid from thine eyes. (Luke 19:41–42)

And so, judgment and mercy at Palm Sunday! That is the meaning of the strange pageantry of our Lord's entry into Jerusalem on the humblest of animals and midst the roaring hosannas of a great mass of people, waving their palm branches. All who look upon the coming of the Lord Jesus to Jerusalem and who hear the multitude want to rejoice. We want to enter into the spirit of gaiety and celebration, taking our own palm branches and lifting our voices to join in the thunder of the multitude, crying, "Blessed be the King that cometh in the name of the Lord" (Luke 19:38).

Only there is a shadow over it all. We know now that not a week would pass before these happy cries would turn to frenzied screams for the death and end of the strange, quiet man who moves in the midst of this tumult and excitement. The sun shines brightly on Palm Sunday, but grim things are in the offing. So quickly the awful fury of all hell will be loosed in the midday midnight of Calvary's hill, engulfing all, Jew and Gentile alike, Caiaphas and Pilate, in the horror of the death of the Son of God. With what a shudder would these happy shouts end, making many to understand the lament of some simple people whose words haunt the world. "Sometimes it causes me to tremble, tremble, tremble." Yes, in the midst of the merriment and the note of deliverance drawn nigh, a solemnity and a sadness hang over Palm Sunday, determining that the mood of the church on this day of happy shouts is somber, grave, measured.

184

In this, Palm Sunday is much like life. There is a brightness, a sparkle in our day, and thank God for it. We are often merry. There are days almost cloudless when our families are all about us and our strength and health within us and the road rises to meet us and the morning wind blows gently in our faces. Thoughtless must be the person who does not sense in all of this, oh, not morbidly, that there are shadows over life too. There are hard duties, sometimes harsh ones, which must be met, burdensome responsibilities which must be shouldered, and parts of the journey which are uphill and taxing. Yes, and in this life there are sorrow and sin and sickness with all the dividends of misery which they bring. Over our dearest and tenderest loves there hovers another shadow, far off, we hope, but certain. It is the awareness that no matter how close we are to those whom God has given us to love, we must part. The mood of Palm Sunday, then, with merriment and sadness mixed is an authentic sample of our lives with their lights and shadows.

At the center of this odd procession which we call the triumphal entry is the figure of Jesus, facing the city of David, Jerusalem. Adoring and pious Christian art has painted him as gentle, tame, inoffensive — Jesus, meek and mild. The Palm Sunday procession where judgment and mercy meet hardly shows such a bland, passive soul. The figure at the center of Palm Sunday has a splendid dignity, a royal purposefulness, a grand determination, an almost austere majesty, as he faces the city of Jerusalem. He considers this Palm Sunday entry to be one last offering of himself, one final chance, too, for his people to embrace his way before a terrible and awesome visitation of death and destruction would come upon the city. The awful option of life or death hangs over this day.

Jesus has the courage to face the city, Jerusalem, your city, my city, and every city. He does not run from, he moves toward human attempts to fashion some kind of community. He knew that there are hazards, fierce ones, where men and women of good intentions and evil intentions come together, but such are the terms of community. Jesus faced people in community. He did not flee from that enterprise.

A person is no friend, no follower of Jesus Christ who looks with contempt and disdain upon our old, faltering, admittedly imperfect, attempts to establish community, to build a livable society. There are those who seek their security and salvation in separating themselves from the pain and stress of men and women together in a community. Well, of course people disappoint us and disgust us. Well, we disappoint and disgust them too. Still, does it not seem that Jesus, facing the city, on Palm Sunday, not fleeing it, is saying that our peace in the earth will never be found in denying our common humanity? In that way lies an endless hell and destruction, as so much of our history tells us, and in blood, over and over again. Something else is needed, at whatever price, at whatever peril, at whatever pain. Edwin Markham speaks of it when he describes one who

> drew a circle that shut me out—
> Heretic, rebel, a thing to flout.
> But Love and I had the wit to win:
> We drew a circle that took him in.

Our hope is in community. It is truer now than ever that "we must all hang together, or assuredly we shall all hang separately" — and on gallows of what varied and indescribable agony. Jesus faced the city, offering it light and life, offering it himself.

It was with no sickly sentimentalism, no pious pap, no pale politeness that Jesus faced the old, grand capital of religion — Jerusalem. Coming upon the ancient city, our Lord spoke words of judgment, of God's overseeing inspection and superintending examination. "If thou hadst known, even thou, at least in this thy day, the things which belong unto thy peace!" Did he behold more than the ugly, massive power of Rome, perhaps evil incarnate in its refined cruelty and never-to-be-satisfied lust for conquest? Did the piercing insight of Jesus see also a community in which angry divisions, brother against brother, sister against sister, would be more destructive than the alien warlords of Rome? Such became the history of Jerusalem before its fall in A.D. 70.

So the eyes of God search any city, any community, any nation, any individual soul. Do we believe that our human affairs, international, national, local, individual, any of them, go on with no eyes to gaze upon them and to judge them save our own? Do you think there is no review of our human doings? No other court except the petty tribunals we set up of dying men and women whose dust will soon be blown by every vagrant wind? History speaks otherwise. There are many evils left in the world, but every great group guilt has been judged by history and history's God. Massive, entrenched institutions of evil have not gone unchallenged, unpunished. The divine right of kings, sweatshop labor, oppression, slavery, doctrines of Aryan supremacy. There is an all-seeing eye. God is still on the throne. This, Jesus was saying to his city and to your community and mine. Do we need to do anything other than search the events around us, crime, the lust for things, the international uncertainty, to hear what is being said to us, to see what is laid out before us? Is not greed strangling our society? Are drugs and guns, crime in our streets and offices the final epitaph to be written on our society, so advantaged in so many ways, so promising even in its darkest hours? One senses that this nation is intended of God not to be as the old notion had it, a melting pot, but a concert of ethnicity, each bringing the rich notes of his, her origins to the great music of the American undertaking. One wonders if slothfulness, an empty swagger, and slavery to every passing fad are to be the fate of our black community in America where fathers and mothers and theirs before them embraced a bright vision of our destiny and toiled on toward it so gallantly and against such overwhelming odds? The words of Jesus, "If thou hadst known . . . the things which belong unto thy peace," sound so powerfully, solemnly over us.

How is it with you? You will know better than I what gifts of mind and heart you brought to the living of your days and what you planned to do with those gifts. No one can know as you can how far you have fallen short of what you meant to be and what you intended to do. Someone has told of meeting a disheveled beggar in one of the worst sections of London. Asking for a handout, the poor, broken shell of a man said, "I know I don't look like much, but you've no mind the man I meant to be." On a day to be forever regretted someone gave up on integrity and honor and decided that one plays the game, and that's all there is to it. You thought that you were wise, smart, knew your way around when you turned from the God of your fathers and from the old, dear lessons of home and church and school. Now you have only a nameless sadness as you try to push out of your mind the mystery, the loneliness, the uncertainty, the pathos of life with no sense of God to steady you and to keep you. How piercing sound the words of Jesus over our brokenness, the end of our flight from God, "If thou hadst known . . . the things which belong unto thy peace!"

The judgment is searching and disarming, but something else appears to sound, also, in the charge of Jesus. One seems to hear in these solemn words a stubborn refusal to write if all off. "If thou hadst known . . . at least in this thy day, the things which belong unto thy peace!" Surely there is a limit, a cutoff point, a terminal line in the time of privilege and opportunity. It runs out somewhere, but I think I hear a reluctance here to close the case, to ring down the curtain forever on opportunity. Still, while darkness comes on, there is a last faint light before the night falls, and on some of us forever. "If thou hadst known . . . at least in this thy day."

I will not hint it. I will say it boldly. The old, pursuing, persisting love of God has not given up on you, on me, not yet. Jesus left Palm Sunday and headed on his sad and lonely way toward Calvary, the place where he declares in his own death that it is not over, not yet. The sands have not run out, not yet. There in the darkness on Calvary where Jesus died, God made a statement. It is that a way is opened, and a highway. Calvary is the hill of another chance, the mount of a new beginning where the love of

God goes all of the way for us people and our salvation. Palm Sunday's sorrow leads to Crucifixion Friday.

It is all there in essence on Palm Sunday, a searching judgment and an endlessly tender mercy. That mercy, that care comes into full view as the pauper King leads his ragtag retinue toward the city of a thousand sacred memories, Jerusalem. The procession comes at last to the southern slope of Olivet, and suddenly the city in all of its stately beauty lies smiling in the morning sunlight. The immaculate marble of the temple and the pinnacles of the city's palaces make Jerusalem a strangely touching sight to the Savior, as his vision beholds, also, the pain and pleasure, the bright friendships and the ugly cruelty, and the things which break souls that transpire in the city's avenues and alleys. Looking across the ravine of Kedron, Jesus beholds the city with its missed opportunities, its pretense toward love of God; he sees what might have been, and from the soul of the world's Savior tears come. Could it be? Is the strong Son of God moved to tears by our poor mortal failure? A hush falls on our souls at this inexpressible sight. It slowly dawns on us that this is no slip, no chink in the armor, an embarrassment to be quickly glossed over. This is the very heart of God laid bare before our eyes, and that heart is infinitely tender and cares about you and about me. Dare we look on this heartbreak and remain unmoved? It is enough to melt the stoniest heart. For Jerusalem, for your city, for mine, for you, for me, the great Savior weeps, and the sobs send visible shudders through his work-hardened, strong body. Ends of the earth, see your Savior weep. Yes, Calvary is at the gates of Palm Sunday.

I trust myself to these tears of a sobbing Savior; do you? I throw my frail heart, with all its doubts, at the weeping Son of God. I place my hopes, all of them, in the strong hands of him who openly grieves and sobs for me. Christ weeps, my heart melts. Christ weeps, my will is broken. Christ weeps, my head bows, my knees bend before him. Christ weeps, my life is his. Christ weeps! That wins me forever. Does it you?

⌒ 32 ⌒

GETHSEMANE: THE PLACE OF VICTORY

[The date of this sermon is unknown but thought to be before 1981.]

> Then cometh Jesus with them unto a place called Gethsemane, and
> saith unto the disciples, Sit ye here, while I go and pray yonder.
> And he took with him Peter and the two sons of Zebedee, and
> began to be sorrowful and very heavy. Then saith he unto them,
> My soul is exceeding sorrowful, even unto death: tarry ye here,
> and watch with me. And he went a little further, and fell on his
> face, and prayed, saying, O my Father, if it be possible, let this cup
> pass from me: nevertheless not as I will, but as thou wilt. And he
> cometh unto his disciples, and findeth them asleep, and saith unto
> Peter, What, could ye not watch with me one hour? . . . Rise, let us
> be going. (Matthew 26:36–40,46)

We were driving to California. Arriving in an Iowa town we
studied the map and discovered that by driving north nearly a
thousand miles we could come to where the Mississippi River
began. Having been born almost within sight of the Mississippi
River, I was anxious to make the trip. We did and on a clear and
sunny day came to Lake Itasca far up in northern Minnesota. At
the beginning of the Mississippi River, it is a tiny stream about
a foot wide. One can stand, as I did, straddling the Mississippi
River. It is a mile wide by the time it reaches New Orleans, has
touched thirty-one states, and has as its tributaries the Ohio and
the Missouri Rivers, but its source is a small rivulet so narrow
that a child can stand with a foot on one side and the second foot
on the other side.

As in the case of the mighty Mississippi's beginning in a
tiny rivulet, most great public occasions have their source in
private, apparently small events. A distinguished teacher of English lawyers used to say to his students that "cases are won in
chambers," meaning that private preparation and transactions determine public decisions. Games of athletics, any coach will tell

you, are not really won on the playing field but in scrimmage and practice. God help the preacher who depends on the inspiration of the moment in public worship to give him what he shall say. Along this line, each of us needs the private practice of godly and Christian exercises of prayer and meditation which prepare us for public testing and living.

Calvary is looked upon as the place of our Lord's great victory, the overcoming point in the struggle for God's supremacy and human redemption and deliverance in the earth. Calvary, said the old preachers, was the place where God in Christ took on himself our sins before a sorrowing heaven and a sinning earth. Calvary represents the central event in our Christian gospel, the focus of all divine history as far as the sons of men can see. There the Lord Christ lured the powers of hell into a fatal misstep and an over-reaching of their evil designs and ways. Calvary is the supreme public event in the divine purpose.

I am suggesting this morning that that great public victory, that unspeakably enormous event which we call Calvary, has its source immediately in a private and solitary act in a garden called Gethsemane, where the seed, the essence of the public victory was won in a lonely, secret struggle in prayer. The supper we now call the Lord's Supper is just past. That will be the last tender, serene occasion in our Lord's life until the glories of resurrection morning. As the disciples and their Master file out of the upper room, the last golden rays of pleasant sunshine depart from the skies of our Lord's soul. All beyond that is composed of gathering, deepening, threatening clouds and darkening skies, except perhaps for a bright moment in Gethsemane where Jesus prayed for strength and resolve and final commitment to the Via Dolorosa, the way of sorrow, which lay before him unto death. In Gethsemane that prayer was answered, and the Savior moved on his appointed way.

As they leave the upper room we follow the little band, already looked upon as outlaws, as they walk slowly through the streets of Jerusalem. Now the disciples pass likely out of the fountain gate in the east wall of the city of Jerusalem, and then across Kedron Brook they make their way. Once among the gnarled olive trees of Gethsemane garden, the Master stops a moment and then bids three of his followers, those closest to him, the inner circle, Peter and the two sons of Zebedee, James and John, to go on a little farther into the garden. I seem to hear in the Master's next words a strangely tender, pathetic, almost pleading note. He unburdens his soul a little to them. How slow many of us are to reach out to others for fear that they will not understand or accept or appreciate our need. How the Master must have felt that if any of these twelve, no, now reduced by one, these eleven, could sympathize with the great secret spiritual issues which confronted him, surely these three would understand. He said to them, opening the hurt and anguish he felt in these hours, "My soul is exceeding sorrowful, even unto death."

We greatly need somebody to whom we can reach out in the hope that there will be acceptance and perhaps understanding. If Jesus with all of his strength needed that, then we do too. "Our lives through various scenes are drawn." There are dark nights of the soul, times of testing and loneliness. We need someone to whom we can turn and hope for a little encouragement and a little cheering along the weary way.

Jesus exposed his heart to his disciple and revealed his lonely need. Dr. Alexander Maclaren expressed the opinion that the Lord may have been the loneliest man who ever lived and loved people. He tried so hard; they understood so little. There was this need in him of some soul to stand close. If that be in you, do not call it foolishness; your Lord needed that. It was said of his very selection of these men that he chose them "that they should be with him." The dear Lord had so few, really. Does he not still have so few? One looks out upon any congregation of people and wonders how many are really with the Lord? Does there blaze within you or me the desire to be well-pleasing to him, to hold up his arm, so to speak, in this world which hates him and always has hated him, in this world so prone to scorn his way? Will you hear the Lord of your life and mine saying, "My soul is exceeding sorrowful, even unto death: Tarry ye here, stay with me and watch with me"? Tarry and watch with me (Matthew 26:38).

Do you not understand that? Have you never been to that place? It is the place where we seem to have done all that we can and then find that it is not enough. It is the place where we have spent ourselves and apparently in vain. If only someone would just come up to us then and put out a hand or say a kind word. "Watch with me, stand with me, sit with me a moment," we want to say. Dr. Elisabeth Kübler-Ross, author of *On Death and the Dying* and one of the world's outstanding authorities on dealing with dying people, says that people who are critically sick and who are facing death may just need someone to enter their room as a human being, not claiming to have the answers. Such a person, says Dr. Kübler-Ross, may need more than anything someone who will simply ask if there is anything the critically sick person wants done. In other words, our greatest need in extremity is to have someone to be with us, whether or not there is anything that can be done for us.

Before we mount up to the place of victory in prayer, let us complete the human equation. The Master retreats, and when he returns, his friends on whom he counted and whom he asked to stand sentry for a while, had failed him. Maybe he wanted to have this last little time to get ready and needed to be protected from sudden appearance and surprise attack by his enemies, who were already making their way through the chill night to arrest the Savior of the world. At any rate, I seem to hear an almost unutterable sorrow rising like a hurt cry up out of the depths of the soul of our Lord. "What, could you not watch with me one hour?" Was that too much to ask? He had comforted them and strengthened them and guided them, and now in his hour of need they failed. Let that question pass quietly among us on this Lenten Sunday morning. Let the presence of this preacher be wiped out, let this voice be lost in another. Hear your Lord ask you: "Was it too much to ask you to watch with me one hour? Did I ask too much when I asked that you be regular in worship one day a week? Do I go too far in saying, 'Every man according as he purposeth in his heart, so let him give; not grudgingly or of necessity: for God loveth a cheerful giver.' Is it too much that I ask you to show a little kindliness to my little ones, to those who are old and tired, to those who are sick and in pain, to those who are alone in prison?" "Look," he says now to us, "look at these nail marks. They are there for you. Do I ask too much?" In that piteous cry of our Lord I hear a word from the sixty-ninth psalm, "Reproach hath broken my heart; and I am full of heaviness: and I looked for some to take pity, but there was none; and for comforters, but I found none" (Psalm 69:20).

The secret victory, the gathering of his soul into a unity of purpose which would have its dramatic triumph on Calvary was not found in the garden because of friends, for people will fail us in a trying hour. He went back again and knelt and talked it over with God. He confesses, my dear Savior showing himself tempted as we are, that he does not want to be humiliated and shamed and spat upon and scorned and pushed and shoved. He did not want the excruciating physical pain and shrank from spiritual abandonment and traveling some far stretches of God-emptiness never before encountered by the sons of men. He pleads, listen! The Son of God, the Son of Man pleads, "O my Father, if it be possible, let this cup pass from me." So! It is natural for us not to want to face great trials and hard tribulations. We have a right to ask God to spare us, please, daunting sorrows and bitter trials. And then, as we listen, not once but three times he reaches his hand and heart out toward God asking for willingness in his own soul to be ready for whatever God wants. "Nevertheless, not as I will, but as thou wilt."

God heard and answered. The victory was won right there. Friends slept, but God neither slumbers nor sleeps. God heard. Men may have failed, but God did not. Luke says that Jesus prayed in an agony of desperate pleading until sweat like drops of blood fell from his brow. God got him ready. Luke puts it so interestingly. He says an angel came and strengthened him. I know that angel. It is the presence who says to the trembling believer, "Be still, my soul, the Lord is on thy side." I know that angel, I have met that presence outside operating rooms, when hearses roll and hearts break, when jobs are in jeopardy and friends forsake. I know that angel.

Jesus got up and faced forward, as if saying, "It's all right now. Let enemies come. Let friends forsake. It's all right now, let courts lie and governments oppress, it's all right now. Rise up, let us go on. There is a heavy cross on ahead and beyond that a bright crown. Let us go to meet it." And so prepared by prayer, we may face our times of trial and testing, sure that victory is on beyond.

∽ 33 ∾

THE GREATEST LOVE AFFAIR

March 8, 1981

We love him, because he first loved us. (1 John 4:19)

The pastor of the old Fort Street Presbyterian Church in Detroit was driving me to his city's airport. He had been preaching on the parables of Jesus. Suddenly he put the question bluntly to me, "Where do you think Jesus got all of those stories?" As we talked, it came out that some must have come out of his God-illumined imagination. Others were perhaps suggested by incidents and events which he observed around Nazareth as he grew up. He may well have known shepherds who had searched through the hills day and night for a lamb which had strayed from the fold.

It is conceivable that not far from the carpenter shop of Jesus' father there was this house where a boy broke his father's heart by announcing one day that he was leaving home. Perhaps it was the talk of the town and many a sympathizing sigh was turned in the direction of that home so marked by loneliness. People waiting in the carpenter shop for work they had ordered from Joseph may have recounted to each other how day by day the father could be seen peering down the road his youngster had taken, with the hope written in his face that the form of his boy facing home would show itself far down the road — and one day the father did see that familiar stride.

Later Jesus would seek to penetrate the hard disbelief of people about the mystery of God's love by telling of the love of God being like that of the father who watched so long for his boy to come home. Jesus kept telling us that the only way we can somewhat grasp the wonderful and unspeakable relation God bears to us and we to him is by illustration, example, by comparison,

196

by "like." And so our Lord said that God's reign and our place in that reign are like first this thing and then another. He says in Matthew 13:33, "The kingdom of heaven is like some yeast which a woman worked into a bushel of flour." Or the "kingdom of heaven is like unto a treasure hid in a field," and again he says that those who hear and heed him are "like a man which built a house and digged deep" (Luke 6:48).

Thus, all through the Scriptures God's relationship to us is set forth in likes, in similarities to the various kinds of love relationships we know in this life. This word *love* both in its noblest and its puniest meanings may well be the most potent word in human language. Tanks, rockets, nuclear warfare — whatever — have no power to win the soul's inward yes. The powers these words represent may rape and batter our will into obedience and force our external agreement. Neither one, no, not all of them together, can command an eager willingness, a glad yes in our inmost souls. There is a door marked "private" inside of us through which no armaments of force, government, church, school, social order, whatever, can find entrance. It is locked tight against them when they come with nothing more than their key of authority and power. At that door, that inmost door, marked "private," love needs no key, need not even knock, since the door is flung wide and the heart within waits eagerly. This word *love* is, I believe, the most potent word in the universe. It is the theme of young courtship, the atmosphere which gives beauty to the marriage altar, a young mother's heartbeat, the death-defying bond of friendship between strong men, the life-giving fire to all our worship, the saint's bright delight, and the bridge by which the church on earth keeps "mystic sweet communion with those whose rest is won."

Love in all its forms is used in the Bible to illustrate God's interest in us and his care for us. Hosea, either out of a stunning reversal and humiliation in his own marriage or with an incredible imaginativeness, saw God's love affair with us as similar to that of an eager young man who woos and entices a maiden into the consent of marriage. For that the Greeks had a word, *eros*, out of which our word *erotic* comes and which describes what Hollywood has been principally about. The Old Testament suggests that at least in one instance, that of Moses, a man might be said to be a friend of God, to whom God spoke, says Exodus 33:11, "face to face, as a man speaketh unto his friend." Greek people of New Testament times would call that form of love *philia*, the association of mutual interest and appreciation which we call friendship.

The great New Testament word for love is neither *eros* — sexual love — nor *philia*, mutual respect or friendship, but *agape*. It is what we meet in our text. It is best defined as an outgoing goodwill, a drive, an urge toward reunion of the separated, a care without self-interest, and in God's case is a manifestation of "what is most God in God." And so it could be flatly stated "God is love." It has not to do primarily with worth of its object, and Isaac Watts was eminently correct when he asked in music:

> Alas! And did my Savior bleed?
> And did my Sovereign die?
> Would he devote that sacred head
> For such a worm as I?

The ablest of New Testament expositors has said to us that we need not rush to complete the primal and causal thought of our text. "He first loved us." We might well leave ourselves out of it for a moment and say "He first loved." That would mean that love was operating, God's love, far back in the misty, nebulous, indescribable nonregions of eternity. Even then God's love was at work. "He first loved" when there was nothing to love except his own intention. This is our ground for believing that this universe is keyed to love. First of all things was God's love, at the beginning of all things is God's love. Out in the farthest precincts and outposts of God's creation, love is central. God first loved. I read this week that a galaxy has been discovered which is ten billion light years from the earth. I am staggered by being informed that light emanating from that galaxy takes ten billion years to reach the earth though it is speeding through the great oceans of space at a speed of 186,000 miles a second. I do not know how far ten billion light years are located in distance from where I stand, but God's love touches that part of his creation, for "he first loved."

What a moving word it is when I go on to say that "he first loved us." This was before we thought of returning any flickering devotion toward God. "He first loved us." He loved us first — before anybody else loved us, fathers or mothers or wives or husbands or children. "He first loved us." I wonder if you would substitute "me" for "us." He first loved you, first loved me in all of my unworthiness, in all of our rebelliousness and selfishness. Can you say that to yourself right now, "God first loved me"? How understandable that would be if you and I were creatures of such moral purity that we merited God's favor. That word in the New Testament, "grace," means that we enjoy God's love, but we do not merit it. How much less difficult it would be for us to understand God's love if we were models of kindliness, patterns of godly conduct, examples of pure thoughts, exemplars of good deeds. Even then it would be a startling condescension that God would direct his interest and affection toward us.

We cannot pass such a test. If I were competent and were allowed to examine each one of you this morning, who would pass the test? Could you say no, if I asked you have you thought any ugly thoughts this week? Who among us could answer yes if I asked if you have only had goodwill toward everybody you have met? If someone here claimed that he or she has done everything right this week, thought only the best thoughts, wished only good to everybody, you would convict yourself of another terrible charge. I would have to brand you as the biggest liar in Brooklyn.

He first loved us. Does someone ask how we know? Well, first we are here, clothed, as they say, and in our right mind. There was food on our table this morning, and the light of God was in the sky when we awoke. Prophets have told us that God loves us. But then there is that hill called Calvary. No matter how people look at it, never mind what explanations they give, we know that

God was at work there, in our interest and at a great cost. And for us, of all people!

Somewhere there is a story of a village ne'er-do-well and idiot who fell into a raging river. Standing on the bank with his friends was the handsomest, smartest, tallest lad of noble birth in that whole region. Seeing this human form thrashing around in the water and about to go under, this brave, talented lad leapt into the water and saved the other, pushing him to shore. In rescuing the drowning man, our hero was pulled under by an eddy in the water and was himself drowned. When they dragged the corpse of the handsome, brilliant lad to shore and laid it alongside the reviving form of the town idiot, the dead lad's friends not only mourned his death but also said in bitter sorrow, "And to think he gave up his life for such trash as this. What a waste!"

A fairer one than any village lad threw himself into death's awful waters for you and for me. Fairer? Fairer by far, for this one of whom I speak is "fairer than ten thousand." Christ died for you and me. There is not much we can do in return, we are so limited, so frail, so feeble, but we can turn back to him some faint reflection of his great love and say and mean it, "We love the Lord." I hope you can truly say that while you may not be all you ought to be, but you do love the Lord. And we can show that love for God by the care we give and the interest we take in each other. Where people are hungry in Africa and homeless in Italy and families mourn and a city lies in fear near Atlanta, there our hearts and our prayers and our material interest ought to be offered. Yes, and here in New York, where our black community has become almost completely powerless politically, more so than anywhere in America, we ought to exercise our Christian love to God by loving each other to empowerment. The upkeep of our communities, the schooling of our children, the handling of funds at state and city level will all be determined by who puts people in office and who takes them out. Protest meetings are good, but people are not put in office by protest meetings, nor removed by name calling, nor withdrawal, but by votes. Yes, love of God demands love of people and helping people to their true and God-given strength is love. Read my text in the Revised Standard Version of the Bible and it leaves off "him," in "we love him." It states "we love because God first loved us." All of our love worth being called by that name spring from this central sun throwing its great warming and healing rays on our unprofitable lives. We love, love fathers, love mothers, love wives, love husbands, love children, love fellow human beings because Christ first loved us.

That is the central theme of the Bible, that is the central theme of the universe, that is the central theme of life. "God loved us and loves us." This is the simplest, sweetest speech that infant lips can try, "He first loved us." This is the sublimest music that reaches the majesty on high, "He first loved us." The little child may lisp in early faith what Karl Barth said was his central word after a lifetime of theological scholarship: "Jesus loves me, this I know, for the Bible tells me so." Ask the convert dripping from baptismal waters, and these ought to be the earliest words: "He loved me and gave himself for me. He first loved me." Ask Christian pilgrims midway through their journey home, and they ought to cry, "What manner of love the Father hath bestowed upon us that we should be called the sons of God. He first loved me." Ask the saint on a dying bed, and he ought murmur through lips hot with life's last fever, "Having loved his own, he loveth them to the end. He first loved me." Eavesdrop on the praise of the redeemed in the city of our God, in the new Jerusalem, and they are singing "unto him who loved us, and washed us from our sins in his own blood and hath made us kings and priests unto God" (Revelation 1:5–6). "He first loved us."

I think that this is the supreme theme I would want to sound as a New Testament preacher. Last Monday in Detroit, I had what was to me a gratifying experience in old Fort Street Presbyterian Church talking to nearly one hundred ministers of that city and from many denominations about the art of preaching. And may I say that I am gladdened that this strange business to which my life has belonged is coming again to the fore of the church's interest. In a discussion period toward evening a young pastor, still in the tender freshness of his ministry, asked me a question which I had never been asked before. "Tell me, sir," said he, "if you had only one more sermon to preach in life, what would it be?" I was startled, for such may reasonably be the case any time now. When I recovered, I said, "I think it would be there is a Father who made us and loves us and whose children we are, and there is a Savior-brother who loves us and who died for us. There is a Holy Spirit who loves us by companionship and guidance. And there is a home where some day we shall all be together." It adds up to "He first loved us." I put that first. Above God's greatness, "he first loved us." Above his majesty, "he first loved us." Above his holiness, "he first loved us." Above his omnipresence, his equal attendance everywhere at the same time, "he first loved us." Above his omnipotence, his power without limitation, "he first loved us."

↷ 34 ↶

A TERRIBLE WARNING

November 15, 1981

Remember Lot's wife. (Luke 17:32)

This verse is the second shortest verse in the Bible with one word more in it than the shortest, "Jesus wept." When Jesus spoke these words, he illustrated an unforgettable depth of care about the eternal destiny of men and women. Jesus was in solemn earnestness where people's relation to God is concerned. There is not the slightest evidence in the Gospels that Jesus ever took lightly the will of God or the awful choice people must make as for or against God.

Earnestness, seriousness, determination can spring up out of different sources and roots. Sometimes we are intensely earnest because our own interest is involved or we do not like to be made out to be wrong or because our own self-regard, our vanity is tied in with our opinion or our action. There is an old story in the Scottish church of a day when the general assembly reached a decision which had provoked much discussion and no little heat of temper. Feelings had run high, and when a decision had been voted on, someone was called on to pray. The prayer ran, "God, grant that we may be right, for thou knowest that we are determined." It will not be the first time that we have put what we want before what we think God wants. Along this line we often first decide what we want and then start looking for high and holy reasons why we are right. Sometimes we tie God into what we know in our deepest hearts he has no part. Charles Haddon Spurgeon, bless his great pulpit gift, is said to have dared to reply to a criticism about his use of cigars by saying, "I smoke to the glory of God." Hardly.

The burning earnestness of our Lord was built on other foundations. He was serious, earnest, solemn, determined, pointed, uncompromising about people's relationship with our Father in heaven because he knew that our eternal destiny depends on how it stands as between us and God. This passion, this blazing earnestness in our Lord has nothing to do with his own vanity but rather with the love of God and what an awful thing it is to reject his love and go marching off into the darkness without God, without hope, without anything.

The text, "Remember Lot's wife," grew out of some stern and urgent words our Lord was speaking about judgment, eternal destiny, the final things, the summation of it all. We make much of the bright, blessed words our Lord spoke, and they are supremely tender and incomparably sweet. Who on earth ever spoke more endearingly about us poor humans, but who on earth ever spoke more witheringly about us as did Jesus? "Fear not, little flock," he said so tenderly to some humble people. "Ye workers of iniquity," he said to others. To some, Jesus said, "Ye blessed of my Father"; to others his word was "Ye whited sepulchres." Never accuse Jesus of sailing along, gently blown by every vagrant wind. There was about him an intensity and a blazing moral earnestness.

The urgent words Jesus spoke had to do with events of judgment when God in mighty, winnowing power comes sifting the wheat from the tares. It is not for me to try to call any of you to any fearful considerations which some might think belong to another generation. Think not to say to me that you have no interest in any final destiny of where you are going to spend eternity. It is a matter between you and your God. I only know that Jesus speaks most pointedly about the future, about judgment, about souls being welcomed by God and others sent away. Where they go, whether you care about this, is really not my business. I seek not to try to frighten you or pull any pulpit scare tactics. Still it is truer that at other times of warning such as those which surround our text, our Lord uses language which makes us shiver.

He speaks of "hell," "hell fire," "the damnation of hell," "everlasting fire," "outer darkness," of a condition where "the worm dieth not," and where "the fire is not quenched."

Old-fashioned talk, did you say? Some quaint phrases from a long-gone day before our science and modern knowledge and skills came? Is that so? Maybe you ought to read your daily newspaper. The atomic bomb which we dropped on Hiroshima toward the end of World War II killed hundreds of thousands of people and horribly disfigured all that it did not kill, burning human bodies until flesh dropped from the bone. That was in 1945, and we are told that that bomb in comparison with what we have now, and what Russia has, is as a firecracker to a stick of dynamite. For the first time since these awful things were invented, leaders of government, including our own, have actually begun talking about possible use of these things. Up until now, this was too horrible a subject for nations to talk about.

You may dismiss the word of Jesus as quaint and primitive, but the "everlasting fire," "the fire that is not quenched" is present in our new weapons of destruction. If you tell me that you cannot do anything about this, I may agree. You can do less about rain falling from heaven, but you can get an umbrella. If you tell me that you are not afraid of a storm, I will call you brave. If you say to me that you want no shelter in case of a storm when the dark clouds grow ever more threatening, I say that you are a fool.

We have a shelter and a hiding place and a way through the fiery trial. We can know someone who says, "when thou passest through the waters, I will be with thee; and through the rivers, they shall not overflow thee: when thou walkest through the fire, thou shalt not be burned; neither shall the flame kindle upon thee. For I am the LORD thy God" (Isaiah 43:2–3).

Jesus was so deeply moved, so passionately earnest, so completely consumed with the time of judgment that he reaches back over the waste of many centuries, bridges a thousand years and more, and takes his hearers back to the destruction of the wicked city of Sodom, that wild and riotous community of unbridled pleasure and godless living, to that most wicked of all cities which has given its name to acts which shame forbids us to describe. The Book of Genesis tells of how Lot journeyed with his uncle, Abraham, as that patriarch searched for a new land. A difference arises between Lot and Abraham. The older man gives his nephew first choice of land to be occupied. Lot was bewitched by the sights and sounds of Sodom and what seemed a rich and inviting community. One hears an ominous note and sees a gathering and threatening shadow in the words about Lot's decision, for the Scriptures say that Lot "pitched his tent toward Sodom" (Genesis 13:12).

Sodom seems to have been a scene of luxuriant vegetation, an oasis surrounded by barren and rocky country. In Sodom, tropical vegetation was found in lush abundance. Palm trees waved gently in the desert breeze. Lovely flowers spread their fragrance by night and day. Work was not demanding, and every pleasure of life could be found in plentiful supply. Night became day in the Sodomites' search for delights, and good times never ended. Sodom was the capital of loose living, unbridled pleasure, and anything-goes entertainment.

Such was the city to which Lot brought his wife and children and his family. How sad and tragic it is for us to put ourselves and those whom we love in the midst of wicked and enticing temptations. Lot apparently was able to withstand the temptations of this most wicked city in the world, but his family found it not so easy. Lot was warned by angels that Sodom was about to be destroyed. He received notice that the sin city had passed the limits of Divine patience and long-suffering. There is a point of no return. Lot was warned to get out. Never mind the thoughtless laughter which rose from dens of iniquity where people wasted their strength; Lot was to leave at once. Get out! Forget about investments and important papers. Get out! Does that word speak to someone here who is in some evil condition? Get out!

Lot was reluctant to leave — maybe things were not as bad as they seemed — but the angel of God took him by the hand

and his wife by her hand and the hands of the two daughters and almost dragged them out of the city. The escorting angel told them to make haste and "look not behind thee. Be done with this evil. Cast it out of your heart and cast it out of your mind. Look not behind thee" (see Genesis 19:17). Lot's wife could not help remembering the ties she had in the city about to be destroyed. Some of her family were likely there, mocking their old folks for talking silly talk about the judgment of God and the ruin to so fair and so permanent a city. Lot's wife remembered her lovely home and the wonderful times she had had in Sodom and so looked back. Did she stumble? And was it in the mad rush for safety that the others did not immediately miss her? Fire and brimstone or a sulfuric storm fell on the fair city of Sodom and, yes, on Lot's wife with her backward glance. And Lot's wife became a petrified form. Lot's wife died leaving Sodom.

Jesus picked up the account a thousand and more years later telling us that we must turn from what is low and foul and never look back. This was not the only time our Lord spoke in this manner. He said on another occasion, "No man, having put his hand to the plough, and looking back, is fit for the kingdom of God" (Luke 9:62). There is a life outside of God which we must give up — it is a Sodom which is to be destroyed no matter how delightful it may seem. Turn from anything or anybody who stops you from loving and serving the Lord. True repentance is *metanoia*. It means about face, turn around, stop going the way you are now going and go in the opposite direction. From doubt, turn toward faith. From fear, turn toward trust. From filth, turn toward decency. From fleshiness, turn toward spirituality. From people's opinions, turn to God's Word! From the valley, turn toward the mountain.

And we must never look back. Whatever anybody leaves for the Lord is well worth leaving. What you do for Jesus is all that will matter in the final totaling of things. "Remember Lot's wife," says, Jesus, "look up," fix your gaze on things ahead. Set your affections on things above. There is nothing evil or selfish we have given up which is worth looking back upon one single time.

Rather thank God that the future is open, shining more and more unto the perfect day. Thank God there is a bright side somewhere, and don't you rest until you find it. On ahead, the sun is shining. On ahead, the angels are singing. On ahead, friends are waiting. On ahead, we are to become what we long to be. And one day we shall pass through the last valley, climb the last mountain, weep the last tear, suffer the last hurt, endure the last criticism, feel the last pain, know the last disappointment.

Remember Lot's wife.

～ 35 ～

A FULL-GROWN CHRISTIAN FAITH

November 30, 1981

> Now that I speak in respect of want: for I have learned, in what-
> soever state I am, therewith to be content. I know both how to
> be abased, and I know how to abound: every where and in all
> things I am instructed both to be full and to be hungry, both to
> abound and to suffer need. I can do all things through Christ
> which strengthened me. (Philippians 4:11–13)

Early Christians recognized that there are stages in Christian
discipleship. Everybody was not of equal rank in the knowledge and faith of Jesus Christ and therefore could not be held
equally responsible for loyalty to the Lord and for obedience to
his word. There were classes of believers, higher and lower levels of disciples of Christ in the early church. For instance, the
lowest level of Christian belief was composed of those who were
called catechumens. You may notice a similarity between this
word and *catechism*, the book of instruction and questions which
some branches of Christianity follow — such as Lutherans and
Roman Catholics. You may recognize from the word *catechumen* the term *catechizer*, the person who questions candidates for
ordination to the ministry of Jesus Christ.

The catechumen in the first-century church was one who was
interested in the faith of Christ, an "inquirer" who had been
accepted but was going through a period of preparation before
baptism. Many remained for years in the class of hearers or catechumens who were apprentices, learners, seekers, not yet ready to
take on full discipleship and who were not admitted to the inner
mysteries of the faith such as baptism and the Lord's Supper.

In a sense we are all catechumens who have not yet reached
to full-grown Christian faith. Most of us who are baptized would

have to say that we are still immature believers. This does not mean that we do not love the Lord; it only means that we are not yet complete in our Christian development. Paul recognizes such immaturity even in the household of faith when he tells some Christians in 1 Corinthians 3:1, "And I, brethren, could not speak unto you as unto spiritual, but as unto carnal, even as unto babes in Christ." Monsignor Ronald Knox translated that last as "little children in Christ's nursery." Paul goes on to say, "I have fed you with milk, and not with meat: for hitherto ye were not able to bear it, neither yet now are ye able" (1 Corinthians 3:2).

How grown are you in Christ? How mature have I become in the Lord? Do you wish some gauge to see how we measure up? Are you wanting an examination of how you may be graded? If so, I have the test which will tell each one of us how far we are advanced and where we stand in our development of Jesus Christ. Writing from a prison house in Rome to the church he loved the best, the one at Philippi, Paul gave us a good test, a litmus paper to determine the quality of our growth in Christ. Listen to these words from a full-grown Christian: "For I have learned, in whatsoever state I am, therewith to be content. I know both how to be abased, and I know how to abound: every where and in all things I am instructed both to be full and to be hungry, both to abound and to suffer need. I can do all things through Christ which strengthened me."

You and I will recognize from this test stated, so to speak, by Paul how far we are from bring full-grown Christians. Nor should we be discouraged because we cannot now utter the words which the great apostle states here so confidently. We are in the right school, and we have enrolled in the right course, and we are studying under the right master of instruction, Jesus Christ. We need rather to find out how it was that any person could make so wonderful a statement as this, leastwise one in prison, even house arrest, and under circumstances which must have begun to seem to him quite capable of bringing him to his death. And who among us would not give almost anything to be able to say these words truthfully: "I have learned, in whatsoever state I am, therewith to be content. I know both how to be abased and how to abound....I can do all things through Christ which strengthened me"?

Take note, if you will, first that Paul hints that he had not always known such inner calm and such poise of soul. He says, "I have learned," so once, just as is true with us, Paul must have been nervous and anxious, jittery and apprehensive, seeing insurmountable dangers and crushing circumstances all around. Most of us live lives of quiet desperation, reeling and staggering from one crisis to another, terrified by first one fear and then another. Such does not have to be the case. In the school which Christ keeps and where the Holy Spirit is instructor we may learn not to be threatened and overborne by every trouble which comes our way.

This full-grown Christian says, "I know how to be abased, and I know how to abound." I know how to be at the bottom, and I know how to sit on top of things. That is a versatile, competent, mature human being. Some of us know, instinctively almost, one or the other of these two things.

Some are fairly well at home when things are wrong. Indeed, there are people who seem to enjoy being in trouble. They never stop talking about what is wrong in their lives. If there is one speck of cloud in the sky, that is what they see, never mind the sun blazing away in the heavens. They never weary of describing their aches, and their pains are the constant conversation with anyone who will listen to them. They describe their surgery down to the last stitch. They are walking complaint bureaus, souring everyone they meet until friends guiltily try to avoid them. Others are only satisfied when everything is on their side. They feel like it is their birthright to walk on the sunny side of the street, and they can function quite well when they've got the world in a jug with the stopper in their hand, as the old saying went. When things go well, we strut and brag and prance and pose and act as if the whole world should come to us and stop and stoop and salute and surrender.

Paul speaks of a larger, fuller capability into which he had been initiated. He knew how to be down and how to be up. There were others who practiced a certain resignation and hardness toward the good and the bad. They were the Stoics, who set their jaws, bit their lips, gritted their teeth, and determined to take quietly and uncomplainingly whatever happened to them. This was their resignation, a kind of "brave, unyielding despair," as Bertrand Russell put it. You have known people like that as I have, tough, hard-nosed people who will not crack and will not collapse. We admire such people, but if this is all one has, and it is considerable, then something is missing. They resign themselves to whatever must be.

This full-grown Christian, Paul, is not merely bowing his head to what must be. This man has drive, determination. In prayer he speaks of a doggedness, "three times I besought [begged] the Lord." He speaks elsewhere of a kind of athletic effort: "I press toward the mark." The contentment of New Testament Christianity is rather what grows out of a deep confidence that one is moving within the will of God and has gone to the limit of human effort. Out on that boundary of our capability, surrendered to God's use and God's purpose, contentment is born in the knowledge that the Judge of all the earth will do right and the faith that our times are in his hand and are more than safe there. In God we are to find quietness and strength when things seem against us and when they are favorable.

The Christian realizes that we have here no abiding home, that we are pilgrims and, therefore, the scenery changes. If we are in a low place at the moment, we shall soon reach an elevation. As the hymn has it, "Our lives through various scenes are drawn." Through it all the Lord is leading us, sometimes in the valley in the darkest of night. We can be content if we know that the Lord is leading us. Christians know that difficulty cannot always be their lot, for God has arranged that "this, too, shall pass away."

Many are ruined when they "abound." Success may have destroyed more human beings than failure has. How many people have been warm and radiant Christians until the Lord blessed them and prosperity became dearer than God? Poor souls, they are to be pitied, for success is a fickle lover quickly turning scornfully away from us, not to be lured back to our embrace by all of our pleadings and efforts. Success is doubly a joy if we remember to thank God for what has happened to us.

Every Christian is in process of becoming a full-grown, adult-enough Christian to be content in all conditions. Full-grown Christian discipleship means that one is a person for all seasons. In Christ, we may hope for this. We may not have reached it. God knows I have not, but I do believe — no, I know — I am on my way. I long to reach that place. Christian history tells of many who have learned to be content in all conditions. One such was Basil of Cappadocia. Born to a wealthy and cultured family in A.D. 329, Basil became bishop of Caesarea and metropolitan of the province of Cappadocia. In a doctrinal dispute, the Roman emperor, Valens, threatened Basil with confiscation, seizure of all that he possessed under the power of supreme authority which resided in the emperor. If confiscation did not break Basil, the emperor said that he would issue a bill of banishment, exile from home and friends. And if this Christian leader would not bow at that, then the emperor would order his execution, death. Basil replied, and God knows I want to come to this, by saying, "Nothing more? Not one of these things touches me. His property cannot be forfeited who has none; banishment I know not, for I am restricted to no place and am the guest of God, to whom the whole earth belongs; for martyrdom I am unfit, but death is a benefactor to me, for it sends me more quickly to God, to whom I live and move."

I want that, I pray for that full-grown Christian faith for each of us, where whatever the world does leaves us calm and content, safe in the arms of Jesus. Paul sums it up: "I can do all things through Christ which strengtheneth me." "I have strength for all things in him who gives me power. I am ready for anything through the strength of the one who lives within me." I want that, do you not? To be so possessed by the Lord so that the world can do me no harm, to have that peace which the world cannot give and the world cannot take away.

We cannot do this ourselves. We can steel ourselves, harden ourselves, but something will hurt us and cut us to the quick. We cannot reach unto this by our decision, determination, deliberations, or discipline. Christ can give it to us. Paul says, "I can make it through Christ." Not by power and not by might, but through Christ. Not by luck and not by pluck, but through Christ. And so the Christian may say that if the world pushes me back, Christ will bring me forward. If people talk against me, Christ will speak up for me. If people hurt me, Christ will bind up the wounds. If trouble shakes me, Christ will steady me. If the world puts me down, Christ will pick me up. If people slander me, Christ will praise me. If people frown, Christ will smile. If the enemy comes from this side or that, Christ will be all around us. Think of it! Tables in the presence of enemies. The valley of the shadows so lonely, so dark, but someone is there right at our side. If all human support is taken away, underneath are the everlasting arms. Nothing but blazing heat — no, one thing more, the shadow of a rock in a weary land. A dry and barren land — yes and more, rivers of water in dry places. The enemy storms forward and we have no defense? Not so! Lead me to that rock that is higher than I; thou hast been a shelter for me.

✦ 36 ✦

TRUE WORSHIP

February 7, 1982

O come, let us worship and bow down: let us kneel before the LORD our maker. For he is our God; and we are the people of his pasture, and the sheep of his hand. (Psalm 95:6–7)

The subject "True Worship" suggests that there is a false worship. And to be sure, there is. False worship is a detestable and horrible thing because the act of worship is so holy and so precious. That brings us to a serious principle which we all ought to know and observe. The preciousness and holiness of any relationship or attitude determine how terrible and damnable is its misuse. As an example, it is wrong to mistreat anyone, but as the relationship gets closer and dearer, mistreatment becomes more diabolical and satanic. It is wrong to mistreat anyone, but to mistreat one's mother is worse than wrong. We make some difference between the poisoning of a dog and the poisoning of a human being. The preciousness of anything is the measurement of how awful can be its misuse.

We all witness false worship. It showed on television the other night. Thousands of people, young people, were shown at a college which calls itself a university and which is located in South Carolina. These thousands of people, most of them young students, sang the old, well-loved hymns. The name of Jesus Christ was called again and again. Some of these young people appeared on television and said that they went to that particular school because they wanted to serve the Lord Jesus Christ. In this school there is no drinking, card playing, or television watching. In the midst of all of this, human worth is defined by color and racism, thick and deep. It is almost to sicken one at the stomach to hear the dear Lord's name called in connection with the filth of racism

215

and the idolatry of color. That is false worship, and it is an abomination before the Lord God. It must sicken heaven above and cause hell below to rejoice. There is a false worship which substitutes showmanship for spirituality and exhibitionism for sincerity and which entertains but does not edify.

False worship is bowing down before anything we make, or human beings like us make. If you want a test of what is false worship, it is found in assigning too much value to what we ourselves create. Anything that a human being can consciously produce by ingenuity and skill is something less than what ought to be adored and knelt before as an object of reverence and praise and obedience. Do not make me draw up a list of such things, for I shall surely forget some item. You must make your own list.

Our worship can go in another sad and pitiable direction. It is to accept as divine what has proven unable to help those who have already put their trust in that object. I do not want anybody to read any tarot cards or my palm or the stars to tell me how to make money when that person is living in the midst of sleazy curtains and a dirty storefront and grasping for every dime he or she gets.

There is a startling example in the Scriptures of the worship of gods who have already failed. In the twenty-fifth chapter of 2 Chronicles, the account is given of Amaziah, king of Judah, who went out to fight the Edomites, who went forth to battle calling on their heathen gods. The Edomites were roundly and soundly beaten. What did Amaziah, king of Judah, servant of Jehovah, do? Having just defeated the Edomites, he went and got their gods and brought them to his palace and "set them up to be his gods and bowed down himself before them, and burned incense unto them" (2 Chronicles 25:14). These false gods had not protected the Edomites, and Amaziah, who defeated the Edomites, then took their gods, which led Dr. Harry Fosdick to preach a sermon from this incident, entitled "Serving the Gods of a Beaten Enemy." I will not worship anything people make, can make, or which they have when it has not delivered them.

True worship means adoration of and submission to the God who has made us, and so declares the ninety-fifth Psalm. This is one of the songs raised by those who came up to the joy of worship in the temple. To the Old Testament Jew, Jerusalem was the holy city and Mt. Moriah, the most hallowed of its mountains, for it carried the national memory back to Abraham's offering of Isaac. Atop Mt. Moriah stood the glory and grandeur of the temple, the earthly residence of God. There was no joy like that of families and neighbors coming up together to Jerusalem for one of the great feast days. Fathers and mothers told wide-eyed children who were on their way to see the holy city for the first time of how it was "beautiful for situation, the joy of the whole earth." No matter how many times older people had seen the hill of God, excitement raced through the pilgrim ranks as they sang their songs and made their way to Jerusalem, to Mt. Moriah, and to the temple.

Is it foolish fancy to imagine that too many of us approach the time of worship as a dull prospect void of any enthusiasm? Is it a trick of memory when one thinks that once people came to the house of God with far greater expectancy than is now the case? Of course, if we come to God's house with no eagerness and no spiritual preparation, then it is almost inevitable that nothing will happen to stand our spirits on tiptoe. If you see nothing here but the walls and roof you have seen so often, you can hardly be asked to be excited. On the other hand, if one sees prayer and faith and the testimony of gallant souls who have lived and died here in Jesus, shining out of these walls and from that roof, then excitement can be ours. If the people we meet here are just "old so and so" and "what's his name" who work over on Twenty-first Street or in Brownsville, that is one thing. On the other hand, if all around you are kings and priests unto our God, friends of Jesus, intimates of God, experts in prayer, living examples of sins forgiven and souls set free, then we have something that can excite the dullest of us. Did you know that right where you sit in that pew one day a soul looked up and saw the Lord and repented and believed and was baptized here into the family of Jesus? Right there in that pew where you sit one day another soul beheld the Lord God on his throne. Did you know that right there on that pew where you sit, one day another soul found strength to go out of here and die the death of the righteous? So seeing and so understanding where we are this hour in this temple of the Most High God, we will cry with Jacob, "How filled with God is this place! This is none other but the house of God, and this is the gate of heaven" (Genesis 28:17).

And so, excited and expectant, the people of Israel came up to Jerusalem singing, and this was one of the songs they sang. (And I do pray that many of you will come to this place week after week with a singing eagerness in the soul.) Can you hear their footfalls, a dozen, fifty, a hundred, a thousand people going up to Jerusalem to worship God together in the great temple with its lifted arches, its stately walls, its reverent atmosphere, its sacred memories? What is it they are singing? What is this burst of praise, resounding with the joyful noise of hearty thanksgiving? "O come, let us sing unto the LORD: let us make a joyful noise to the rock of our salvation. Let us come before his presence with thanksgiving, and make a joyful noise unto him with psalms" (Psalm 95:1–2). And then our text, "O come, let us worship and bow down: let us kneel before the LORD our maker. For he is God; and we are the people of his pasture, and the sheep of his hand."

Did you hear what went before? "For the LORD is a great God, and a great King above all gods. In his hand are the deep places of the earth: the strength of the hills is his also" (Psalm 95:3–4). I know of no way to account for this world and all that is in it other than by the name of God. I care not what theory you may hold of the origin of this vast theatre in which we move and call the cosmos. Be a creationist, if you will, and say that by one sudden lightning like swiftness of God's word the heaven and the earth were created and we ourselves. In his hands still are "the deep places of the earth: the strength of the hills is his also. The sea is his, and he made it: and his hands formed the dry land." Hold, if you will, to the hypothesis of gradual evolution and say that human life began as twisting slime in some marshy backwater and evolved through millions of years. In God's hand still are "the deep places of the earth, the strength of the hills is his also. The sea is his, and he made it: and his hands formed the dry land." Believe if you will in the punctuation theory of evolution, which holds that forms of life continued for long ages and then, suddenly, bang! new and different species appeared. Still in God's hand are "the deep places of the earth: the strength of the hills is his also. The sea is his, and he made it: and his hands formed the dry land." Take God out and you have an explanation of this universe's existence as sensible as the notion that a tornado could blow through a junkyard with a 747 airplane as the result.

True worship involves adoration and praise and thanksgiving and petition before God whose signature is on all that is. The God we serve was not made by any human hands or conceived by any human mind. He is Creator and Owner and therefore has a right to make demands on who we are and what we have. God owns all that is. We read that when Columbus came to the New World, he planted the flag of Spain on the soil of the new land to claim it for Queen Isabella and the nation of Spain who financed the voyage. Likewise, the American astronauts and the Russian cosmonauts vied for who would be the first to reach the moon. Our television made much of the American flag being planted on the moon. Nothing but empty ceremony! Neither America nor Russia can own the moon. Why, in my own native state it is known by every schoolchild that ten flags have flown over that territory, each believing itself to be permanent, final, lasting. All of the earth is already spoken for. "The earth is the LORD's, and the fullness thereof; the world, and they that dwell therein" (Psalm 24:1). The banner of the Creator flies over the whole earth. And so we may say lustily and thankfully, "O come, let us worship and bow down: let us kneel before the LORD our maker. For he is our

God; and we are the people of his pasture, and the sheep of his hand." And let us not harden our hearts when we hear his voice.

E. B. Pusey, regius professor at Oxford University, worshiped well in another generation when he cried unto God, and so may we cry.

> O most merciful Savior, O blessed Creator, Everlasting Redeemer, all that I have, all that I am, my soul, my heart, my mind, my strength, thou hast given me. Therefore with all thou hast given me, I would bless and praise thee and with all thy holy angels glorify thy great and matchless name.
>
> O God, my God, it were fitter far for such as I to lie down in the dust before thee, ashamed for my many sins. Yet since thou willest, I will arise and worship thee, ashamed for my many sins. Yet since thou willest, I will arise and worship thee, and praise thee, and glorify thy great and matchless name, that thou art so good, and so good to me....
>
> I adore thee and worship thee, for thou art all holy, all perfection, all majesty, all excellence, all blessedness, without beginning and without bound. I worship thee. Amen.

So, the soul, like an angel on mighty wings, mounts up everwidening circles, seeking an ever ampler range, and searching for an ever vaster sweep, reaches up on pinions of faith and praise until it glimpses blessed spirits in the great cathedral of eternity, all worshiping the great triune God — angels and archangels, thrones and principalities and powers, the seraphim and cherubim, the multitude of the redeemed that no one can number. And thus in his sanctuary we worship him who dwells in the midst of his holy church, from everlasting to everlasting.

"O come, let us worship and bow down: let us kneel before the LORD our maker. God is in his holy temple. Let all the earth keep silence before him."

～ 37 ～

DOWN PAYMENT AND WILL CALL

November 16, 1986

[In Christ] also we have obtained an inheritance, having been pre-
destinated according to the purpose of him who worketh all things
after the counsel of his own will: that we should be to the praise
of his glory, who first trusted in Christ. In whom ye also trusted,
after that ye heard the word of truth, the gospel of your salvation: in whom also after that ye believed, ye were sealed with that
holy Spirit of promise, which is the earnest of our inheritance until
the redemption of the purchased possession, unto the praise of his
glory, who first trusted in Christ. (Ephesians 1:11–14)

I have said before that New Testament people wrestled with an
enlightened, pagan world for the souls of men and women and
in so doing they seized vocabulary for the faith, the language of
Christian beliefs from wherever they looked, from the old Jewish
system, from the Olympic games, and from the whole system of
Mediterranean commerce, the marketplace, trading, business affairs. They took the language, the words of these various aspects
of the life of the empire. Armies, warfare, whatever, wherever
they found, words and acts that they could seize and baptize them
for the use of Christ, they did so, until they built the vocabulary
of the faith, the language of grace, and this morning I come in the
Book of Ephesians to a commercial term. For the ancient world,
though we do not think so sometimes, was highly commercial.
Business transactions were at a greatly developed and sophisticated state. Sometimes we attempt to look upon these ancients as
being primitive and unlearned. I must say to you again that most
of the thoughts we have today came from them.

And so I use the phrase "Down Payment and Will Call." I
begin here at the twelfth verse "That we should be to the praise
of his glory, who first trusted in Christ." But particularly these

two verses, "In whom ye also trusted after that ye heard the word of truth, the gospel of your salvation: in whom also after that ye believed, ye were sealed with that holy Spirit of promise, which is the earnest of our inheritance until the redemption of the purchased possession, unto the praise of his glory."

In that first chapter more than once and perhaps more intensely in that first chapter than anywhere else, the word, one of the most widely debated words of Christian history occurred: predestination. Now, hearing that word, predestination, do not let your minds wander off saying, "Aw, he is dealing with something far out and abstract." Theologically, the doctrine of predestination states that by number God has already decreed that a certain number of people are predestined, foreordained, already scheduled for everlasting life. And by the same token, a certain number of people, no matter what they might do, are scheduled for hell and damnation. That is the doctrine. But do not say that it is something far off and that I am dealing in something way out and philosophic. All of these old doctrines sift down into the street where we live, and they take on everyday language, but they're the same old doctrines. The trouble with our modern people is we are so "unsmart" that we think that the things we are saying all started with us. "You're not going to go until your time comes." That's a neighborhood expression of predestination. We think it started with us because we do not know.

I drove this week from Richmond to Charlottesville because I had long wanted to see Monticello, the estate of Thomas Jefferson. On my way I stopped far toward evening at a barbershop in Lynchburg. You hear strange things in barbershops and, I am told, in beauty parlors. The barber's name on Fifth Street where I stopped was Joe. I do not know his last name. Another man came in, and Joe said something to him, and he said, "I didn't know that, Joe." And Joe said something I hadn't heard in a long time. He said, "What you don't know would make a whole other world. And a big one, too." I guess we would all have to admit that what we do not know would make another world, and a big one, too. We think that these sayings all started with us. "You don't go until your time comes. It's when your number is up." Or that song that came from the Spanish idiom some years ago, "Que Sera, Sera, whatever will be, will be." Those are neighborhood expressions, down-to-earth versions of the doctrine of predestination. Of course, I would think that anybody who believes in the doctrine of predestination, that you don't go, to put it in a homespun way, until your time comes, crossing Fulton Street ought not to look up and down the street since you don't go until your time comes.

There may be some truth in the doctrine of predestination. Some people are more spiritually sensitive than others. They are born that way, naturally. Some people are firmer in determination and character than others, naturally. Some people are less sexually motivated than others, naturally. To that extent we are born with certain inclinations, but to say that God has already decreed that some shall go to hell does not gibe with the New Testament. For it says that God willed that *all* people should be saved (1 Timothy 2:4). To say that some *cannot* be saved is to make our Lord's death of limited value. For again the New Testament says that Christ died a ransom for all, and to say that some people cannot qualify for the kingdom is to make a lie of what Jesus said, "Whosoever will, let him come." No, there is a part we must play in the plan of salvation as is clearly expressed here in the Book of Ephesians. There is something that God will not do for us. I had almost said that God cannot do for us.

The first human responsibility occurs in this, well, this transaction, this exchange of values which is, I take it, the meaning of a contract. There are some things God cannot do, will not do. First, the writer of Ephesians says, "In whom ye also trusted after that you heard the word of truth." So somebody is called upon to make God's Word "hearable." I don't know whether this is a good and proper word or not. Somebody is called upon to make God's Word "hearable," to make it heard. The church is called on to do that. When I speak about the church I'm not talking about some entity, some embodiment, some thing that is separate from you and from me. The church is not something different from you; the church is you. When the old Concord building burned down, the first thing I said to the people of this church was that Concord Church did not burn. The building in which Concord Church met burned. So you and I, the church, are called upon to make the Word of God "hearable," and this is a great responsibility. One of the reasons we give our money is that in such a way we make the Word of God "hearable." We give our money that there might be a place where the Word of God might be proclaimed. But that is the least, for you and I are called upon out of our experience of the Lord in our lives to make the gospel *hearable* by our witness.

If you walk up and down the streets of Brooklyn, talking about everything and everybody except the Lord, you are failing in your responsibility to make the gospel "hearable." To make it heard, to let it be heard. The apostle spoke of the Lord Jesus Christ "in whom you trusted after that ye had heard." Somebody spoke about the Lord, and these people in Ephesus heard it, and they believed after they heard.

There's an old story, perhaps all of you have heard. It's a little legend, but a lovely legend. It says that when the risen and triumphant Spirit of the Lord returned home, angels asked him, "Where have you been?" and he said, "I've been down to the earth to win people, men and women and boys and girls, back to God." "What did you do to do that?" said the angels. "I died on Calvary's cross," the risen Savior said. "How will they know about it?" and he answered, "I left some people with whom I had been in touch and asked them to spread the word." Then an angel asked, "What if they fail to tell the story?" The Savior answered, "I have made no other plans."

That's the responsibility on you, that's the responsibility on me. Whenever the Lord has touched somebody's life in whatever way, if he has fixed us when we were out of fix, if he has straightened us out when we were bent and crooked, if he has lifted us when we were down, if he has brought us in when we were out, if he has made us something when we were nothing — then we've got a story to tell, and the Lord has made no other plans. He has so much confidence in you and in me that he has put the whole thing in our hands. What a responsibility! What confidence! Had you ever thought of that, that the salvation, the eternal destiny of the souls of men and women, boys and girls, is in your hands? Not mine alone! I must remind you of your responsibility.

Most of the things I talk about are things that have come to me, filtered through my own mind and imagination, from those preachers I heard in my earliest years. Following my preaching forebears I have imagined how else the Lord might have spread his gospel. How might he have done it?

He might have written, put it like you want, tattooed, cut, carved the word of the gospel in the leaves of the trees, "God is love." He might have written that on every tree, on every leaf, on every limb in every tree, in every forest. And autumn winds, blowing leaves hinder and yon, would have spread the word that God is love. But leaves blow only in the autumn. To get the word, someone would have to come up to the leaf, so God did not do that. He might have skywritten "Christ died for you" and emblazoned those words on the face of the sky that people looking up to wonder whether the day would be cloudy or sunny would read in the heavens "God is love. Christ died for you." But if you did not look up you would not get the gospel.

Ah, I have imagined that God might have made it an audio gospel, purely by hearing, not by sight. And he might have put the good news in the music of old ocean as the waves everlastingly pound against the shores and the great breakers roar in and out. He might have put the sound in the waves of the ocean, "God is love." But people far inland would have never heard the gospel. You would have to be a coastal dweller to hear the gospel. Or he might have put the music of grace in the winds, so that the winds blowing through the trees might have sung, "God is love." But the deaf would have no chance at the gospel. What did he do?

He touched you and he touched me. He picked us up, turned us upside down, and then put us right-side up again, placing our feet on solid ground and putting inside us a witness that God cares for us. That witness is inside of me and inside of you.

Then he said to us, Now that you've got it, let the infection of grace spread wherever you go. Let there be a contagion, for there's something in you, something that, if you let it brush up against someone else, it will infect that person's soul. For spirit bears witness unto spirit. That is our purpose and our privilege. A "secret service Christian" is no Christian at all. Anybody hiding the fact that the Lord has been good to him or her is ungrateful and unworthy. Anybody who has been blessed by the Lord and makes believe that the Lord has done nothing for him or her does not merit God's favor. That's the first part of the responsibility.

The second part is that having heard, we believe. Now do not tell me that you are a hard believer and such is most difficult. We are all believers. I don't think that life could be lived a single day without belief. I think if anybody did not believe in anything, that despair, hopelessness, would so surround that life that it could not survive even one day. As a matter of fact, we're all believers. We believe all of the time, every day, every night. Let me go from the ridiculous to the absurd. If there were such a thing as somebody who did not believe at all, then you would believe in your unbelief. For we are believers. We believe in so many things. We believe in traffic signals, in sales slips, in property deeds, in airplane pilots, in bus drivers, in barbers, in beauticians, in contractors, in plumbers. Belief, that's all we are. Your life is nothing but a network of belief. From morning until night, you believe when you turn the switch in your house that the light will come on. All kinds of beliefs. When you open a can of whatever, you believe that it has been canned properly. Belief, belief, that's all we do, it's the only way life can be lived, and when you go to a bank and put your money in you believe that when you go back there, it will be on hand. Do you talk about being a believer? A believer? My God! That's all we are, and when we die and leave wills, we believe. It may not work out, but we believe that the terms of the will will be honored. So we leave here believing.

But here is the highest belief that we can have: to believe in God. To believe in him because he has already shown us how good he is. Do you realize that you have never learned how to breathe? You never went to school for that. I'm not sure anybody could've taught you. They might teach you to breathe properly and to breathe as a singer or speaker, but to breathe, no! When you knew you were breathing, you were breathing. As a matter of fact the only way you could know you were breathing was that you were breathing. God has been good. Put it at that basic elemental level. God has equipped us to breathe. He has somehow made air that is adaptable to our lungs. He has made water that matches our thirst. God has been good. He has made food that satisfies our appetite. You don't even need a Bible to believe in God. Oh, thank the Lord that we have the Bible, but look around anywhere, raise your hand, shut your eyes, open your eyes, draw in your breath. Yes, God is good! That truth is everywhere.

And you're called and I am called upon to believe in the Good News of God's love and of Christ having died for you and for me. This is no fad we are believing in, this is no new thing that came along. This has survived two thousand years. Poets have rhymed their meter around it. Musicians have rhapsodized their melodies upon this theme. Some of the noblest minds of the world have written about it. Preachers, some of them of consummate gift, have tried to comment upon it. It has lasted and millions and millions and millions of humble believers have lived out their days in the trust that God would provide and their witness thunders through the ages that God does provide! The Lord will provide! Has provided! Does provide! That is one side of the contract. Let me quickly bring you to the other side.

Once we have done that, God pays down on our full possession. He does not complete the contract yet. He gives us the seal of the Holy Spirit. That's the promise, that's not the finished contract, that's the promise, that he will at last possess us completely.

Now you and I know that the Lord does not own us fully yet. You may claim so and you may say so, but you know that the Lord does not yet have full possession of your life and he does not have full possession of my life. I am going to be talking next week about the Holy Spirit, but he seals us with the Spirit, the witness inside of us who corrects us when we are wrong, who comforts us when we are sad, who strengthens us when we are weak, who encourages us when we despair, gives us the spirit in us as the mark that we belong to him! But that's not the full possession.

Our niece who lives and works in Las Vegas visited here some months ago and worshiped in this church. She visited Atlantic City, and since they have the same kind of industry in Atlantic City that she works as a croupier in in Las Vegas, she came out of Atlantic City with a large profit. When we took her from this church to carry her to LaGuardia, she said, "You must stop me by such and such store, because when I came from Atlantic City yesterday I paid down on a new mink coat and I must go to 'Will Call' and pick it up." And sure enough she did. She modeled it for us out at LaGuardia Airport. Well, the Lord has paid down on us. He has claimed us for himself, but the transaction is not finished.

Now the world shakes us, but God has put down earnest payment, a pledge against, the redemption of the purchased possession. And now the world may shake, but it will not shake us always, only until he claims us completely for himself. Now infirmity may be upon us, but not always. When the transaction is completed, we shall be released from all that weakens us and all that enervates us and all that stops us. Now the night, until the morning comes! Now the fever of this life, until the kiss of eternal health is upon our brow! Now we weep, until God himself shall wipe all tears from our eyes! I know, said Paul, whom I have believed, and I am convinced that he is able to keep that which I have put in his hands (2 Timothy 1:12). I know whom I have believed. The pledge, the earnest, the promise of our completion in Christ has been made. He will claim us from "will call."

⌐ 38 ⌐

WILD WORDS AND
BRIGHT CONCLUSIONS

March 1, 1987

...that ye, being rooted and grounded in love, May be able to comprehend with all saints what is the breadth, and length, and depth, and height; And to know the love of Christ, which passeth knowledge, that ye might be filled with all the fulness of God. (Ephesians 3:17–19)

The work of the Christian preacher can be very difficult and often frustrating. If there are preachers who hear me this morning, as there often are in this congregation, they will sense something of what I mean. I do not say this in order to seek your sympathy. In matters of public discourse, if I may say so, I do not feel the need of any human sympathy. I, rather, say it to indicate, to suggest the vastness, the magnitude, the scope of the gospel with which any preacher seeks to deal.

Let me read some words from that Christian who has influenced the Christian centuries, I think, more than any follower of Jesus other than the apostle Paul. I refer to the church father, Augustine, who lived in the fourth century. He says,

My preaching almost always displeases me. For I am eager after something better, of which I often have an inward enjoyment before I set about expressing my thoughts in audible words. Then, when I have failed to utter my meaning as clearly as I have conceived it, I am disappointed that my tongue is incapable in doing justice to that which is in my heart. What I myself understand I wish my hearers to understand fully. And I feel that I am not so speaking as to effect this. The chief reason is that the conception lights up the mind with a kind of rapid flash, whereas the utterance is slow, lagging, and far unlike the thing it would convey.

229

Thus, the frustration. It is the scope of the gospel, its hugeness. If I were an orator in any other area, in public affairs, for instance, our responsibility would be simple. I would need only to digest my subject, marshal my facts, organize my material, appeal to your logic, to your minds, to your grasp of things. Use some relieving and, perhaps, reinforcing wit and humor. I need only to follow the procedure I have mentioned, appeal to your judgment, good sense, and I would be done.

The Christian preacher cannot have that kind of confidence. He or she deals with the things not only of time, but of eternity. Not only the affairs of people, but the doings of God in the life of humankind, and that is different. And the words by which the Scriptures themselves try to set this forth, this pressure that all of you feel sometimes in your life, this hankering, this disquiet, this edification, this ennoblement, staggers the mind. The Bible itself tries to deal with this in language that sometimes escapes reason. For instance, there is the word "He that seeketh to save his life shall lose it." Now, when I use that and appeal to your common sense, I confuse you. Or when those great words that shine through the centuries are uttered, "God so loved the world that he gave his only begotten Son that whosoever believeth on him should not perish, but have everlasting life," the mind is dazed.

Sometimes, when you try to put into language what the Lord has done and is doing and has promised to do, you realize how hopeless it is. I suppose that you could take nine brief statements and list the whole meaning of the entire biblical account — God's creation, humanity's fall, Israel's struggle toward nationhood, the prophets and their words of God's righteousness and his demands, the birth of Jesus, his preaching and teaching and healing, his death and resurrection, his ascension, his promise to come again — and claim that the whole gospel has been uttered. But has it? So that where one has tried to fashion into language, though it were the language of Milton and Shakespeare, the things that God has done and is doing and will do, the gospel seems to smile at you and say to you, "How pitiful. You don't really think that describes me, do you?"

And so the frustration, but there is a thrill in it, also.

We have these wild words set down here before bright conclusion in the Book of Ephesians, and the writer starts where all of us might well start: "I bow my knees unto the Father of our Lord Jesus Christ, that he would grant you according to the riches of his glory." But a chapter before the writer has spoken about the "unsearchable riches." What a contradiction! That God would grant according to the riches of his glory, as if the writer has measured those riches, the resources of God. "According to the riches." But before this the writer has spoken of "the boundless riches of Christ." What wild talk is this?

I read somewhere else in the Scripture that Christ says, "I go to prepare a place for you. And if I go and prepare a place for you, I will come again." But here I read that Christ may "dwell in your hearts." Put those together in your mind and see where your reason comes out. The Scriptures say to me that we were born in sin, and here I am told that Christ's people are "rooted and grounded in love"? But I was born in sin! I'm rooted in sin! If you use your mind alone, you will never grasp this gospel. The height of Christ's love? How high is that? The breadth of Christ's love? How wide is that? The love of Christ "surpasses knowledge." This is a wild word breaking out of the bounds of our power to comprehend. A consummate scholar could not get hold of this with the mind alone.

And the length! How long is God's love? I read that "the Lord will perfect that which concerneth me" (Psalm 138:8). How long does it take to make you perfect? What stretch of time is involved in bringing you and me to where we are at last to know and experience the length of God's love? The length of God's love is beyond our reckoning, but we are assured that he who has begun in us a good work will "perform it until the day of Jesus

Christ" (Philippians 1:6). The length and the depth! The depth of
God's love! How deep down does God's love go? What sin is it
that you and I might commit that is below the sweep, the down-
ward reach, the nadir, of God's love? By grace, you and I are to
know the depth of God's love. I read somewhere in the Scripture
that he descended into hell. It does not say that that is the depth
of God's love. It merely says that he went that far, but it doesn't
say that that is the depth of God's love. Still, we are to know, to
comprehend all of this! What a gospel!

And the height of God's love. How high is that? Maybe I
should ask an even larger question: how high is highest? And by
what does one measure what is highest? The height of God's love!
You would have to penetrate the mystery of eternity and you
would have to trespass upon the divine heart in order to know
the height of God's love. How wide is God's love? How long is
God's love? How deep is God's love? Unless the Holy Spirit interprets all that I've been saying, your mind will never grasp it!
This is deeper than mental process. Another agent, another presence must enter, and, for that matter, a research scholar will not
be able to understand this, but I have seen illiterate, backwoods
believers aglow with what I'm talking about. While the preacher
cannot make it clear, the presence of the Holy Spirit can make
it plain.

And so, what I'm saying this morning I say to your minds only
to the extent that they may be a gateway, but I must ask that the
Holy Spirit enter into your hearts and glorify these wild words
that do not make sense to our minds. That they may feed you
and nurture you in the things of Jesus Christ. Ah, Holy Spirit,
come here! Anybody who is to be lifted up will not be so lifted
by the preacher, but by the Holy Spirit. If anybody is to be called
out of darkness into the marvelous light of God's grace, it will not
be by the finished phrases of any preacher. Holy Spirit, do your
work! Holy Spirit, move in this place and make clear what is not
clear and explain what cannot be explained.

And so the preacher backs away and the writer backs away and says, "Unto him be glory." I must retreat. I will never make it clear to you. But now unto him! Now unto him who is able to make plain what is not plain! Now unto him who can lift up what is fallen down! Now unto him who is able. Now unto him who is able to do and — here is some questionable grammar — "exceeding abundantly (somebody has translated that "super-abundantly") above all that we can ask or think," to him be glory and praise. He alone can make it all plain.

Rumor of Life

[The date of this sermon is unknown but thought to be before 1988.]

Their words seemed to them as idle tales, and they believed them not. (Luke 24:11)

The rumor which seemed like an idle tale was the word of life, the resurrection of Jesus, which some women brought to those who mourned the death on Calvary of their favorite Friend and treasured Teacher. It was a rumor of life which they brought from the place of death. They were returning from a cemetery to say that One who had died was no longer dead.

The word of resurrection, the rumor of life, which these women brought was not a new notion. The notion of life being stronger than death is an old one, and we run across it almost wherever and whenever people have lived. The idea that death, which seems so final, is not ultimate is textured and woven into the very fabric of human life. The notion of life beyond life is so universal that we might say it is instinctual, like breathing or knee jerk or the batting of the eye. One looks in vain where men and women have lived to find a society which has not in some way believed in this rumor of life.

The American Indians placed arrowheads and earthen vessels by the side of their dead that they might have weapons with which to hunt and utensils with which to cook in the happy hunting ground to which their departed spirits had gone. The Greeks, a continent away and centuries apart, put a silver coin in the mouth of their corpses that they might pay Charon, the ferryman, to cross them over the river Styx. The Egyptians, brooding beneath the colossal Sphinx and within shadow of the lofty pyramids, looked across the burning desert and, musing on the rumor of life, placed in the coffins of their dead that which they called

234

"the chest of the living," the book of the dead. These books contained the prayers the dead were to utter and a map to guide them through the unseen world. The Laplanders of the frozen northern Arctic buried flint and tinder with their dead that they might have light for the dark journey. The Norsemen, fierce fighters of ancient Europe, buried the fallen warrior's horse and armor with him for the dead hero's triumphant ride into Valhalla. The Greenlanders, I am told in support of the rumor of life, when their male children died buried a dog that the lad might have a guide and friend in death.

There is a rumor of afterlife among all people. Philosophy, religion, and ethics bring their testimony of faith. Plato in the *Phaedo* argued for immortality from the alternations of opposites; life must follow death as death follows life. Religion cried out in Job's question which confronts the darkness and mystery of death, "If a man die, shall he live again?" (Job 14:14).

Plants and flowers repeat the rumor of life. In late winter we look out of our windows and everywhere we see the world of nature sleeping in a tomb of ice and a grave of snow. No green grass tells its story of life; no flower blushes in living color. Death seems everywhere. We look a few weeks later, and the rumor of life whispers in the greenness of the grass and the first brave sprouts that shoot up from the thawing earth.

The rumor of life is in our sense of right and wrong. To be sure, there are some very smart souls who scornfully talk of this precious notion of eternal life as an escape from our struggle for justice here and now. This is a prostitution of the blessed hope. The abolitionists who gave their lives for freedom died because they believed a human being is an immortal soul and, therefore, must not be a slave. I know of no group of people in any land who have striven harder to rise in this world than Christian people. "Yes, and when all of your scorners have finished their sneers, you will find that on balance Christian people are far and away ahead in trying to live decent lives, trying to educate their children, buy property, set good examples for their children, and affect affirmatively the society of which they are apart," William A. Jones has pointed out.

Fight for what is right we must, but when we have fought the best we know, there is still injustice and oppression. Sneer with the cynic about the rumor of life, if you must, and talk of the hope of the resurrection as "pie in the sky by and by." Still, as Dr. George Buttrick once said, there ought to be some pie somewhere for children cheated of life by an atomic bomb as in Nagasaki or by poverty as in slums of certain American cities or in parts of rural America. Somewhere the things that are wrong in this life must be made right, or there is no justice in the universe. There must be an "after awhile" and a "by and by" if God be God and truth be truth.

Now in this rumor of life we all have a stake. Some are at the age where we recognize our part and place in this old and wistful hope. Others occupied with the fresh breezes and exciting scenes of youth think of the whole matter of Easter and resurrection as a remote and insignificant consideration. Nonetheless we are all involved. We are on that journey which leads from the cradle to the grave. For some it is a long journey, while for others it is a short walk, as witness our obituary notices.

> That infant not yet able to use his limbs to walk, lying asleep in his mother's arms has already begun this journey; the old man continues it when his limbs are too feeble to bear him across the room. It is a journey we carry on while we sleep as well as while we are awake. We never halt till we stumble into the grave which lies at the end of the road. On and on we go, moving incessantly toward that certain and particular hour — moving night and day, like the hands that circle round the hours, the heart beating on like the ticking of the clock until it has run down and its hands move no more.

All of us have a stake in this rumor of life. In the twelfth chapter of the Book of Ecclesiastes, Koheleth, the Preacher, was talking about our mortal journey. This unknown seer in Israel, once thought to be Solomon, beheld the sea of mystery which

washes the shores of time and laps against the coasts of disillu-
sionment. Thus the book is a brooding, melancholy elegy. In the
twelfth chapter the writer tells us all why we have a stake in the
rumor of life. The author tells us we had best remember our Creator in the days of youth when evil days come not (Ecclesiastes
12:1). For the days of weakness, the evil days do come. How
graphic and true are the lines of the description. As a preacher
in the long ago put it, "The keepers of the house shall tremble."
The arms that held the wheel or guided the plough shake with
palsy. "Strong men shall bow themselves." The limbs, those pillars of the frame, shrunk and shriveled, totter and stagger beneath
their weight. "The grinders cease," the teeth decay and drop from
their sockets, warning that we shall drop into the grave. "Those,"
he said, "that look out of the windows be darkened" — the eye,
that window from which the soul and brain sit peering out upon
the world, grows dim with years, and man and woman enter the
shadow of the tomb because its darkness closes around them.
"He shall rise up at the voice of the bird" — the sleep of the cradle is calm and undisturbed, but old age brings broken slumbers
and wakes with the slightest sounds of the birds who sing in the
dawning. "They shall be afraid of that which is high," with heart
enfeebled, people close to the grave dare not try high hills but
creep along the flat shore or the level ground, walking cane in
hand (Ecclesiastes 12:3–5).

The next description that Koheleth, the Preacher, gave touches
me with the most tender memory of a dear, departed friend. The
writer said that we come to the place when the "grasshopper shall
be a burden," such is weakness, though the tiny insect leaping
from blade to blade scarcely bends the grass beneath its weight.
That passage touches me because of an evening among the Mexi-
can hills when my late and dear friend Marshall Shepard and I sat
on the porch of our villa in Ixtapan. Our friendship had stretched
for more than twenty years. I knew him as the most intensely
alive man I had or have ever known; his energies ran out in many
directions; his love of life had been something beautiful to watch.

Now, he was infirm, the onset of blindness had dimmed his vision, and his body moved slowly and laboriously. That evening's scene is still fresh in my memory though nearly two decades have come and gone. The hills of old Mexico were silhouetted in the gentle darkness. Around the everlasting hills the encircling sky seemed like a faint pink shawl. My friend began ruminating and then, speaking of his own weakening frame, he said ever so sadly, "Partner, I have come to the place where the grasshopper is a burden." He meant that age had brought him to that place where to walk was a task; to see he had to squint and peer.

So we all wonder if this be all. For so quickly we come to old age and infirmity; how quickly the blithe days of youth and morning pass! So soon our steps are slowed, and vagrant pains tell us of approaching weakness. Is there anything to the rumor that life is mightier than death? We may believe in the rumor of life if we follow with faith some women as they made their way to a cemetery. They had passed through the devastation of Friday and the death of their friend, Jesus. The lonely march from judgment hall to judgment hall, the heavy cross upon his shoulders, the steep climb outside the city's walls, the hill shaped like a skull, the cursing soldiers, the weeping women, the trembling earth, the silent skies, the darkened heavens, the blessed prayer, "Father, forgive," and the lonely cry, "My God, why?" (Luke 23:34; Matthew 27:46). Those who watched saw the dying thief, the intervening Savior, the drooping head in the locks of the shoulders, and heard the valedictory shout, "It is finished" (John 19:30). They had witnessed all of it!

As Sunday comes, let us follow the women to the cemetery where there breaks forth again in Scripture the rumor about life that shall endless be. One finds that rumor in Genesis, "Enoch walked with God: and he was not; for God took him" (Genesis 5:24), but it is a far-off word. The rumor of life and resurrection is repeated in Job, "I know that my redeemer liveth, and that he shall stand at the latter day upon the earth: And though ... worms destroy this body, yet in my flesh shall I see God" (Job 19:25–26).

One can read the rumor in Isaiah, "Thy dead shall live" (Isaiah 26:19). "Kings [shall come] to the brightness of thy rising" (Isaiah 60:3), but the rumor had not passed beyond hearsay until Easter morning.

Friday at last became Sunday morning, and the old rumor took on new life. Two persons, strange creatures with dazzling raiment, were at the grave. Matthew said it was one person who said, "Fear not...he is not here" (Matthew 28:5–6). Could this be the same heavenly creature who at the birth of Jesus said, "Fear not: for, behold, I bring you good tidings" (Luke 2:10)? At any rate, the word was, "Fear not...for he is risen." The women went to spread the rumor.

The disciples would not believe it. They were hiding in somebody's house. "Keep that door locked," someone said, for they were afraid. They let in the women, who blurted out, "He is risen." Mockery must have followed, only to be faced by the women's stout insistence, "He is risen, indeed." They crucified him, but "he is risen." They put him in the grave, but "he is risen." They put soldiers around, but "he is risen." They said it was all over, but "he is risen." The disciples could not believe it until they looked up and saw in the room their Master, who said to them, "Peace be unto you" (John 20:19). When the actuality of the rumor got hold of them, they began spreading the resurrection gospel, and now it covers the whole earth.

The resurrection rumor has been confirmed. Let the ends of the earth hear: the Lord lives! We have now a hope in Jesus as the years go slipping by. We need this hope as the frost of age falls on our heads. We lose so many who are so close, and their absence makes us cry out for the resurrection word. Thus the grandest news the world has ever heard, which started in ages long past as a rumor, is now confirmed by the risen Lord and his living presence among us here and now. Death's ultimate power is vanquished, and Christ is Lord indeed.

∽ 40 ∾

STRUGGLING BUT NOT LOSING

[The date of this sermon is unknown but thought to be before 1988.]

We are troubled on every side, yet not distressed; we are perplexed, but not in despair; persecuted, but not forsaken; cast down, but not destroyed; always bearing about in the body the dying of the Lord Jesus, that the life also of Jesus might be made manifest in our body. (2 Corinthians 4:8–10)

You may not realize it, but you are out every day to find out what life is all about. Every person, whether the case is stated or left in silence, is trying to find what this life is all about. We look for clues as to the nature of life; we search for some sign of a pattern; we believe that there is a design. I heard my father long ago preach a sermon on "The Riddle of Life." In it he reflected upon what he called the "fascinating legend of the Sphinx at Thebes." In that legend the creature with a lion's body and a human head terrorized the people of the city of Thebes by demanding the answer to a riddle taught her by the Muses. Each time the riddle was answered incorrectly, the cruel Sphinx would devour a human soul. At last, Oedipus gave the correct answer. He was enthroned by a grateful citizenry, and the Sphinx thereupon killed herself.

So! an old and fascinating legend, but in some way or another in the days of our years the riddle is put to us in the events of our existence, What is life all about? What is its nature? Does it have a pattern? Can you solve its riddle? Are you able to see a design, a meaning?

You will misread it if you decide that life is a picnic, a frolic, or a party. It has carefree hours, but they are the exception. Life is a struggle, that is what it is, a struggle from the day we are born until the day we die. Follow it, children are barely born, and right where life begins there is a struggle between life and death. How

240

is the baby? How is the mother? are the questions we ask, and in so saying we recognize that there has been a struggle. The infant struggles to walk. Would you like to know, by the way, what the riddle was the Sphinx at the ancient Egyptian funeral city of Thebes asked of its citizens? It was this, "What is it that has one voice and yet becomes four-footed and then two-footed and then three-footed?" It is, of course, a human being with a single voice who first struggles to crawl on all fours, then struggles to walk on two feet, and then struggles at last to stay upright by leaning on a cane.

You and I will never understand what this life is all about until we see it as a struggle. This struggle is all tied up with our capacity to suffer. Frederick Robertson, the English preacher of the mid-1800s, described our human plight and perhaps his own short and tortured life. He said, and some of you will say it is all too gloomy and melancholy a reading of life, that our universal heritage is woe. "Men of poverty we are not all, men of weak ability we are not all — but the man not of sorrows is as yet unborn" — and I may add, his mother has already died.

All that is about us is subject to injury, which opens the way for struggle. The skin of the human frame can be broken, bringing forth blood. There runs beneath the skin, crossed and crisscrossed in layers unbelievable, a network of nerves, every fiber, every inch, every scintilla of which may become the home of pain, and so easily. There is no gap in all of those nerves into which the finest needle may be thrust without producing pain. In a sense which the psalmist hardly meant, we are fearfully made.

The mental machinery, Robertson continued, is even more sensitive. The inner mind is more exposed to shock and wounds than the outer skin, and the sensitive network which comprises the mind is a thousand times more alive to agony than the physical nerves that quiver and ache when they are cut. There is such a thing as disappointment in this world, and we all taste it sometimes. There is such a thing as affection rejected and hurled back on itself. There is such a thing as slight, insult, scorn, and sarcasm which cuts the spirit and then rubs salt in the wound. There is such a thing as sickness, sin, and sorrow. Robertson, himself so troubled, seemed to be describing himself.

Could I but mention another aspect of our being which makes us liable for suffering and struggle? We are creatures made to love, to give our hearts in trust and surrender one to the other. This is as natural with us as breathing. Withholding love and trust are unnatural impulses. This capacity for love opens us to so many hurts and to so much struggle, bitter, anguished, raw, bleeding suffering. The moment you give your trust in friendship or love, you open yourself, expose yourself to betrayal and humiliation. This is the theme of so much that is most touching in music, poetry, and theater. Have you not seen such love and trust rejected and trampled upon? Is there anyone who has not passed through this or who is not passing through it now? I have wept inwardly with so many young women who have been abandoned at a fearful time and whose sad word was, "I trusted him." I have listened to scores of men who have said, "I tried to give her everything, and now this!" I will not peer down the street where parents lament the indifference of their children and whose wail is fashioned out of their love.

So! we get hurt, run risks, and must struggle day by day, for life is a fight. And if you are not careful, it is a losing fight, yes, a losing fight! The struggle can leave one numb, cold, bitter, and cursing, off in a corner — sobbing, or on some skid row looking for peace in the bottom of a bottle, or somewhere else shooting poison into the veins, trying to drive sorrow and struggle away.

There is an antidote for this poison, true and tried. Hear, if you will, this Scripture all laden and heavy with suffering, struggling, and something else, or better still, somebody else who makes all of the difference. This is one man's litany of suffering and struggle. "We are troubled on every side,...are perplexed,... persecuted,...cast down."

It is a Christian man, Paul, talking — the world's best-known proponent and promoter of the gospel of Jesus Christ. When will fools stop talking about the faith of Christ as something soft and innocent as to what life's hurts are all about? You are a Christian: you don't know what the world is like. I have known very, very few Christian people who have not known intimately how ugly and brutal life can be. Our faith is not a hothouse faith, off somewhere in a never-never land of innocent contemplation. The church of Jesus Christ was not born in a quiet ivory tower, isolated, insulated, and protected from reflection. It was born in bloodshed and brutality, midst nails, spears, hammers, lies, curses, gambling, and dark betrayal. The church came to be not by serene meditation alone, but was jostled and pushed by the mystery religions of Egypt and Asia Minor, the hard-nosed, relentless logic of Greek philosophy, the harsh legalism and enmity of those who would not see and would not believe, and the brutal cruelty of the most ruthless empire the world has ever known: Rome.

The man who wrote my text knew what it's all about. You know, the biggest fools are those who think that all which they think is smart got started when they were born. "Mom, Dad, you don't know what it's all about." How vain and foolish can youth be! Some do not realize that there is no mom or dad who was not once their age. All of these smart operators on their way to jail in government think they started it all. Check the encyclopedia and you will see that about 1100 B.C., investigations revealed large-scale plunder and corruption in high places, strikes, and power grabbing in the ancient Egyptian funeral city of Thebes.

The man who wrote the words I have quoted was no shielded, insulated child of privilege. As a young man, he had watched and supported the death of Deacon Stephen by stoning. Think of rocks and stones being hurled at a human body until bones are crushed and life is literally knocked out of the frame. You are onto something more brutal than stabbing or shooting. Here was a man talking out of twenty-five or more years campaigning up and down the empire, sailing, walking, and riding. Look at the labels on his baggage! Tarsus, Damascus, Antioch — all for Jesus. Look again at the luggage of this lonely pilgrim for Jesus preaching, arguing, defending, and explaining the gospel in many strange and hostile forums: no family; enemies, suspicion, attacks, jailings, and desertions. Look again at the labels on his baggage: Lystra, Derbe, Iconium, Perga, Ephesus, Corinth, Athens, Thessalonica, Philippi — twenty-five years alone, traveling, talking, and working. He knew the unreliability of friends. He was so sick one night, maybe in Troas, that maybe they sent for a doctor whose name might have been Luke. Cold shouldered by a church he planted and loved, talked about unkindly by people to whom he taught Jesus and whom he baptized, I think he qualifies in the University of Hard Knocks.

Now listen to how Paul talked about suffering and struggling but not losing. The difference between winning and losing in his life was Jesus Christ. It was the gospel which put joy bells ringing in his heart and singing in his soul, the love of Jesus which shed abroad bright sunshine in his spirit. "We have this treasure in earthen vessels." Paul was saying that he was not much, but he had a great possession. He was very weak, but he had a friend who was very strong. "We have this treasure in earthen vessels.... We are troubled on every side" — all around there is a hard struggle — "yet not distressed." "We are perplexed," puzzled, confused, sometimes, "but not in despair; persecuted, but not forsaken; cast down, but not destroyed," struggling but not losing (2 Corinthians 4:7–9).

One translator, Charles B. Williams, translated that last part in the language of the prize ring, "always getting a knockdown, but never a knockout." Yes, the believer in Jesus gets knocked down but never knocked out. Every time we fall, he picks us up.

There is no place for defeat in God's plan. I used to hear my father say, and God knows I have found this true, that Christians are like rubber balls. The harder you throw them down, the higher they bounce. We may be sure that we shall overcome!

"Thanks be to God, which giveth us the victory through our Lord Jesus Christ" (1 Corinthians 15:57). "For whatsoever is born of God overcometh the world: and this is the victory that overcometh the world, even our faith" (1 John 5:4). In Jesus we shall triumph over every foe, overcome every malady, every pain, and every sorrow. In 1952 the Concord Church structure covering the length of a city block was consumed by fire. The first sermon in the new and larger edifice was taken from Psalm 126. "They that sow in tears shall reap in joy. He that goeth forth and weepeth, bearing precious seed, shall doubtless come again with rejoicing, bringing his sheaves with him" (Psalm 126:5–6). Every Christian can be confident of such an outcome.

God is going to win, and we who enlist in his army are going to win because we are his and he is ours. When our warfare is over, we shall claim the triumph, and we shall go stately sweeping to the great coronation, waving palms of victory in our hands and shouting, "We have overcome the wicked one." We shall march on through floods and flames, through sufferings and sorrows, until the great victory banquet of the Lamb. We shall come up from every side, from the north, south, east, and west carrying our crosses, bearing our burdens, weeping our tears, suffering our sorrows, limping with our hurts, and nursing our wounds. When the journey is past, we shall live, love, learn, and labor in that sunlit land where the flowers never fade, the day never dies, and the song never stills.

ᔓ 41 ᔒ

THE SAVIOR'S FINAL NAME

February 11, 1990

And I saw the dead, small and great, stand before God; and the books were opened: and another book was opened, which is the book of life: and the dead were judged out of those things which were written in the books, according to their works. (Revelation 20:12)

Worship, when it is grand, has no comparison, and we have had that this morning in the music of these several choirs. Such worship lifts the soul, people are not going through some motions at a poor dying rate, and the great God and his Christ are lifted up. Trumpets sound in the soul, spirit stands on tiptoe, banners are unfurled within, the redeemed say so — that's what great worship does. I thank God for that in Concord Church. Great worship, grand worship. We have come almost to the end of the clouds and darkness, and except for two brief, slender clouds in Revelation. We shall see such in the twenty-first chapter at about the eighth verse and another hint of a shadow in the twenty-second (Revelation 22:15). We shall see no more clouds in this book beyond these. But today we do, for we come to the last judgment.

I don't suppose there has ever been a boy, and perhaps never a girl, who has not known the meaning of judgment. One knows that whenever mother with that particular look in her eye, or father, says, "There's something I want to talk to you about." That's judgment. I have, I am sure, told some of you this account, but it's too good to tell only once. It is the story of my great and good friend, Mr. Rudolph Thomas, who was for a long time head of the Harlem YMCA. During his childhood, his family lived in Orlando, Florida, on Church Street in that city, if some of you come from there. It was his mother's custom, he has told, to bake

246

a fruitcake at about Thanksgiving. She would treat it with suitable liquid and then put it under her bed for Christmas. He said that a little after Thanksgiving, his baseball or marbles or whatever rolled under the bed, and he crawled under to get his ball and saw that rich, brown, luscious fruitcake, dotted with nuts and fruit. And he said that he figured he would take just the slightest pinch; nobody would miss it. And he did.

The next day about the time school let out, he said all he could think of was that fruitcake under the bed. So when his mother was not looking he crawled under again and turned the fruitcake around to another side and took just the slightest pinch off. Then the next day this fruitcake preyed on his mind during school hours, and he crawled under the bed and took another piece of it. Then after that, more every day; the more he ate of it, the larger the gouges came out of the fruitcake. He said he knew it was wrong, but he could not resist going at the fruitcake. Then he said that about five days before Christmas, his mother said, "I guess I'll take my fruitcake from under the bed." My friend said he knew judgment had come. Days and weeks had gone by, but Judgment Day had come. And he said, sure enough, it had. When she got through with him with the peach tree switches, he knew what judgment was.

Judgment happens every day. That pert, pretty teenager sitting on the third row in the history class, day after day, is shortly facing judgment: examination final. That young man making his way at the department store or at one of the utilities is facing judgment: evaluation time will come soon. Judgment goes on, and if it does not come in any other way, it comes evenings in that period between going to bed and falling asleep, when conscience hauls out the deeds of the day and in the quiet dark of night we are excused or accused. For judgment goes on all of the time. The Bible, however, tells us that there are not only these constant testings of who we are and where we are, but that at last there is a final arbitration, a concluding examination.

Donald Barnhouse, who was a mighty expositor in his day, said that he thought that this account in the twentieth chapter of the Book of Revelations was all too stark, too simple for such a huge event, that it was an understatement, too lean, too laconic. "And I saw the dead, small and great, stand before God; and the books were opened: and another book was opened, which is the book of life: and the dead were judged out of those things which were written in the books, according to their works" (Revelation 20:12). Well, it may be that there is no way that language can report such a huge event, the final summing up of things when earth's last stroke has been painted on the canvas. He said that this account is so stark, so unadorned, that it is almost like someone telling of a great battle in which a noble knight meets a mighty opponent and they wrestle and fight to the death. And then when the final stroke has been made and the enemy has been destroyed, the only thing that can be said is that the opponent died, which seems like a great letdown. I do not find it so here.

There are intermediate trials all along the way, but at last the one final striking of the balance, this is a "Katy-bar-the-door" time. The end of attitude time, as these young rap singers are singing. The nitty-gritty time, and everything is brought at last to a final conclusion.

Last time we were together I spoke about God's mercy running out, and someone appropriately enough raised the question about this. I know that Psalm 103 particularly states that the Lord's mercy is from everlasting to everlasting. But you must be careful and read the rest of that. It says "to them that fear him." And we dare not try to evaporate the reality of consequence and the finality of judgment in some kind of vague universalism. There is to be a final testing. I know again that some time ago I sought to speak to you from that passage in Peter in which it says that the Lord went and preached to the spirits in prison as if there is a second probation, and there might be. But there is to be a judgment. The Bible is very clear about that. Jesus our Lord, looking into the very jaws of death, into the cauldron of his own destruction, physical destruction, spoke in this manner.

In the twenty-fifth chapter of the Book of Matthew he said it clearly; the words that fall from his lips seem almost too severe to come from someone whom we have called meek and mild. He said, "Depart from me." He condemns some into everlasting fire, prepared for the devil and his angels. And, again in the thirteenth chapter of the Book of Luke, he says to some people gathered around that "unless you repent you shall all likewise perish." It's too clear for us to make a mistake about, and maybe I ought to somewhat amend what I said last time about the mercy of God because it may well be, and I think all of us ought to take notice of this, that it is not so much that God's mercy is exhaustive, though I am prepared to argue that. But the exhaustion of that mercy may take another form. It is, I believe, possible for someone to refuse repeatedly the overtures of God, for one to steely set himself or herself against the clear teachings of Scripture. It is possible, I believe, for one to refuse the offerings of grace. I believe that it is possible for one with such determination to turn his or her back upon our Lord's offering of Calvary. I believe it is possible for one to so scorn the Lord's great sacrifice of himself, to look upon it so casually and so indifferently that one at last becomes too spiritually desolated, too isolated from spiritual reality to recognize the voice of God. I speak to you this day with an utmost earnestness and sincerity. You say that the thief on the cross had gone about as far as a human soul can go, had wandered out to a terrible barren precipice, out at the very edge of doom and destruction. And he had, and he was saved, but as old Maclaren said in his time, we ought never forget that there were two thieves. And as far as we know only one was saved.

What was the difference between the saved thief who died on one side of our Lord's cross and the other thief? Might I not say that one, as far as he had gone, still stood within the range of conscience? Out on the precipice, where he could but hear the voice of God faintly, only faintly, but he could. Am I prohibited from saying that the other, dying the same death, had gone so far, had laughed at spiritual reality so long, had scorned the outstretched hand of God with such determination that at last even in the presence of a dying Savior his heart could not respond? How else are you to explain that? That one in the same plight, under the same sentence, was saved and the other.... One had still the spiritual sensitivity to look at the dying and Lord and say, "When thou comest into thy kingdom, remember me" (see Luke 23:42). The other had gone so far that he could only rail at the dying Savior.

There's a story, perhaps Anatole France has told it, I forget whom, about Pilate, who one night stood in the presence of the Savior of the world. Think of it, he was in the presence of the Lord Christ. Retired and at a watering place in Switzerland, so this old story runs, his whole body filled with arthritis, and someone at the spa asked him about a trial that happened during his procuratorship in Judea. Pilate, sunning himself after the baths at this watering place in Switzerland, said, "What trial?" And the man said, "It was one Jesus." Pilate tried to travel back through the cobwebs of memory, to put his hand upon it, and finally said, "I cannot remember." Think of it. He stood in the presence of the Savior of the world. Jesus, the Christ! He could not remember it!

So, I will not say clearly that the mercy of the Lord runs out. I will say that I believe that we can so rebuff the Holy Spirit, we can so grieve the Holy Spirit, we can so refuse the terms of grace and become so hardened in our hearts, that we cannot hear God's voice talking to us. Oh, hear me this day! If you are drifting, playing fast and loose with spiritual reality, think very solemnly this day. What an awful destiny to come to, what a terrible plight, at last, not to be able to hear God speaking. I think I have seen it at least once. It was in the first church that was kind enough to call me pastor, or foolish enough. Don't you laugh, because you are the last of four. And you know what they say, there's no fool like an old fool. But in that church, I never knew his full name, this is fifty years ago, but Pops Swinton we called him. I can still see him across the years. He was a dapper little man, always immaculately groomed and dressed. In the height of what was the style then, he wore spotless black-and-white combination shoes, a bowtie, there was a boutonniere often in his lapel. He hung out at the Elks Hall in that little town which was the center of whatever worldliness that community knew. Ah, I remember how the people not only of the church where I was, but all of the churches in that little community labored to get Pops Swinton to turn to Jesus Christ. And you know something? I believe with all of my heart that he tried. They said that he had been what we called a "rounder," a good-time fellow, a hustler. And I saw him as people gathered around him time after time, at revival time, and prayed for him and, my God, how earnestly did they pray for him.

It seemed to me, and the years have not diminished that conviction, that Pops Swinton tried, almost physically tried. But he never did. I cannot say for sure, but given the earnestness of those people, and how they dealt with him spiritually and how he seemed to be trying so hard to accept the Lord and couldn't, I thought then, and I think now, that Pops Swinton had gone so far that he could not get back. Oh, hear me today! Do not let any cloud grow so thick between you and the Lord that his face is shut from view. Do not let any habit get a hold on you so that the Lord's voice can no longer be heard in your life. Keep an ear tuned for the Lord. Listen to what he has to say. Trust him for his grace. Trust him when he speaks to you. Answer him when he calls. Today, today is the day of salvation!

The Scriptures say almost ominously in the "day that you hear my voice, harden not your heart." Ah, today I would to God that I could plead with you to realize that at last all of us, must stand our trial in judgment. What does it say here? "The dead, small and great." No exemptions: prince and pauper, preacher and pimp, beautiful belle and repulsive hag, banker and beggar. The small and great shall stand before the judgment seat of God. Where will I be when the first trumpet sounds? When it sounds so loud as to wake up the dead. Why, surely as I stand here and extol, as the Word of God is true, the day will come when there will be no more time for praying, no more time for preaching, no more time for singing. . . . It will all be over. Time will fall exhausted at eternity's feet, and the dead small and great shall stand before the judgment seat of God to receive a reward or punishment for the deeds done in the body. There is to come a day! How many ages have gone by, but at last a finish. How many centuries have passed through the sieve of history, but at last no more. How many generations, how many years? But at last, the judgment with no chance to repent, no chance to turn around, no chance to ask for mercy.

There is a promise here in all of this. The Lord says, also, at least by suggestion, that there is to come a day when death, which disrobes us all, and sin, which disgraces us all, will be no more. Ah, I cringe almost from thinking about it. A day when time will have seen its last sin and the last tear will have been shed. When the last fever will have scorched the last burning brow, there is to be a day. There is to be a day when the last load will have been lifted, the last misunderstanding will have been borne, and the last cruel word will have been spoken and the last heart will have broken. There is to be a day when no cloud will touch the sky, when morning will know no evening. There is to be a day! And let us now thank God that there is still time, still time to call his name, still time to ask him to forgive our sins. We still have time to plead at the mercy seat, still time to mend our ways, still time to seek the Lord while he may be found, to call upon him while he is near. Ah, thank God that we are still on praying ground.

I saw the dead, great and small, stand before the throne. And the books, the books, were opened and another book was opened, the Book of Life. And the dead were judged according to their works, as recorded in the books. God have mercy!

ISBN 081701428-4